Wheel

of

Stars

**THE ANCIENT BIBLICAL CALENDAR
OF THE FUTURE**

Andrew Gabriel Roth

Printed in the USA

ISBN: 978-1-934916-09-4
(1-934916-09-9)

Copyright Notice

All versions of Scripture, unless otherwise stated, are from Andrew Gabriel Roth. First Covenant/Tanakh quotes are from the ongoing **Ma**soretic-**Tar**gumic Amplified Edition (MATARA) project. New Testament quotes are from the Aramaic English New Testament, both copyright © 2010 by Netzari Press LLC.

WWW.WHEELOFSTARS.COM

NETZARI PRESS

Table of Contents

Acknowledgements

Over the years many have asked me for Pesach, Shavuot or Yom Teruah dates. Little did I know that those questions would result in this publication becoming a reality. So, I must extend my heartfelt thanks to everyone who has shown an interest in returning to the Ancient Calendar to clarify the future.

There was a team that came together to add their talents, gifts, insights and abilities to this undertaking. First I must thank akhi (my brother) *Bill Welker* who "crunched the numbers" like no one ever has before. *Bill Welker* is a Physicist, a military man, very disciplined, and honest in his approach to this kind of material. Bill and his wife *Carmen Welker* have been the driving force behind this book. I would like to thank akhi *Marty Herz*, a Messianic (Netzari) Jewish Bible scholar, well studied in Hebraic concepts, for taking on the draft copies with the aim of making every idea and concept easy for students of the calendar to understand.

I also must thank *Bill Sanford*, a calendar expert and Torah teacher for providing questions, ideas and graphics. Special thanks also go to Aaron McGill and Richard Leduc for their help with the illustrations.

Peace & Blessings

Andrew Gabriel-Yitzkhak bar Raphael
Andrew Gabriel Roth

WHERE WE BEGIN

WHAT IS MAN THAT YOU TAKE THOUGHT OF HIM, AND THE SON OF
MAN THAT YOU CARE FOR HIM? YET YOU HAVE MADE HIM A LITTLE
LOWER THAN ELOHIM (GOD), AND YOU CROWN HIM WITH GLORY
AND MAJESTY! YOU MAKE HIM TO DOMINATE OVER THE WORKS
OF YOUR HANDS; YOU HAVE SUBJUGATED ALL THINGS UNDER HIS
FEET, ALL SHEEP AND OXEN, AND ALSO THE BEASTS OF THE FIELD,
THE BIRDS OF THE HEAVENS AND THE FISH OF THE SEA, WHATEVER
PASSES THROUGH THE PATHS OF THE SEAS. O YHWH, OUR MASTER!
HOW MAJESTIC IS YOUR NAME IN ALL THE EARTH!
PSALM 8:4-9

Prologue: Our Place in the Cosmos

Haven't we all gazed into a starry night with awe and wondered how we
fit into such vastness? It has been true of physicists and astronomers,
atheists and philosophers, little children and great artists like Vincent Van
Gogh and his famous *Starry Night* painting.

Our Universe, like the Master Who designed it, meets us where we
are. The constellations call to us through the ages, letting us know that,
however large we might think we are; they are larger. Scientists cannot
put the Universe on a slide and observe it from the outside, we live inside
that which we observe and study. We are part of it, and the Universe
is part of us; atomically, chemically and spiritually. It beckons to us
and says, "Remember where you came from. Come home." This is a
common heritage and legacy for all humans, but the vast knowledge and
information that flows from that common source depends on the path
each of us has individually chosen.

We humans have plenty of competing sacred and scientific traditions.
Even a denial of all such spirituality is a possibility in the realms of
atheism, agnosticism and secular humanism; yet, all these choices must
be welcomed in this discussion. However, all of our choices are borne
from a common human legacy, reflected in what is referred to as Scripture

(the Bible). What each one does with this information is their choice. I offer it for dialogue, debate and inspiration.

Apocalyptic fervor and New Age speculation appear to be ubiquitous, pointing to that common human need to know. A lot of the, for lack of a better word, "shine" that these philosophies offer has to do with how spartan and austere traditional monotheism seems in comparison to science, astrology, magic and so on. By knowing, we all hope to gain some control of the future, but just because a methodology may be suspect, doesn't necessarily mean all ideas behind them are.

I respectfully submit that science, astronomy and physics operate exactly the same way. The physicist knows he or she can't observe the Universe as something outside of his own paltry five senses and knows our senses limit what we can perceive. We also know via the Heisenberg principle that whatever we study could, in fact, be altered by the very fact that it is being observed. How can we know that what we are seeing is how it actually would behave if we were not looking at it? Scientists know that we can't, and they admit it.

We can't even traverse our own solar system, but scientists make a compelling case that the laws of physics in our corner of the Universe are exactly the same as in the deepest reaches of the cosmos. Granted, telescopes like Hubble, Chandra and Spitzer can see backwards in time to an astonishing extent, perhaps even back to the Big Bang, but even at that, only a tiny sliver is being observed. Not all space in every conceivable direction can be monitored simultaneously. How do we know, for example, that just as physical laws may change in the presence of a super-massive black hole that they are not turned upside down in a multiplicity of unforeseen ways in places too distant to imagine, let alone observe? Again, they don't, and they admit it.

My point is: There is also an element of "faith" operating within the sciences, and I realize that "faith" has a variety of definitions. The most common is a belief in that which is unseen and incomplete as Rav[1] Shaul

---

1 Rav is an honorary title within the Jewish community that means teacher. The Christian world extends their respect to his Apostleship.

(the Apostle Paul) says, so there must also be a lot of science in faith. In 1 Thessalonians we are instructed to *"test everything, hold on to the good, and reject all evil"* and this is the core of the scientific method itself. Genesis 1 has the first command of YAHWEH: *"be fruitful and multiply, fill the earth and subdue it"*. How can you subdue something as massive as the earth without understanding it? How can you understand it without observing its patterns in the first place? Disciplined observation and empirical processing of data is what science does. It is also what YHWH commands, because the heavens *declare* His glory.

As I write, a group of physicists representing the world's best minds are in Switzerland smashing atoms for clues to the Universe's origins. They are looking for "the God particle". My contention: Great, keep looking, but while you are at it you might want to also look for "The YAHWEH Equation" because what I have found in more than 30 years of research is this: The greatest witness in the real world for the existence of YAHWEH, whom the world calls "God", is in the mathematics at the core of the Universe itself. And the guide for showing this math as you will see is, you guessed it, the Holy Bible.

What about the "holy books" in Hinduism, Buddhism, Islam and all the rest? Certainly, if adherents to these traditions find something similar, then please let them offer it to the world with such a publication! What you are about to see is a most amazing mathematical and astronomical code from the ancient Hebrew and Aramaic Bible. It's not that I say these things are only in the Bible, I don't know. I have not spent 30 years studying the Koran or other works and can only do such a study like this one Scripture tradition at a time. That being said, I've seen much evidence suggesting that most of man's traditions are derived from the common source of Babylon.

There is one group I must address: Not only Christians, Jews and members of other faith traditions and human philosophies, and not just members of the scientific community, but those in my own Nazarene-Messianic faith. I must say to you: The Biblical calendar has been a kind of "spiritual third rail", as it will shock whoever touches it, however they touch it. As much as this book brings ideas together, there is no place where I can stand without stepping on toes, and yet, the Master YAHWEH commands us to make a choice and defend that choice for *the faith once delivered*, and to the best of our abilities.

I'm sure there will be concerns with barley or equinox issues, the new moon and so on. I ask your forbearance and fortitude to read past these differences to the end of this book for two extremely important reasons: My research has uncovered four unique calendars that are all equally important. If you want to comprehend the Wheel of Stars, it is imperative that you understand how the other three calendars relate to the one you are currently using. Only then, with the full spectrum of information, relating, and resonating, can you see the bigger picture of this presentation.

The second, and by far the most important reason, is that our community is fraught with division on the calendar issue. There are even leaders out there who make their calculations of Feast Dates a "salvation issue". Amazingly, some "believers" are putting other "believers" in hell for not following their choice of Feast dates! Families, marriages and friendships are being stressed by the theological pride of being on the "right dates". Communities are being divided and spoiled, losing huge potentials for blessings, because of a lack of understanding regarding the nature of the Israel of Elohim, and YHWH's calendar(s). Therefore, it is imperative that each soul has patience and tolerance for all who haven't had access to this type of material, or the conviction to study it as deeply as we will here.

Wheel of Stars shows how all the celestial phenomena: the sun, the moon, the stars and their constellations, work together with the earth and the barley and all other elements within the Biblical calendar. Most assuredly, the pattern herein has profound ramifications for humanity's future, not the least of which, Mashiyach's return. If these "macro trends" interest you, then I urge you to investigate the full pattern.

And finally, in recent years we have seen two periods of great Apocalyptic speculation rule countless millions of peoples' lives. We saw this with the dawn of the 21st century and the "Y2K" phenomenon which attached significance to the years 2000 and 2001. Now the conspiracy folk are beating the Mayan calendar and the December 2012 drum. Such a fertile "playground" is already leading many into hurtful, dangerous, and demonic speculation.

To the multitudes of fable-making materialists and their followers who assert that YAHWEH and His Holy Writ are a corruption of record and foolishness, let them understand the math. Even the most ardent materialist and humanist might well begin to understand that cosmic design points to a far greater human destiny than that of this material universe!

So let the journey begin.

Chapter 1

Four Calendars

I WILL GIVE YOU THE TREASURES OF DARKNESS
—THE SECRET WEALTH OF HIDDEN PLACES—
SO THAT YOU MAY KNOW THAT IT IS I, YHWH,
THE ELOHIM OF ISRAEL, WHO CALLS YOU BY YOUR NAME.
ISAIAH 45:3 (MATARA)

Reading the End from the Beginning

When I first began calendar research more than two decades ago, I was confronted with a bewildering array of what seemed like irreconcilable choices, mechanisms, and possibilities. I'm certain that most researchers who have studied Scripture for time clues have experienced similar frustration. We all understand the sun, moon, and the stars keep time and mathematical patterns in the Bible. Numbers like 7, 10, 40, 100, 1000 are the results of that timekeeping. We also all understood that some parts of the calendar spoke of sacred observances and others of prophecy and still others had the potential to resolve long standing scientific and religious debates.

All students of Scripture have contemplated such things.

But when we look at the collective output of those efforts, those irreconcilable choices can also hit the researcher like a tsunami of doubt and frustration:

Barley or Equinox?
Lunar, Solar or both?
Rabbinic or no? Why or why not?
Sight or calculate the moon? Darkness or sliver?
Keep it according to where you live or via Jerusalem?

These are just a few of the questions common to all systems, but there are countless others. But, we know that YHWH[1] is not the Author of confusion, so whatever the answer, it has to, at least in its broad contours, make sense and follow His rules as revealed in His Word. This is where I began, with the Word. I had no idea how these disparate parts would work together or how the components of all systems were incorporated into the final product. I had no stake in terms of any denomination/sect as to how it came together or even if others would agree or not.

In addition, this topic is so vast that it has taxed my abilities beyond anything I've previously embraced. When I used the calendar research to answer a huge question, such as: when Mashiyach might return: even then, that was relatively straightforward compared to the rest of the research. Each answer inexorably led to another question and another complicated mechanism or process to deal with.

Perhaps the most confusing "macro" issue was this: Many times I would look at extremely thorough and intricate systems on the web that were backed up by computer programming and algorithm engines. I could see they were "right", but yet they disagreed fundamentally with one another on the details. I began to wonder why YHWH led me to this issue and even despaired for a time of ever finding an answer through one unified calendar.

The answer, as it turns out, is that no *one* calendar can do all the things needed, and in the process, answer the majority of questions from nearly a dozen separate study disciplines (linguistics, astronomy, etc). I knew I would *never* find that *one* calendar…

I did however find four calendars that were interrelated but also retained distinct functionalities! They are, in the broadest of terms:

1) **Prophetic:** This is the calendar used by YHWH to encode some of the deepest mysteries of time and space that He has allowed us to discover. It is this calendar that suggests the possible range of Messiah's return.

1 See Name of YHWH in appendix.

2) Solar Pre-Metonic: This was the way the solar and lunar year was inter-calculated from before Moshe's time when the moon was not required to synch festivals. A more complete name is the "Pre-Metonic Lunar Regression", indicating that the lunar year drags behind its solar counterpart and must be adjusted accordingly. This calendar ran Tishri-Tishri (the seventh Hebrew month - autumn to autumn) and was used by Adam, Noah and Abraham, among others. While similar to the Rabbinic calendar in adding leap months about every 3 years, the Rabbinic system was based on the work of a Babylonian astronomer named Meton who lived a thousand years after Moshe. In many ways, the Solar Pre-Metonic is the same as the Prophetic in its synchronizing mechanism that has at its base, a 360 day year which balances to the 365.2422 day year even better than our own modern Gregorian. The main difference is that while the Prophetic was meant to track YHWH's times for deliverance, the Solar Pre-Metonic was meant to keep the yearly cycles on time. The fact of the matter is that this calendar was adapted with minimal changes by almost all ancient civilizations and also synchs to Biblical dates.

3) Equinox Pre-Metonic/Moedic: This calendar was largely instituted for timing the spring and fall festivals that YHWH established for Israel. As a result, it is a calendar instituted by YHWH to Moshe when He proclaimed it directly with the shifting of months from Tishri (autumn) to Abib (spring), as recorded in Exodus 12:1-2.

4) Priestly: The Priestly Calendar, like the Moedic, is synched to the month of the first Passover. However, while the Moedic is a lunar-solar calendar, the Priestly is purely solar and will return to the exact solar date of the Vernal Equinox cycle but in much longer time cycles that form what I will refer to as The Constellation Clock, or "Absolute Zodiac." This latter term is meant to differentiate YHWH based astronomy from pagan based astrology which not only divides the sky up but also worships those regions as animals or gods. The process of 24 courses[2] throughout

---

2 "Courses" refer to the 24 family groups or divisions of priests that each take turn serving in the Tabernacle or Temple for a week, "sabbath to sabbath". They are first mentioned directly in 1 Chronicles 24 and, as we will see later, are meant to mirror the 24 hours in the solar day.

the millennia "floats" and has a striking mechanism that moves forwards and backwards at the same time and in one motion; truly something only the Master Architect of time could accomplish!

Calendar Mechanisms (General)

Each calendar has a guiding principle followed by applications to bring that principle about. Here's how each one worked:

Calendar Type: Prophetic

Beginning Point: Creation of Adam

Ending Point: (Probably) Mashiyach's return, but theoretically could go on forever.

Balancing Mechanism: 360 day year, 12 months 30 days each with 30-day leap months added as needed and based on Biblical mathematics.

Purpose: To point to the eternal nature of YHWH and the redemption of His Son, Y'shua the Mashiyach.

Calendar Type: Solar Pre-Metonic

Beginning Point: Creation of Adam

Ending Point: The time of Exodus 12:1 just before the liberation of the Israelites from Egypt, at which point it folds back into the Prophetic as far as YHWH's elect and Israel are concerned; yet continues to be used by other nations. Only a select few in Israel will see its patterns in Scripture after the time of Moshe as they relate to the eternity of YHWH and the return of His Son Y'shua the Mashiyach.

Balancing Mechanism: 360 day year, 12 months: 30 days each with leap months added as needed and based on Biblical mathematics.

Purpose: To allow ancient man to keep the proper solar year for planting and harvests, so they could "be fruitful and multiply, fill the earth and subdue it." However, while ancient man may have had his own harvest festivals, YHWH wasn't concerned with them until He set the real harvest festivals to coincide with a fixed time that had to be perfect every year. He (YHWH) ordered the change from the Solar Pre-Metonic to the Moedic system which demanded that the lunar cycle also needed to be accounted for when setting the months of the year.

Calendar Type: Equinox Pre-Metonic [Moedic]

Beginning Point: The start of the month of the first Passover (Abib 1)

Ending Point: Mashiyach's return or some unknown time afterwards, but certainly not prior to the end of this age.

Balancing Mechanism: Signs, Seasons, Days and Years, with Vernal and Autumnal Equinoxes synched to Pesach and Sukkot feasts, months starting from one New Moon to the next. Additionally, the count for the week is an absolute hard count from YHWH's first day of creation before the sun and moon were made. The year is forever expressed as 365.2422 days for man's use and 360 days for YHWH's.

Purpose: To allow mankind to keep the eternal festivals of YHWH.

Calendar Type: Priestly

Beginning Point: The start of the month of the first Passover.

Ending Point: Unknown.

Balancing Mechanism: The eternal cycles of the Constellation Clock which will be explained later.

Purpose: Largely unknown, but generally meant to freeze the time of the Exodus in solar terms. Not meant for festival observances in Israel. For our uses however, seems to assist the faithful in reconciling some of the more difficult Biblical chronological puzzles. In other words, it is a gift from YHWH but with the full ramifications still unknown. Please note, however, that the Practical or Actual Priestly calendar that the sons of Aaron literally used for their historical services to YHWH is a main topic of my next book, *Y'shua Year by Year*.

Research Approach

As I will detail later, my focus is on ancient resources in astronomy, mathematics, linguistics and Scripture. My goal is to use Scripture inductively, rather than contradict it or weigh it down. When I arrived at places that seemed open to interpretation, I considered the words of ancient sages but the math *always* had to remain perfect.

The Simplest of Beginnings

Before we get into the many nuances and majestic grace of the Heavenly Calendar or "Wheel of Stars"[3], let me open with a bold, simple and provable statement:

The calendar you are about to see is mathematically perfect and never loses time.

For reasons we will discuss later, one of the more simple and practical iterations of this work involves a calendar that is balanced to not lose a day until 100,000 years have passed from the Creation of Adam. After 100,000 years this calendar can easily be calibrated and balanced

---

3 See Illustrations in Appendix.

so it doesn't lose time for trillions of years, making it, essentially, an eternal system. In another mechanism, *the Constellation Clock*, we see a calendar that is, in fact, more accurate than our current Gregorian calendar including the calibration with losing a leap day every 4,000 years, the much celebrated Mayan[4] calendar and in any other calendar system derived from the mind of man.

Having said that, and in spite of the multiplicity of sources employed here, you are seeing a "Sola Scriptura" (Scripture alone) system. I have also vigorously checked this work against other Scripture-only systems, such as www.torahcalendar.com and www.360calendar.com. Although, I found out through continuous and evolving research that the repository of ancient knowledge was in the Scripture all along and passed down through the millennia by learned sages whose work was to keep prophetic and practical/sacred timekeeping synchronized. When I reached an impasse as to how to apply Scriptural data, I reviewed works like Josephus and Philo who had special priestly knowledge that Scripture also confirms which helped show which methodology was used at which periods of history.

Similarly, in our modern internet age, the Christian, Jewish and Netzarim (Nazarene) scholars who are doing this research each bring their own validating mechanisms to the table, and all are needed to give light to understanding the Scriptures and glory to the Name of YHWH Who revealed them to mankind.

So for example, those who did a magnificent job on www.360calendar. com are clearly coming at the task from a mathematical perspective, and the mastery of numbers is very evident. But, while looking at the numbers, I then reviewed Hebrew and Aramaic[5] linguistics to flesh out Scriptural meanings and directions that might not be immediately apparent in English, but, nevertheless, validate the work.

Finally, like the calendar I am describing, this research is ongoing, I don't expect that every small nuance will be immediately apparent to everyone

---

4 See Understanding the Apocalypse in Appendix.
5 See Aramaic Basics and History in Appendix.

on their first reading of this book. A lot of that issue; the vast majority of it, I chalk up to my own limitations as a writer, as I am constantly challenged by how to emphasize and characterize complicated Biblical questions. But I promise this: I will make the best effort possible to walk you through virtually every difficult chronological puzzle that Scripture throws at us. For the remainder of what might not be clear after that entire process is completed, I look to YHWH to guide us all to His ultimate truth in His intended timing.

Understanding the Book of Signs

My normal presentation style is to offer broad elements and then get increasingly more specific as the evidentiary foundations are laid, one at a time. However, the challenges presented by this intricate and interlocking material cross nearly half a dozen disciplines, which forced me to rethink that approach.

So, in this case after giving an overview, I will skip to the end so to speak, and provide more conclusions. By doing so, my hope is that larger lines of evidence will make more sense since you will have already "previewed" them. Then, near the end of the book we will revisit the whole thesis.

As we will see later, the *"Book of Signs"* is another term I coined for the body of teaching as it might have originally appeared to various ancients, whether in oral or written form, or a combination of both. The "book" is manifest from Scripture instructions and Biblical mathematics, and various individuals throughout the ages would have had different "chapters" for their use. So the *"Book of Signs"* as Adam may have known it would have grown a bit by the time it would have been passed to Enoch; Enoch would have used/worked on it before it passed to Noah and the same would apply to Abraham, to Moshe, David and so on.

In some cases that transition of "the Book" from one hand to the next seems very clear to me, such as in 1 Chronicles 24. It states directly that David put the priests in their proper order based on instructions passed down from Aaron four centuries earlier. Then, adding another four centuries after that, Scripture tells us these identical instructions from Aaron were also preserved into King Josiah's time. After the Captivity, the "divisions" of the priests are confirmed, not as an innovation of David, but trace back to Moshe and Aaron (Ezra 6:18). From there it's an easy reach into Y'shua's (Jesus) time, as even the Maccabean Revolt (167-164 BCE) disrupted Temple services for only two years. Furthermore, Torah itself gives us other hints about the Book of Signs. Again, this must be true because while the 24 priestly courses are never mentioned in the first five books, every other Scripture source says **written instructions** came from Moshe and Aaron![6]

However, in other situations, it may even be possible that some parts of the Book of Signs were lost either due to the fulfillment of prophecy or the circumstances of a given disaster, but the evidence was still in Scripture and still remembered by YHWH and perhaps a select few.

Meanwhile, I intend to give you in written form, the simple rules of the Book of Signs as I understand them, and then encourage everyone to see how these principles work their way through the rest of the book.

And of course, this is a theoretical text. Since I don't expect that an ancient Hebrew or Aramaic manuscript of it will be discovered any time soon, I will endeavor to show how it was derived from The Word and developed for ancient Israel.

My other challenge is to retain a "clinical approach" for fear that spiritual language like: *"thus sayeth YHWH your Elohim"* would cause some to suppose that I might be adding to the Word. I *am not!* Instead, I am applying the Word through Its own principles as YHWH spoke them in the first place.

So, as you read this, please check these statements against every event and person as depicted in Holy Writ and allow me to say very clearly:

---

6 And to all these we must add the traditions regarding Hillel the Elder, whom the Talmud says was the only one to have the Shekinah (Presence) of YHWH rest on him that originated from Moshe. The last person who was described in similar terms before Hillel the Elder's time in 10 BCE was Ezra the Priest, who also happened to make direct reference to this Book of Signs as well. We will talk a bit more, however, about Hillel the Elder later.

I add nothing from Genesis 1:1 through Revelation 22:19, but I *explain* what is in those pages as they relate to a particular issue.

The Book of Signs

These are the instructions to the elect of Master YHWH for proclaiming His glory, His appointed times and His will for all the ages.

To Adam and his descendants:

> 1) The birth of your father Adam is the birth of your race, from which all My promises will be proclaimed throughout time. What Adam has named is its name, but, remember, I am the one Who named him.
>
> 2) The sun, moon and stars are your markers, and they bring to you signs, seasons, days and years, in that order. No season may start without the signs sending My approval. No days will happen until the season starts. No years will pass until I send the signs to return and do My will.
>
> 3) My signs always proclaim My power. My power is shown by their might. I am mightier than all and mightier than the sun. The sun is mightier than the moon; for she has real light and the moon only begs for what light it can get from the sun.
>
> 4) Just as the sun divides the day from the night, evening and morning, so too will the sun divide the year by the time she returns to her origin point easily seen by you in the sky. You will find these equinoxes and use them for now to mark the boundaries of the years. In later times you will use them to keep My Torah.
>
> 5) When the sun gives her approval, you will count 30 days for 12 months and begin the year anew. The next year's first month will be both when the first spring constellation returns, and it will be vouchsafed by the New Moon that happens nearest to the Vernal Equinox.

6) As I rested on Shabbat, the seventh day, so too will you at the end of each week. From now on and forever you will count the week as I did, work for six days and rest on the seventh as I did. Count the seven days without the sun and the moon as I did, the same is the pattern for you as well. As I did from heaven, so shall you do on Earth.

7) You will count your year from the time I created Adam your father, from the month you will later call Tishri, and the middle of that month was set by Me to have begun before the Autumnal Equinox so that you might keep the year by the sun, My messenger and plant your crops on time. This will be done until I set the time for your deliverance from a nation you have yet to know.

8) Your seven cycles will extend from the week and unto the year, the 12 months of 30 days making the year short after six cycles, from which the year will have its rest with an extra 30 days after. As you balance every seventh year this way, so too will you in later times balance the Land every seventh year by letting it rest.

9) Count seven of these seven cycles, unto the time of your short generation of 40 years, and add 30 days for that generation so that it too may rest. In so doing you will find your year will never run short from your days to the time of the Deliverance cycle.[7]

To My chosen sages from Adam to Mashiyach's first coming:

1) I am YHWH your Elohim Who called you out of darkness and doubt to serve Me.

2) To you I give wisdom, understanding and knowledge, to track the Wheel of Stars and know how the constellations bring all into season under My will. You will retain the knowledge of how I have set the heavens to rule over the earth, as I will tell My servant Job.

3) In the fullness of time you will understand the one great unit of time I have withheld, but that interval of years will not be revealed

---

7 Further balancing mechanisms for longer intervals of time, such as 4,000 years and 100,000 years, will be discussed in detail later.

before the First Deliverance.

4) It is also to you and your descendants, both in this age and those yet born, that I will allow to know the great cycles from now until your deliverance and from that calling out to the ultimate mission of My only begotten Son who is the Word and the Message that has come from My mouth and is watching you now.

5) You will until those great days regard the timekeeping of the other nations and you will see with your own eyes how I have shown these things to other nations, but the nations have not understood why and they have perverted My truth through the worship of false gods.

To Enoch:

You have walked with me one year for each day of the solar year; three hundred and sixty five years. Your walk has pleased Me and your example will be known forever, but the knowledge I have given you will passed on only to the elect.

To Noah:

You alone are righteous in your generation and your family will be given the knowledge of Adam through Enoch, through which you will continue to number the days and years as I also ordered them. You will count the 30 day months through the storms and darkness, where neither sun nor moon will shine, and pass your example down in witness to your chronicler Moshe so that all may know the seasons I have commanded you.

To Abraham:

You were born to a people who count the stars. Nevertheless, I have called you to come out and go from that place, but you will continue counting the stars as I have shown you. Within the stars your blessings are revealed, your descendants are as numerous as they, as the grains of sand on the beaches of the world. You will remember My message Abraham: The stars point to the pattern under My direction and the Earth and her sands confirm it as a witness but never a judge.

To Moshe My chosen teacher:

1) I am YHWH your Elohim. Your fathers Abraham, Isaac and Jacob walked with Me and guarded my Torah. To them I promised that you sojourn in a land you did not know for four great cycles of time. I have surely heard your cries and know of your afflictions, and will come with a Deliverer to lead you out with a mighty hand and an outstretched arm, with signs and portents. I will also judge all the man made gods of Egypt to show that I am supreme to their false deities of the sky, sea and air; nay, even their king is said to be a god and I will bring him to ruin in the waters.

2) When your deliverance draws near, I will show and tell you how your timekeeping is to be calibrated and will begin from the beginning of your freedom and from solar year to solar year, forever. At that time you will no longer count from when I created all but from when I freed My people under your staff O Moshe.

3) When the sun sign enters into the constellation that you were freed under (Aries), you will know that the moon will then be allowed to count your days for that year. My sacred feasts of Pesach and Sukkot will be guarded through the middle of those months with the former fixed to occur after the Equinox signs. Your time is forever fixed to memorialize the sky as I set it for you on the great day, not for how it will be in ages to come. This is your Day One and Year One. I am YHWH your Elohim.

4) Your beginning month for each year will always be the New Moon nearest the Spring Equinox, from which Pesach will happen 2 weeks later. The barley you need for the harvest festivals thereafter will always be in green ears as you observe them. Remember that first month of that first Pesach I set for you, when you had not

beheld the barley, for I will provide ripe barley for you each year, when My servant the sun has done as I require.

5) These things you will speak to Aaron and the nation of Israel, and to you and Aaron I give a separate revelation. You will write out all My Words and keep them.

To Aaron with Moshe as witness:

1) Aaron, Moshe your brother will lead you and Israel out of bondage. From there you will be tested to see if you will rely on Me or on your own understanding. If you hearken to Me, all will go well with you. But if you become stiff necked, yes even you Aaron, and try to proclaim images in strange worship even to My glory, then I will deal a terrible judgment upon you.

2) It is your responsibility, Aaron, to maintain my commands for sacred service and pass them down to your children forever. But not even the sons of your body will be immune from My wrath should these Commandments be set aside for even a moment. I will give you the pattern and understanding for how many of your sons serve Me forever from Sabbath to Sabbath, in the Wilderness and in the place where My Holy Name will reside.

To Aaron's sons, Aaron and Moshe as witness:

1) To all who follow in Aaron's office: know that I am YHWH your Elohim Who has consecrated you as a people to serve Me and perform intercession for Israel. You will forever root your service of your 24 courses to the solar day, the first anniversary of your emancipation from Egypt. You will stand in order, continuously, and never waver from that order. If you fall away, you will count from the year of your emancipation which is enshrined forever and maintain 12 year cycles from when course 1 starts the first Shabbat on or after the Vernal Equinox to when he returns to this same Shabbat in twelve years time. All ordering from there will be maintained regardless of how long a period between services

occurs, for I, YHWH, have given you that date and that interval of twelve years in your writing and in the sky, that it may never be forgotten.[8]

2) As priests, I will give you the 12 stones on the breastplate of your leader to be your *Mazzaroth* [Zodiac] that is consecrated to Me. Thus you will never forget to track the year as your forefathers did. You will maintain My annual sacred Moedim (appointed times – feasts) by the seasons of the moon. You will count from one Seventh day Shabbat to the next Seventh day Shabbat as from the beginning of creation, as all elect before you have counted. This is My memorial throughout all your generations.

3) Stay in my service and gain My favor and My wisdom to prosper. Fail to keep my Feasts or deny the Land her Sabbaths and I will take them back and send you into captivity as before, even as some of you witnessed My power in bringing you out of captivity from Egypt.[9]

4) If you fail to keep Pesach, you will also fail for the rest of the Set Times. If you fail for the rest, the Jubilee cycle will be lost to you, but your other knowledge, for the sake of the nation, will remain; although you will forget why you have continued to reset yourselves to the right courses after My disasters have befallen you. Your timing will be faithful so that My Son can come to you

---

8 This is again regarding the Practical-Actual version of the Priestly calendar, or the one used by the sons of Aaron literally. I contend that the practical and spiritual overlays are actually part of the same calendrical system, but this Actual version is detailed in the next book *Y'shua Year by Year*. The reason these mechanisms are part of the same calendar and not--as with the Prophetic and Solar Pre-Metonic--separate calendars, is because there is no real difference in the overall workings between them. With the former set, Prophetic will measure the additional interval of the 50-year Jubilee whereas the Solar Pre-Metonic will not. By contrast, these Priestly versions are on the identical system with the only difference being one of magnitude of the same cycles, i.e. one year versus 276 years per course. These differences will become apparent as you read through this study. While the Constellation Clock that we will explore later assumes a pure floating eternal mechanism for the heavens, Y'shua Year by Year will explain why, in practical terms, the real sons of Aaron made a hard adjustment to recycle the first course to the 12th spring, regardless as to where the floating courses would have been at that same period.

9 We will look into exactly where and why this knowledge may have been lost in the concluding section.

at the promised occasion; but not for your benefit alone.

5) My Mashiyach will be sent to proclaim My Torah, as it should be, but if you reject him your house will fall again. Just as you rejected My prophets which caused Jeremiah to weep for you as the first House burned. From that time onward your knowledge will wait until the Temple may, yet again, rise and the tabernacle of David will be restored through My Son the Lion of Judah, Y'shua your Master.

Please remember that this format was simply *an intellectual exercise*, not the constitution of a faith document or the start of a new religion or textual tradition! I write in this style for the reader to understand how these calendars relate to specific people and times. However, I do not see a separation between theory and the facts that underlay its foundations.

The reader should understand that I am simply making an opening statement, before providing the evidence for your careful consideration. The preceding are my conclusions and beliefs, but what follows now is the proof of those beliefs or the end from the beginning.

Background Information and Research Methodology

"Can you bind the beautiful Pleiades? Can you loose the cords of Orion? Can you bring forth the *Wheel of Stars*[10] into its seasons and stand in the path of Ayish/Iyutha (Aldebaran) and her satellites (Hyades). Do you know the laws of the heavens and can you establish their rule over the earth?...Have you given wisdom to the Lance Star (Antares) or intelligence to the Bow Star?" (Hebrew & Aramaic Job 38:31-33, 38, cross referenced to the translation of T.K. Cheyne: Journal of Biblical Literature, Vol. 17, No. 1 (1898), pp. 103-107)

---

10 The original translator writes "Zodiac", but this can be a confusing term. The NAS Old Testament Hebrew Lexicon defines the Hebrew word *mazzaroth*, "the 12 signs of the Zodiac and their 36 associated constellations." It is important that a clear distinction be made between the Zodiac/Wheel of Stars as an absolute marker for a region of the sky as opposed to the dwelling places of false deities.

All versions of Scripture agree that YHWH says it is He Who brings the Zodiac / constellations / Wheel of Stars into their seasons, and that He has placed the laws of the heavens above the laws of the earth, with both heaven and earth forever submitting to His authority.

The "Wheel" is actually a fixed marker for regions of the sky and has nothing to do with the fact that constellations have shifted from our view because of the precession of the Earth's axis. Yet, it is also the case that the Wheel contains within it a backwards mechanism that reproduced the same precession during it's forward motion.

The current Rabbinic Jewish calendar is a fixed model that came into its final and current form long after Hillel the Second in 359 CE. While tradition tells us that it was Hillel's doing, the first full accounting of the Rabbinical calendar, in all its details, does not occur until the time of Maimonides many centuries later. There is no way to definitively prove that intervening epochs did not *add* substantially to what Hillel the Second began, and Jewish tradition is replete with examples of ascribing more recent ideas to those of the distant past.

Let us be generous, and assume that all the details of the Rabbinic calendar were fixed perfectly in 359 CE, understanding also that it was built on a Babylonian intercalculated pattern that was based on the work of the famous astronomer Meton ca 432 BCE.[11]

If we were to place the intercalculated system about 800 years before Hillel the Second, as far back as it can go[12] we still have a major problem. There are more than a thousand years of Jewish history to connect with

11 The captivity in Babylon is considerably earlier, 586-515 BCE, so it is possible that the intercalculary system Babylon adopted did not extend that far back, although there is good reason to believe that it did.

12 Meton (5th century BC) is generally credited for discovering the 19-year cycle, however some suggest that the Chaldean astronomer Kidinnu (4th century BC) discovered the 19-year cycle. The Babylonians may also have learned of it earlier. They measured the Moon's motion against the stars, so the 235:19 relation may originally have referred to sidereal years, instead of tropical years as has been used in various calendars. Ancient astronomers did not make a clear distinction between sidereal and tropical years before Hipparchus discovered precession of the equinoxes c. 130 BC. (Quoted from Wikipedia online) The point is that if we fix this calendar to this timeline, we are still far from the time of Moshe and Abraham.

the calendar Moshe used; and of course much more if we intend to go back to Abraham, Noah, and so on.

Part of the Jewish calendar has always been lunar. Since Moshe's day, those lunar calculations have also been tied to agricultural festivals. Viewed on its own, a lunar calendar will fall out of season if a 354 day lunar year is followed. Furthermore, the instructions of Genesis 1:14-19 clearly mandate the sun, moon and the stars in the role of keeping the time.

Many say that the Babylonian Captivity was a huge influence on the timekeeping of the Hebrews albeit this event is relatively brief and quite late in their history. How much more influence could the ancient Egyptian Captivity have had, since they kept a 365 day solar calendar and forced the Hebrews (including Moshe) to follow it for more than 400 years?

The intercalculated system would have then been in existence long before Meton. Interestingly, the Karaites[13] and other Torah observant groups claim they have an easy answer. Follow the Torah and check the barley for green ears, and you will always know when the first month is. However Torah-based and simple as this approach may appear, there are many questions left unanswered, and this will become apparent as we progress.

Lest there be concern or contention that external sources outside the Malchut (Kingdom of) Elohim (God) should not be consulted, let's clearly understand the differences between YHWH's *astronomy* and pagan-corrupted *astrology*:

> And when you look up to the sky and see the sun, the moon and the stars, all the host of heaven, do not be tempted into bowing down to them and worshipping the things that YHWH your Elohim has

---

13 The Karaites are a group of Jews (and converts) established in the Middle Ages who broke with nearly all Rabbinic tradition. Their name is likely derived from the Hebrew *karet*, or "to cut out", as in cutting away the oral traditions that they felt were added to Torah. While the Karaites may be a relatively modern group, many of their positions reflect ancient minority voices. Therefore it is necessary that current Karaite views not be dismissed by the misperception that positions they hold are not also ancient.

given to all the Nations under heaven. (Deuteronomy 4:19-Matara)[14]

If a man or woman residing with you in one of the towns that YHWH has given you is found doing evil in the eyes of YHWH your Elohim by going around and past[15] His covenant and against My command bowing down to other gods, bowing down to them or the sun and the moon and the stars of the sky, and this [violation] has been told to you, you must investigate it thoroughly and then, behold! If it is true and the verbal account has been established that such a detestable act has been done in Israel, take the man or woman who is guilty of this offense to the city gate and stone them to death. Deuteronomy 17:2-5 (Matara)

Going even further, those who attempt to divine destinies from the stars, as opposed to waiting on YHWH who named the stars and controls their movements (Psalm 147:4, Jeremiah 31:35), they are the *"stargazers"* who are strictly condemned:

All the counsel you have received has made you weary! ***Let your astrologers*** [*havri shamayim* **הֹבְרֵי שָׁמַיִם**][16] ***come forward, those stargazers who prophesy month by month and let them save you from what is coming against you. Surely they are as stubble that a fire will consume. They cannot even rescue themselves from the power of the flame!*** They have no coals to warm anyone by and no fire to sit by. Thus have they become to you, these people with whom you have worked with and traveled with since you were children. Each of has continued in their error and there are none who can save you! Isaiah 47:13-15 (Matara—see also Jeremiah 8:1-3)

---

14 Matara is the name for my ongoing translation of the Tanakh.

15 The Hebrew word *aibar* (עָבַר) is ironically the same word for "Hebrew" and literally means, "to cross over; go around". So people either cross over the right way, keep YHWH's commands and become "Hebrews" or they cross to the wrong side and "go around" or beyond, the strictures of the covenant, which is the literal meaning of "to transgress".

16 This phrase literally means, "those who have divided up the heavens". However as we read further for context, it is not that act alone that YHWH condemns. Rather it is dividing up the heavens and then worshipping them in place of He Who made them in the first place.

Conversely, when the stars witness to their Creator, it is a holy and blessed event (Psalm 19:1-6). Furthermore, when men use them properly in accordance with YHWH's instructions, they are declared righteous (Psalm 8:3-9, 136:9). In many places, Genesis 22:17 being one example, the stars are used as a teaching aid and comfort from YHWH. *YHWH-based astronomy has absolutely nothing to do with the precession of constellations that were named after pagan deities.*

Torah astronomy examines a section of star lit sky as it appeared, for example, during the Patriarchal Age through to the end of the Late Prophetic period that closes the Tanakh. So, it's really about what appeared in Moshe's day, not what might appear now. By "freezing" the canopy of stars as a memorial to a divine event, we eliminate the problems associated with the motions of the earth, precession and the *sidereal* versus *tropical year* debate.

For these reasons, let's, tentatively, refer to this system as the "Absolute Zodiac" with a clear proviso again that we are in no way honoring names such as Aquarius, Cancer, and so on, but the One Living Elohim, YHWH, who created the heavenly host to serve both Him and us.

Let us now proceed to a list of the basic sources used, as well as a brief analysis of why some material should carry more weight than others. The rationale for categorizing reference materials is for the simple reason that no individual is above YHWH's instruction or correction.

In order of stated importance:

1) Scripture – Hebrew and Aramaic authorities for the Tanakh and New Covenant Writings form the most authoritative source material available.

2) Ancient Primary Source Material – The general rule is that the older the source material and/or the nearer to events it described, the better. One of the major areas where we could use expert testimony is with respect to priestly procedures and service cycles. The most authoritative source we would consult would be as follows:

1. Fully established in the Second Temple period, as opposed to harking back to it from centuries later.
2. A written manuscript record that is beyond dispute.
3. A witness who is a position to provide comment from direct personal and professional experience concerning the events described.

As most who have studied the time period know, there are two authorities that have impeccable Pharisaic and priestly family connections. Both were well respected in their day and have shown great devotion to righteous living in Torah.

Josephus Bar Matthias and Philo Judaeus remain our best sources for just about anything happening from the Persian period to the destruction of the Second Temple in CE 70. What's more, and in complete contrast to the Rabbis of the Talmud, who commented on these times centuries later,[17] Josephus and Philo confirm each other's details, and in one case, the former writes about the latter as a man of high esteem in the Jewish community.

Philo is sometimes accused of being far too eager to combine pagan, and Greek philosophy with Torah. However, his endorsement by Josephus goes a long way to mitigate this accusation.[18] If Josephus, a devoted

---

17 On a few occasions our only source for certain relevant information is the Mishnah and, where needed, these are taken into consideration on a case by case basis.

18 Josephus mentions Philo Judaeus here: [259] Many of these severe things were said by Apion, by which he hoped to provoke Gaius to anger at the Jews, as he was likely to be. But Philo, the principal of the Jewish embassy, a man eminent on all accounts, brother to Alexander the alabarch, {b} and one not unskilful in philosophy, was ready to make his defence against those accusations; [260] but Gaius prohibited him, and bade him begone; he was also in such a rage, that it openly appeared he was about to do them some very great mischief. So Philo, being thus affronted, went out and said to those Jews who were about him, that they should be of good courage, since Gaius' words indeed showed anger at them, but in reality had already set God against himself. (Antiquities 18:259-260)

Another man, dubbed "Philo the Elder" is mentioned in Against Apion 1.218, but this is not the same man as Josephus clearly links him with other pagan Greek philosophers that he expects another Greek pagan anti-Semitic historian, namely Apion himself, to have been familiar with. The first Philo is "the principal of the Jewish embassy" whereas the other one, this "Elder" and these other Greeks "have not greatly missed the truth about our affairs; whose lesser mistakes ought therefore to be forgiven them; for it was not in their power to understand our writings with the utmost accuracy." Surely that could not apply to one of the greatest Jewish representatives of the generation that saw the birth of Josephus himself!

Pharisee, who spent most of his life in Israel and who fought against the Romans can back Philo, it is also very likely that Philo enjoyed normative status by Jews in Israel.[19]

Granted, Josephus is not immune to some scorn in Israel, either. Even today many rabbinic authorities have leveled a charge of "switching sides" against him. They note that his own biography admits that he fought against the Romans, then helped the Romans by interpreting surrender terms to the Jews, and finally moved to Rome where he spent the last three decades of his life after the Jewish War. In all fairness, the counterbalancing facts are that even the father of Rabbinic Judaism, Yochanan ben Zakkai, also cooperated with Rome as the price for preserving the faith. ***However, if support for a plain reading of Scripture is questionable from these sources, it simply will not be quoted.***

On the other hand, if the quote is a logical and very short extension from those plain readings and still not contradictory, then this constitutes valid commentary from these two learned men on the Torah as they understood it.

Finally, Philo could easily be equated in like manner to Rav Shaul (Apostle Paul), who used quotations from Greek playwrights, philosophers and popular culture to clarify his original Hebraic points.[20] Philo appears to use his surrounding culture to enable his audience to better understand the genuine and final authority of Torah. He neither bowed to Hellenism, nor suggested the merging/addition of their holidays to those given by YHWH. This speaks volumes towards him being a Pharisaic Jew of the Diaspora.

3) Mishnah - the Torah commentary that grew out of Rabbinic Judaism, is used here with a proverbial "grain of salt". The reason for the extra care is, generally, that we are looking at a body of work centuries removed from the primary sources of the period. Furthermore, the Mishnah frequently has codified information which, while generally correct, is

---

19 Rather, to be precise, that Philo's direct interpretations of Torah were not that off the mark from those in Israel or the Diaspora. It should be noted however, that Philo's veneration of the LXX would have been met with sharp resistance in Israel.

20 In fact, both Philo and Paul quoted Menander of Ephesus, a very popular playwright of the time.

nevertheless emphasizing only certain aspects to advance the religio-political realities of the time. As the reader will see though, the key facts in the Mishnah are usually adequate, but that the details and the reasons behind what they relate are often suspicious. I beg the reader's exercise of longsuffering and patience while waiting on the examples, since my reasoning for this evaluation will be clarified with further details.

4) The Ephraim Exception – Here is one possible example where a more reliable witness may overrule an earlier one. It has to do with the testimony of Mar Ephraim, a Fourth Century Syrian Saint, and one of the foremost authorities the world has ever known on the Aramaic Peshitta Tanakh and Renewed Covenant writings. In this case, even though Ephraim writes 200 or more years after the time of the Mishnah, I believe his commentary in one area supersedes that of the Rabbis.

The issue has to do with Ephraim's interpretation and identification of stars mentioned in Job 38:31, part of the overall quote that we saw at the beginning of this section. The Rabbis have generally favored a reading of the Hebrew Ayish constellation as "the Great Bear". However, the Masoretic Text (Jewish Publication Society 1999 Hebrew English Tanakh) itself references an ancient Aramaic Tanakh reading that identifies the constellation as Iyutha, believed by almost all scholars to designate the star Aldebaran.

This reading of Ayish as Iyutha/Aldebaran is, in turn, backed up with evidence from centuries before Ephraim's time, going back to Babylonian Jews who would later compile the Talmud itself. Ephraim's contribution then is simply to affirm that very ancient Aramaic understanding.

As a result, it is not just a matter of choosing Mar Ephraim over the Mishnah vs. choosing the ancestors of the original Mishnah editors and Mar Ephraim over those who came later, because the later authorities clearly have a more subjective agenda than their forebears did.

Finally, the three main sources I use on the Mishnaic side are "The Mishnah" by Jacob Neusner (1992 Yale University Press); The Babylonian Talmud by Michael Rodkinson; and the widely respected works of the

19th century scholar Alfred Edersheim. Edersheim's treatises such as *The Temple: Its Ministry and Services* have been indispensable resources in making much of this difficult material more accessible to the wider world.

Now that we have the ground rules, let's move on.

As in Heaven, So On Earth: A Brief Example:

As a primer to establishing an ancient Scriptural mindset, we need to understand the idea of the heavens ruling over the earth, which is a common refrain going forward, but also of the very patterns of heaven being repeated on the earth:

> Now the sum of the whole is this; *we have a High Priest who is seated on the right hand of the throne of the Majesty in heaven: And he is the minister of the sanctuary and of the true tabernacle which Elohim has pitched, and not man*. For every high priest is established to offer oblations and sacrifices; and therefore, it was proper that this one should also have something to offer. *And if he were on earth, he would not be a priest because there are priests (there) who offer gifts in accordance with Torah*: (namely) *they who minister in the emblem and shadow of the things in heaven: as it was said to Moshe when he was about to build the tabernacle, See and make every thing according to the pattern which was showed you in the mount*. Hebrews 8:1-5 (AENT)[21]

These patterns can range from the majestic, to the poetic to the sublime, but the message is always the same as Y'shua taught:

> Therefore, you pray like this: Our Father in heaven. Hallowed be thy name. Thy Kingdom come. Thy will be done. *As in heaven so on earth*. Matthew 6:9-10 (AENT)

---

21 The Aramaic English New Testament (AENT) is a translation of the most ancient original Aramaic sources of New Testament writings currently available at www.aent.org.

Note that *heavens* come first, and Y'shua also told us to watch the heavens for signs of our salvation coming to the earth:

> *And there will be signs in the sun and in the moon and in the stars.* And on earth, distress of the nations and confusion from the roaring of the sound of the sea. And upheaval that casts out life from men, because of fear of what is about to come upon the earth. *And the powers of heaven will be shaken. And then they will see the Son of man who will come in the clouds with much power and great glory. But when these things begin to happen, have courage and lift up your heads, because your salvation draws near*.
> Luke 21:25-28 (AENT)

It's time to pay attention and see what Scripture has to teach us! One thing is for certain: In Scripture there is no such thing as a meaningless detail!

> If a man dedicated his house as something Set-Apart unto YHWH, the Cohen will judge its quality as good or bad and as the priest judges its value, so will it be valued. If the man who dedicates his house redeems it, he must add one fifth to its value and it will be restored to him. *If a man dedicates to YHWH part of his ancestral land, its value is to be set according to the amount of seed needed for it: A homer of barley seed at fifty shekels of silver.*
> Leviticus 27:14-16 (Matara)

Perhaps you may be thinking, "So what? Fifty shekels for land and barley—what's the big deal!" The "big deal" is that this is part of the valuation for the Jubilee which is a set interval of 50 years! Not only is that not a coincidence, but the number 50 comes up again here:

> You will make loops of blue thread along the edge of the ending curtain in one set, and then do likewise with ending curtain of the second set. You will *make fifty loops* on one curtain *and fifty loops on the ending curtain* of the other set, and the loops will be facing opposite one another. *Then make fifty gold clasps* to join

the curtains together in order that the tabernacle becomes a single unit. Exodus 26:4-6 (Matara)

The word for "tabernacle" in Hebrew also means "to dwell" and the Israelites dwelt *fifty days* when counting the omer between Pesach and Shavuot.Moreover, wherever people dwell, they need something to eat. *Isn't it interesting that the same 50 shekels is fixed to the price of a homer of barley from which we bake bread?* Wouldn't it be interesting if somehow bread/barley and the number fifty would show up again in one place as it does here here?

> And Y'shua went out and saw the many crowds, and he had compassion on them, for they were resembling sheep who had no shepherd, and he began to teach them many things. Then when the time became late, his disciples drew near to him and said to him, "*This place is barren and the time is late. Dismiss them to go into the surrounding fields and villages, and let them buy bread for themselves. For they do not have anything to eat.*" But he said to them, "You give them something to eat." They said to him, "Should we go and buy two hundred Denarii worth of bread and give it to them to eat?" And he said to them, "Go see how much bread you have here." And when they saw, they said to him, "Five loaves of bread and two fish." And he commanded them to seat everyone by groups upon the grass. *And they sat by groups of hundreds and fifties. And he took those five loaves of bread and two fish, and he looked to heaven and blessed and broke the bread and gave it to the disciples to place before them. And those two fish they divided to all*. And all ate and were satisfied. And they took up the fragments, twelve baskets full, and of fish. *And there were five thousand men of those who ate.* Mark 6:34-44 (AENT)

These men sat in groups of "hundreds and fifties". Of course, fifty divides perfectly into one hundred, but probably more interesting to our purposes is this equation:

50 x 100 = 5,000

This is no coincidence. We start with a heavenly pattern of 50 years for the Jubilee, then go to the earthly pattern of the land involved in the Jubilee with a full value of 50 shekels, all the way to the literal tabernacle having 50 holes, one for each of the 50 days the Israelites "tabernacle" during the omer count. Then, since 50 shekels is also fixed to a homer of barley we can see a place in Scripture where people are fed bread in groups of 50 and 100 equaling a total of 5,000 souls.

This is one simple pattern, but there are countless throughout Scripture. Perhaps the reader will think some of these patterns to be coincidental, but the totality of the many interlocking patterns becomes both majestic and elegant while pointing to a Master Architectural design. With those ideas in mind, let's investigate the literal study of *"signs, seasons, days and years"*.

Mechanisms Common to All Four Calendars: Signs, Seasons, Days and Years

Signs

This first step will likely be the most radical one for most, in that I am suggesting we simply take Scripture at its word:

And Elohim said: Let there be lights in the firmament of the heaven to divide the day from the night; and; and let them be for lights in the firmament of the heaven to give light upon the *let them be for signs, and for seasons, and for days and years* earth. And it was so. And Elohim made the two great lights: the greater light to rule the day[22], and the lesser light to rule the night; and the stars. And Elohim set them in the firmament of the heaven to give light upon the earth, and to rule over the day and over the night, and to divide the light from the darkness; and Elohim saw that it was good. And there was evening and there was morning, the fourth day. Genesis 1:14-19 (Matara)

If we go by a plain and simple reading, we see clearly that:

---

22 Samaritan: "the abundance of greater light".

- The lights in the sky were made to separate the day from the night and give light to the earth. These lights include the sun, the moon and the stars.[23]
- The lights in the sky have a greater one that rules the day (sun) and a lesser one that rules the night (moon).[24]
- The sun, moon and the stars are also to serve as **signs, seasons, days and years—in that order.**

This last point is a key to understanding the biblical calendar systems. Without the *signs*, there can be no seasons, days or years. The other parts of time literally wait for the first marker. Here is another point to bear in mind:

> Do you know the ordinances of the heavens or can you set their rule over the earth? Job 38:33 (Matara)

This is a rhetorical question that YHWH asks Job. The point is that Job, who is trying to judge his Maker, cannot do what YHWH is asking. Thus by understanding that the Hebrew style of this passage is really a statement masquerading as a question, we clearly get the answer we need. **YHWH has set the laws of the heavens to rule over the laws of the earth!** As a result, we see the general pattern that the heavens come first, the earth second, and nowhere is this truer than with **sky signs** and **earth signs**.

The first place we see the pattern is, of course, in Genesis 1:1, where the heavens are made first, and then the earth. But what exactly is a "sign"? In Genesis 1:14, the Hebrew word *owth* (אות) is meant to designate a banner or flag, a graphic symbol of a spectacular nature that is impossible to miss.[25] Let's see some other places where *owth* (אות) appears:

---

23 It is fair to point out that the sun and moon are not directly mentioned. However, there is universal agreement that they are meant by the "and it was evening and it was morning" pattern that pervades Genesis 1. Of course there is also ample evidence that the sun controls the day and the moon the night.

24 For an easy confirmation of this fact, see Jeremiah 31:35.

25 It is important to note that there are other sign types throughout the Scriptures as well. The kinds we are discussing here are what I term "covenantal signs" in that they relate to calendar, covenant or ritual instruction issues. On the other hand, "situational signs" are just what the name implies, relating solely to a person, event, place or message. So, the mark of Cain relates to his

And Elohim said, This is the *sign (אות)* of the covenant which I make between me[26] and you and every living creature that is with you, for perpetual generations. *I do set my rainbow in the cloud* and it will be for a *sign (אות) of a covenant between Me and the earth*. And it shall come to pass, when I bring a cloud over the earth, that the rainbow will be seen in the cloud, And I will remember my covenant, which is between me and you and every living creature of all flesh. And the waters shall no more become a flood to destroy all flesh. And the bow shall be in the cloud. And I will look upon it that I may remember the everlasting covenant between Elohim and every living creature of all flesh that is upon the earth. And Elohim said to Noah, *This is the sign (אות) of the covenant which I have established between Me and all flesh that is upon the earth.* (Genesis 9:12-17-Matara)

So we see here:

- The sky sign (rainbow) comes first and is the reminder to YHWH of His covenant with the earth and man.
- The earth sign comes after the sky sign, and is simply the continued existence of the earth.[27]

Let's look at another example of the same idea:

This is my covenant, which you will keep, between me and you and your seed after you. Every male among you shall be circumcised. And you will be circumcised in the flesh of your foreskin. And it shall be a *sign (אות)* of a covenant between[28] me and you. And

---

complaint that others will seek to kill him, and that is obviously situational. The same can be said for the vision of the pregnant woman in Revelation, as that presages a future event, not a call for obedience/observance. On the other hand, sometimes situational signs can suggest the other kind, such as in Isaiah 7:1-13. In that case, Ahaz is being asked to request a sign for his comfort that can be "as high as heaven" (sky) or "as low as Sheol" (earth), but when the king does not answer, YHWH picks one for him.

26 Onkelos and Jonathan: "between my Word…", also in verse 17.

27 We also see elsewhere in this speech, the definitions that YHWH gives to time in Genesis 8:22: "As long as the earth endures, seedtime and harvest, cold and heat, summer and winter, day and night will never cease." This also dovetails, of course, with a solar year.

28 Jonathan: "Between My Word and you."

he that is eight days old shall be circumcised among you, every male throughout your generations, he that is born in the house, or bought with money of any foreigner that is not of your seed. He that is born in your house, and he that is bought with your money, must be circumcised. And my covenant shall be in your flesh for an everlasting covenant. And the uncircumcised male who is not circumcised in the flesh of his foreskin, that soul shall be cut off from his people. He has broken my covenant. Genesis 17:10-14 (Matara)

The sky sign, in this case is creation itself, as the Hebrew the words for "in the beginning" (*bereshit*- בראשית) and "covenant" (*breet*- ברית) are closely related. It, therefore, can literally be said that the covenant was in creation, and this covenant requires an earth sign of obedience, that of circumcision. Now, let's investigate another way the sky sign of covenant manifests on earth:

Then YHWH said to Moshe, speak to the Israelites: You must **surely keep** (**shomer**- שמר) My Shabbats. This will be a **sign** (אות) between Me and you, for all the generations to come, that you may know that I am YHWH who has made you Set-Apart. Keep guard over and observe the Shabbat, for it is Set-Apart unto you. Everyone who pollutes it will surely die, for whoever expands their domain [works][29], that person will be cut off from the midst of their people. For six whole days are for expanding your domain but the seventh there is Shabbat of Shabbats[30]—total rest—that is

---

29 The word here translated as "work" is *melaka* (מְלָאכָה) which is the same word as "kingdom/domain". The "work" reading may seem puzzling since, sometimes, objects used in synagogue service, like Torah scrolls, are heavier than the objects people are supposed to avoid picking up on Shabbat. In later centuries, Nehemiah, and others will define this word as indicating a person's normal, for-profit, endeavors being set aside on Shabbat. This is the intended meaning by Moshe here, that a person should not "expand their domain through normal working activities". What must be set aside can vary from person to person, depending on their occupation. For example, if music is my hobby (and it is) then I may play music to relax on Shabbat. But if music is my profession, I cannot play a concert for money on Shabbat because that's how I make my living on the other days of the week. So the same activity can be allowed or forbidden on Shabbat depending on a person's job.

30 Hebrew phrase *shabbat shabbaton* (שַׁבַּת שַׁבָּתוֹן) is meant to emphasize the double meaning of "seventh" and "rest". When two meanings of the same word/root are jammed together in this manner, it is termed, in Hebrew, a double amplifier. As a result, the "rest" meaning is powerfully brought home as the tantamount requirement for the seventh day, to the degree that one cannot think about one without knowing to do the other.

Set-Apart unto YHWH. Whoever expands their domain through work will certainly be put to death. So the descendants of Israel are to observe the Shabbat throughout all their long cycles of time[31] as an eternal covenant. It will be a *sign* (אות) between Me and the Israelites for all time, because in six days YHWH created the heavens and the earth, but on the seventh, He ceased working and was refreshed. Exodus 31:21-27 (Matara)

In another very clear reference, the creation itself is the sky sign. YHWH chose six "days" of creation, and then rested on the seventh, to consider His great work, and bless it. Without the creation/sky sign, there would be no Sabbath. As for the earth sign, it is the **observance of the Sabbath** by man.[32] This idea, of course, leads to why the Hebrew word *shomer* is highlighted, which is usually translated as "observe". As we will see later, "observe" does not mean as much "to see" as it does "to guard, keep account of". In other words, *shomer* is really about counting as a way to ensure accuracy, although repeated sighted patterns are the foundation behind the counting patterns. In this case, and later, we will see other examples of how we are, literally, counting towards each seventh day to mimic the creative cycle of YHWH per His instructions.

Returning to signs; we need to look at two additional examples from the book of Exodus. The first is when YHWH speaks to Moshe (in Exodus 3). His very presence in the Burning Bush is the sky sign!

But Moshe said to Elohim, "Who am I that I should go to Pharaoh and that I should bring the children of Israel out of Egypt?" *And*

---

31 This word for "generation": *dor* (דוֹר) connotes a longer cycle (Genesis 15:13) of a hundred years rather than the usual forty. It is used here to emphasize the long duration and eternal nature of the statute.

32 It is also fair to point out that the seventh day Shabbat is sometimes described as a *moed*, or appointed time or season. However, the Shabbat is an absolute seven day cycle that is not set by the sun or moon. Rather, in places such as Leviticus 23:2-3, the context is with respect to the Sabbath that happens throughout the year. As such, Sabbaths are bound to occur within the years and months described, even as the lunar appointments count days to sacred festivals. On the other hand, the Shabbat also transcends the year in the sense that the counting does not stop between the last day of year X and the first day of year Y. Instead, we keep counting through the weeks even when the previous year gives way to the next one. So, it is actually both a sign and a season, the latter only being in the sense that Sabbaths occur every seventh day, including the weeks that annual feasts occur.

*He said, "Certainly I will be with you and here is the sign (אות)
to you that it is I Who have sent you*: When you have brought
the children of Israel out of Egypt, *you will bow down to Elohim
on this mountain.*" Then Moshe said to Elohim, "Behold! I am
going to the people[33] of Israel and will tell them, 'The elohim[34]
of your fathers has sent me to you' but then they may say back to
me, 'What is his name?' then what do I tell them? Elohim said
to Moshe, "Ehyeh Asher Ehyeh[35] [I am Who I am; I will be Who
I will be]. You will say to the people of Israel: *Ehyeh [I AM]
has sent me to you.*" And Elohim continued and said to Moshe,
"Thus you will say to the people of Israel, "YAHWEH [He that is],
the elohim of your fathers, the elohim of Avraham, the elohim of
Yitzkhak and the elohim of Ya'akov, has sent me to you." This is
My Name forever and my memorial name for all time." Exodus
3:11-15 (Matara)

YHWH's name - Ehyeh Asher Ehyeh, I am who I am, as well as, the third
person version that man uses (He is = YHWH), are the banner for Moshe.
YHWH's assuring promise "and I will be with you" is also a sky sign
and, just like before, these sky signs are followed by earth signs here:

Then Moshe said, "What if they will not believe me or listen to
me and then say, 'YHWH did not appear to you'?" Then YHWH
answered him, "What is in your hand?" "A staff," he replied. Then
YHWH said: "Throw it on the ground." Moshe then threw the
staff on to the ground and it became a serpent and he ran from it.
Then YHWH said: "Reach out your hand and grasp it by its tail."
Moshe then reached out and took hold of the snake and it changed
back into the staff in his hand. "This," YHWH said, "is so that

33 The text literally says "sons of Israel" throughout, but the intended meaning is the entire
people of Israel, not just the men.
34 "Elohim" is used here as a descriptor, not a title. If YHWH was saying, "I am the Elohim of
your fathers", then it would be properly capitalized.
35 *Ehyeh Asher Ehyeh* is "to be" in the first person, where YHWH says in essence, "this is the Name
I call Myself". It is the fact that YHWH says "My Name for myself is simply that I exist" which is the
extra revelation given to Moshe. However, Abraham was also told in Genesis 13:14 that Elohim was called
"YHWH". In that case, YHWH is really "He is", or the male third person form of Ehyeh. So Abraham only
knew "He is/was/will be" {YHWH} as the Name, but Moshe understood the meaning behind the Name,
that YHWH applies it to Himself directly. As a result, there is no contradiction between YHWH revealing
Himself as YHWH to Abraham and making the meaning of His Name fully known to Moshe.

they might believe that YHWH, the Elohim of their ancestors, has appeared to you." Then YHWH said: "Put your hand inside your cloak and upon your chest." So Moshe put his hand into his cloak and when he took it out it was full of leprosy and white as snow. "Now put it back into your cloak", He said. So Moshe put his hand back into his cloak and when he took it out, it was restored to health, the same tone and quality as the rest of his flesh. ***Then YHWH said, "If they do not believe you or pay attention to the first miraculous sign (אות), they may believe the second. But if they do not believe these two signs or listen to you, take some water from the Nile and pour it on the dry ground. The water you take from the river will become blood on the ground."***
Exodus 4:1-9 (Matara)

Even the tenth plague, the slaying of the first born, can be said to follow this pattern. The instructions of YHWH are the sky sign, followed by the observance of His command to put lamb's blood on the doorposts. Then the presence of YHWH comes from the sky, ***passing over, or sparing the household*** when He sees the earth sign of the blood which is, the sign of obedience. However, lest the reader feels this trend is confined to just the Tanakh, the Renewed Covenant also follows these exact same rules.[36] The most obvious example, of course, the Star of Bethlehem, needs little proof to designate it as a sky sign!

But the pattern is much deeper than that, as it becomes a key part of Y'shua's own discourses:

And immediately after the suffering of those days, the sun will be darkened and the moon will not shine its light. And the stars will fall from heaven, and the powers of heaven will be shaken. ***And then will be seen the sign of the Son of man in heaven, and then all the tribes of the land mourn, when they will see the Son of man who comes upon the clouds of heaven with great power and***

---

36 It is important to stress that the Aramaic Renewed Covenant, in the vast majority of cases, simply carries over the exact Hebrew word אות into its dialect fully intact as the cognate אתא (*ata*). This is the case, for example, in Matthew 12:38-40, when Y'shua discusses the Sign of Jonah. However, another interesting variant meaning closer to the "vision" meaning of sign, as in Luke 1:22. There the Aramaic word *ramaz* (Hebrew, *remez*), which usually means something closer to "hint" or "clue of insight" is used.

glory. And he will send his Messengers with a large trumpet, and they will gather his chosen ones from the four winds from one end of heaven to the other." Matthew 24:29-31 (AENT)

And he (Y'shua) said to the crowds, *"When you see a cloud that rises from the west, immediately you say, 'Rain is coming.' And it happens thus. And when the south wind blows you say, 'There will be heat.' And it happens. Hypocrites! You know to distinguish the appearance of the earth and of the heavens, but you do not know how to distinguish this time.* And of yourselves, why do you not judge right? Luke 12:54-57 (AENT)

There is also a pecking order in heaven with respect to sky signs themselves. Put simply, ***sun signs rule over moon signs.*** Notice the use of the Hebrew word *gadol* (גדול) to describe the sun as the "greater" light. This word does not refer exclusively to the level of light that the sun produces when compared to the moon for a simple reason: YHWH knows the moon does not produce any light on its own! It simply reflects light from the sun. In that sense, the image we are presented with is the sun entrusting the moon with its light.

Another proof of this is how the word *gadol* is used elsewhere. There are some verses where the extent of something's light magnitude denotes a sense of authority. For example, the High Priest is called *kohen ha gadol*, and there is little doubt that the high priests' power as a master over the other priests and Levites is implied as opposed to the extent of his "luminosity". This is the same way the "greater light" gives permission for the moon to rise and take its light.

In addition, Scripture demonstrates this same idea:

This is what YHWH says: The heavens are My throne and the earth is My footstool. Where is the House you will build for Me? Where will My resting place be? Isaiah 66:1 (Matara)

Which is more likely to have royal power, the throne (heaven) or the earth (footstool)?

Jeremiah then adds an interesting twist, linking the heavenly covenant with the earthly one:

> For this is what YHWH says: "David will never fail to have a man sit on the throne of the house of Israel, nor will the Cohenim [priests], who are Levites, ever fail to have a man stand before Me and continually offer burnt offerings and to offer sacrifices." The word of YHWH came to Jeremiah: "This is what YHWH says: "*If you can break My covenant with the days and My covenant with the nights, so that the day and the night no longer come at their appointed times, then also my covenant with David My servant and My covenant with the Levites who are Cohenim serving before Me may be broken!* But I will make the descendants of David My servant and the Levites who serve before Me as the myriads of the heavens are beyond counting as the sands on the seashores cannot be measured. The word of YHWH came again to Jeremiah saying: "Have you not heard what the people are saying—that YHWH has rejected His two chosen kingdoms? So now they despise these people and no longer consider them a true nation." But this is what YHWH says: "*If I have not established my covenant with day and night and the fixed laws of heaven and earth, then I will reject the descendants of Ya'akov and David My servant and will not choose one of his sons to rule over the descendants of Abraham, Yitzkhak and Ya'akov.* For I will restore their fortunes and have compassion on them." (Jeremiah 33:17-26-Matara)

The final Scriptural validation comes from Ecclesiastes, where the power of judgment resides clearly under the sun, with YHWH, of course, as the ultimate authority:

> And I saw something else *under the sun: In the place of judgment* there is wickedness, and in the place of justice, wickedness was there. I thought at my innermost being, Elohim will bring judgment to the righteous and the wicked for there will be time for every delight and a time for every task. Ecclesiastes 3:16-17 (Matara)[37]

---

37   Also see Revelation 12:1-6, where the sign of a pregnant woman has the sun at her head and the moon at her feet, indicating the sun in a superior position.

And Philo adds this insight on the same idea:

> He (YHWH) has assigned to him a complete number, **as the sun is ordained to be the chief of the stars of heaven**, under an appointed number, in the time which came before the period of his repentance, to lead to the oblivion of the sins previously committed; since, as Elohim is good, he bestows the greatest favors most abundantly, and, at the same time, he effaces the former offenses of those who devote themselves to him, and which might deserve chastisement, by a recollection of their virtues. (Questions & Answers - Genesis 1:84)

This representative sample should suffice for understanding the meaning of signs, the first major definition in our study. Let's move on to unlocking the rest of Genesis 1:14-19.

Seasons

The Scriptures tell us the seasons do not begin prior to this phenomenon making its appearance. In Hebrew then, the next word that we need to look at is *moed* (מועד) which, as indicated earlier, also means "appointed time".

The first season of the year is, of course, spring, called *Abib* in Scripture. The characteristics of spring involve the earth returning to a state of greenness, which is why we are told in Exodus to observe that moment of the year as its beginning. Karaites hold that the sign of spring is the tender and green ears of the barley, the first of the produce to ripen in Israel. However, they are incorrect that Abib has started when the barley ripens, at the end of the lunar year. Barley is the earth sign, but it requires the sky sign to precede it before the season can officially begin.

It is important to understand that the first two commands to "observe Abib" don't take place in the Land of Israel. The first Abib occurred in Egypt and the second was in the Wilderness. Such a pattern begs several questions of the Karaite position. Which barley "counts" since it ripens gradually over several weeks? Is one part of Israel superior to others?

What about the places where the command was originally given, that were both outside of Israel? Where is the biblical procedure that tells us where we get the barley? How much barley needs to be ripened? Who does it and who judges the matter?

There are, of course, basic answers to these questions, however such is assumed by the Karaites, who add their own religious traditions and authority to Torah, even while criticizing the Rabbis[38] for doing the very same thing! If we know there is a sky sign that will always point to when the barley is ripe which is in harmony with the Torah in places like Genesis 1:14-19, then no additional procedures are required. We simply wait for the sky sign; the barley will have been ripened by receiving required sunshine, and we're all ready to go!

What we can also say about the *moedim* is that once the time is set, the moon controls the ordering of the sacred festivals:

> "The moon marks off the seasons, and the sun knows when to go down." Psalm 104:19 (NIV)

Philo provides an interesting commentary on this verse:

> [59] And before now some men have conjecturally predicted disturbances and commotions of the earth from the revolutions of the heavenly bodies, and innumerable other events which have turned out most exactly true: so that it is a most veracious saying that "the stars were created to act as signs, and moreover to mark the seasons." And by the word seasons the divisions of the year are here intended. And why may not this be reasonably affirmed? For what other idea of opportunity can there be except that it is the time for success? And the seasons bring everything to perfection and set everything right; giving perfection to the sowing and planting of fruits, and to the birth and growth of animals. [60] *They were also created to serve as measures of time; for it is by the appointed*

---

38 Karaites are a minor (9th century CE) and relatively insignificant sect compared to the Pharisees who trace their origin to the Hasmonean dynasty 140 BCE. The major powerbrokers, when it came to calendar issues were the Pharisees. See Pharisaic Calendar in Appendix.

periodical revolutions of the sun and moon and other stars, that days and months and years are determined. (On Creation 1:59-60)

The moon is still subject to the solar year, because without it, these same holidays that are keyed to harvest and planting will occur out of season. As long as those appointed times stay on track, the moon is in charge. When it needs help to keep the festivals at their proper time, the sun takes over. In so doing, both the sun and the moon mark the year as Scripture says.

Days

Once the sun hands control of time over to the moon to show when spring begins, the sacred days are marked from the beginning of the Synodic month,[39] or in Biblical terms, from New Moon to New Moon. This reckoning, however, is only valid from Moshe's day on, since, prior to that time YHWH did not institute festivals that were timed in this manner.

To study and understand the calendar as it was before Moshe, we must preview what will be a fairly extensive discussion later. There was a 12 month calendar of 30 days each, or a 360 day year. How that synchs to our actual solar year will be addressed later, but, suffice to say, Scripture shows examples of consecutive 30 day months, not possible in a lunar system.

Both Philo and Josephus will testify this was the case, as does ancient archaeological evidence that this was understood throughout Israel, as well as Egypt, Persia and Babylon, to name just a few.

My basic purpose in this section on "days" is simply to show that a 30 day period was the normative reckoning astride the more familiar lunar cycle. In fact, Tanakh and Josephus show us that, even towards the end of Moshe's life, the two systems coexisted. Let's see why:

---

39 Synodic is the scientific term for marking the lunar month from one New Moon to another, or 29.53 days. Other methods of marking a lunation can be shorter by as much as two days. Biblical data only recognizes this method of measurement.

[327] Now Moses lived in all one hundred and twenty years; a third part of which time, abating one month, he was the people's ruler; *and he died on the last month of the year, which is called by the Macedonians Dystros, but by us Adar, on the first day of the month.* [330] *So the people mourned for him thirty days;* nor did ever any grief so deeply affect the Hebrews as did this upon the death of Moses. (Antiquities 4:327, 330, also Deuteronomy 34:8)

[78] Then it was that Miriam, the sister of Moses, came to her end, having completed her fortieth year since she left Egypt, *on the first day of the lunar month of Xanthikos [April-Abib].* They then made a public funeral for her, at a great expense. She was buried upon a certain mountain, which they call Sin: and when *they had mourned for her thirty days*, Moses purified the people... (Antiquities 4:78, also Numbers 20:1)

[84] He died in the same year wherein he lost his sister, having lived in all a hundred twenty and three years. *He died on the first day of that lunar month which is called by the Athenians Hekatombaion, by the Macedonians Loos, but by the Hebrews Ab.* [85] *The people mourned for Aaron thirty days...* (Antiquities 4:84-85, also Numbers 20:29)

As we can see, sometimes Josephus says "lunar month" and sometimes he doesn't. Sometimes the month he names has 30 days (Abib) and other times 29 (Ab, Adar). And yet, in spite of that variety, *the normal mourning period in Israel for a great person passing is 30 days, not just a lunar month! Please notice that all three people died on the first day of that month, and are mourned precisely 30 days!*

Josephus may be mentioning "lunar month" for two reasons. First, in terms of synching to festivals and second, because the Greeks and Macedonians also kept lunar months. Post-Moshe, no one can deny that lunar months were important for festival keeping, but, it was never an acceptable counting method on it's own.

Here is another series from Josephus:

[80] This calamity happened in the six hundredth year of Noah's government [age], in the second month, called by the Macedonians Dios, but by the Hebrews Marchesuan ; for so did they order their year in Egypt; [81] but Moses appointed that Nisan [April], which is the same with Xanthikos, should be the first month for their festivals, because he brought them out of Egypt in that month: so that this month began the year as to all the solemnities they observed to the honour of God.. (Antiquities 1:80-81)

Egypt kept a 12 month, 30 day per month calendar and used the remainder of the year for 5 days of chaos "between years"! If Josephus is right, the Israelites initially ordered their months on this system, though how long both systems existed side by side may never be precisely known. This next quotation from Josephus is particularly revealing for our inquiry:

[318] They left Egypt in the month of Xanthikos, **on the fifteenth day of the lunar month**; four hundred and thirty years after our forefather Abraham came into Canaan, but two hundred and fifteen years after Jacob moved into Egypt. {a} [319] It was the eightieth year of the age of Moses, and of that of Aaron three more. They also carried out the bones of Joseph with them, as he had charged his sons to do. (Antiquities 2:318-319)

This is the first time "lunar month" needs to be mentioned! That cannot be a coincidence, because now we need the moon to track Pesach.
Not to be outdone, Philo also references a standard mourning period of 30 days regardless of the time of year:

[110] Moreover, if, after having taken prisoners in a sally, you should entertain a desire for a beautiful woman amongst them [Deuteronomy 21:10], do not satiate your passion, treating her as a captive, but act with gentleness, and pity her change of fortune, and alleviate her calamity, regulating everything for the best; [111] **and you will alleviate her sufferings if you cut the hair of her head, and trim her nails, and take off from her the garment which she wore when she was taken prisoner, and leave her alone for thirty days, during which period you shall permit her with impunity**

to mourn and bewail her father and her mother, and her other relations, from whom she has been separated by their death, or by their being subjected to the calamity of slavery which is worse than death. [112] And, after that period, you shall cohabit with her as with a legitimate wedded wife; for it is right that one who is about to ascend the bed of her husband, not for hire, like a harlot who makes a traffic of the flower of her beauty, but either out of love for him who has espoused her, or for the sake of the procreation of children, should be thought worthy of the ordinances which belong to a legitimate marriage. [113] On which account the lawgiver has given all his laws with great beauty. For, in the first place, he had not permitted appetite to proceed onwards in its unbridled course, with stiff-necked obstinacy, but he has checked its vehement impetuosity, compelling it to rest for thirty days. (On Virtue 1:110-113)[40]

Elsewhere in the Tanakh we find that, just like prisoners in our own time, punishment is meted out in 30 day increments:

[7] All the chief rulers of the kingdom, the chiefs and the captains, the wise men and the rulers, have made a common decision to put in force a law having the king's authority, and to give a strong order, that whoever makes any request to any god or man but you, O King, *for thirty days, is to be put into the lions' hole.* (Daniel 6:7 BBE)

Or here where thirty days just seems like a really long time to wait for an opportunity:

[11] It is common knowledge among all the king's servants and the people of every part of the kingdom, that if anyone, man or woman, comes to the king in his inner room without being sent for, there is only one law for him, that he is to be put to death; only those to whom the king's rod of gold is stretched out may keep their lives: *but I have not been sent for to come before the king these thirty days.* (Esther 4:11 BBE)

---

40 And the actual reference, Deuteronomy 21:10-13, says "a full month", which Philo calls 30 days long.

This next example requires some explanation:

> [12] And Samson said, Now I have a hard question for you: if you are able to give me the answer before the seven days of the feast are over, I will give you thirty linen robes and thirty changes of clothing; [13] But if you are not able to give me the answer, then you will have to give me thirty linen robes and thirty changes of clothing. And they said to him, Put your hard question and let us see what it is. (Judges 14:12-13 BBE)

> After the plowing is over, the fields are deserted until after the winter rains, unless an unusually severe storm of rain and hail (Ex 9:25) has destroyed the young shoots. Then a second sowing is made. In April, if the hot east winds have not blasted the grain (see BLASTING) the barley begins to ripen. The wheat follows from a week to six weeks later, depending upon the altitude. *Toward the end of May or the first week in June, which marks the beginning of the dry season, reaping begins. Whole families move out from their village homes to spend the time in the fields until the harvest is over. Men and women join in the work of cutting the grain.* – ISBE Bible Dictionary

The reason I put these two quotes together is because Judges 15:1 tells us this happened around the time of the cutting of the grain in the latter part of spring, meaning either the 2nd or 3rd month of the Hebrew year. In the calendar system post-Moshe that we will describe later, it is possible for each of the first two Hebrew months, depending on the cycles of the moon, to have 29 or 30 days. In fact, the first month, Abib, might have 30 days in year 1 and 29 days in year 2, and vice versa for the second and third months. As a result, the variable day lengths that are possible for individual months in this period still seem to be set aside for the normal perception of a 30 day month. Such a reckoning of the months that may be going through the star constellations would have been understood by both the ancient Israelites as well as the Philistines.

Years

And now, as we look at years, very little needs to be said. The days, of course, eventually run out, but the Shabbat count is constant even when the next seventh day runs into the following year.

The year also waits for the return of the signs before it officially "dies". That means that sun, moon and earth signs must all agree that the time is right. We can also calculate the proper interval, regardless of the calendar to which we are referring.

The Balancing of 40 and 7

One of the most important concepts that underlay all the calendars is the role of the number 40. In simple terms, 40 represents the interval of balancing, just as 7 represents the interval of perfection. What I mean by this is, whenever a problem gets out of hand, 40 is the interval that will bring correction and restore equilibrium. This can either be 40 days or 40 years, depending on the issue.

In Genesis we are told that the earth is filled with wicked men except for one and his family; clearly a situation of imbalance! So YHWH saves the righteous man Noah and his family and sends rain for 40 days and 40 nights to cleanse the earth of evil. Some time later, Moshe breaks the first tablets of the Ten Commandments and is ordered by YHWH to carve out new replacements. This was another period of 40 days and 40 nights.

Similarly, 40 years is a frequent marker of "generations" in Scripture. It takes 40 years for Israel to purge itself from the sin of worshipping the Golden Calf "until all of that generation was consumed". After 40 years, balance is restored and they can then enter into the Promised Land. And finally, Y'shua hungers and thirsts for 40 days and 40 nights before haSatan (the adversary) comes to tempt him! Moshe's life is neatly divided across three 40 year periods. Intervals of 40 regularly apply to generations of Israel from the Exodus to Solomon (1 Kings 6:1) as well as the literal life spans of many Biblical figures.

Considering Moshe's relationship with the number 40, we also find he is raised in the Egyptian royal court for 40 years. He spends 40 years on the run in Midian before deciding to free the Hebrews. The last 40 years of his life are spent in the Wilderness leading his people toward the Promised Land. Israel's two greatest kings, David and Solomon, also reigned 40 years each.

The question is, how does the number 40 balance the year along with 7? The answer has to do with establishing a 360 day year for the ancients. When we address this shortly, we will have established 12 months of 30 days each, and there will be a leap month of 30 days at the end of every 6 years bringing us close to the actual 365.2422 day cycle.

The key point here is that in cycles of 4,000 years or more, 7 and 40 work this way in 360 day years:

Year: **1, 2, 3, 4, 5, 6** (add) **LEAP MONTH**

("LEAP MONTH" means one 30 day month has been added that year.)

The leap month must be added because the average number of days per year over the span of 6 years almost perfectly matches the actual length of the year, and the 7th year gets to "rest" a Shabbat (of one month long). This parallels our rest every seventh day(Shabbat) and the Land rest every 7th year. Let's continue:

Year: 7, 8, 9, 10, 11, 12 {**LEAP 2**}, 13, 14, 15, 16, 17, 18 {**LEAP 3**}, 19, 20, 21, 22, 23, 24 {**LEAP 4**}, 25, 26, 27, 28, 29, 30 {**LEAP 5**}, 31, 32, 33, 34, 35, 36 {**LEAP 6**}...

Here we have 6 leap months that occur within 36 years. Now the calendar needs precise balancing to keep the right number of days per year in synch with the sun. Thus, 40 comes to the rescue again to "balance" it:

...Year: 37, 38, 39 {**LEAP 7**}, 40.

We find in this sequence of leap months that the average number of days per year approximates the average solar year of 365.2422. Thus, at the end of the generation, both 40 and 7 bring balance and perfection! Later, we will examine how the math works.

In the Beginning...Darkness

> He reveals mysteries from the darkness and brings the deep darkness into light. Job 12:22 (Matara)

> He has inscribed a circle on the surface of the waters at the boundary of light and darkness. The pillars of heaven tremble and are awestruck at His rebuke. Job 26:10-11 (Matara)

Many tend to think of darkness as a bad thing when studying Scripture and often it is, but darkness clearly has its place within the righteousness of YHWH as well. We are told in Genesis 1 that the day begins in darkness. In fact, darkness is the natural state of all things prior to YHWH performing the creative act in Genesis 1:3. As such, darkness precedes light.

Now, let's extend that idea into scientific parlance. Apparently, our Universe began with "the Big Bang" which is the "light" mentioned in Genesis. Physics tells us that both time and space began in this moment. We must remember that our Eternal El, YHWH, is beyond time and space and, therefore, before time and space.

Darkness is where YHWH hid His secrets (Isaiah 45) and its Set-Apart function is to be the canvas from which light and life were born.

> Have the gates of death been revealed to you, or have you seen the gates of deep darkness? Have you understood the full breadth of the earth? Tell *Me*, if you know all this. Job 38:17-18 (Matara)

Darkness only becomes "evil" when it attempts to re-assert itself outside of YHWH's plan and seeks to supplant the life and light that YHWH created for His purposes.

Once the light comes, however, there is no going back to "pure" darkness per se. Now, every day will be reckoned, not from night to night but from "evening to evening" as in "and there was evening and there was morning, day one". Everything is within its place and time, under YHWH's express command.

> Where is the way to the abode of the light? And darkness, where is its dwelling, that you may take it to its territory and that you may understand the ways to its home? Job 38:19-20 (Matara)

The English word "evening", derived from the Hebrew *ereb*, means a time when light and shadows mix, so forevermore and since the very beginning, darkness has had to deal with the reality that there is and will always be a light somewhere in the Universe. Darkness may dominate the landscape in its season, but it will never be as it was before time. The light, in effect, has forever limited darkness from its former total dominion, which is exactly how YHWH willed it.[41]

We must also consider darkness in its Set-Apart and YHWH-intended form. Darkness is an integral mechanism with light used to mark the seasons and to divide the day and night. The Hebrew day, which is solar, nevertheless, begins and ends in darkness; so darkness is the "bookend" of time itself.

As we will see later, the year also begins and ends in darkness. The last month of the Hebrew year, Adar, means "*to darken*". We will revisit this principle repeatedly in a wide variety of places. This is why the month also begins in darkness, sometime between the conjunction of the New Moon and the appearance of the crescent. The "appearing crescent" is a backwards looking marker to the time the month began as opposed to heralding the beginning of the new month. Since the darkness is allowed as a controlling mechanism for the stars, it must also be the case that the moon sets the Hebrew month.

> He who made the Pleiades and Orion and changes deep darkness into morning, Who also darkens day *into* night, Who calls for the

---

41 As Isaiah points out in 45:7, YHWH created the darkness for His express purposes. Sometimes the darkness is also sent as a harbinger of His wrath, (Joel 2:31).

waters of the sea and pours them out on the surface of the earth? YHWH is His Name! Amos 5:8 (Matara)

Who commands the sun not to shine, and sets a seal upon the stars? Who alone spreads out the heavens and treads down upon the waves of the sea? Who makes Aldebaran[42], Orion and the Pleiades, and the chambers of the south? Who does great things that cannot be uncovered and extraordinary works without number? Job 9:7-10 (Matara)

Tracking the 360-Day Year Pre-Civilization

Another way to look at how primitive man may have perceived the length of the year as 360 days in practical terms, before the rise of settled farming communities, was offered by my dear friend Bill Welker. Bill Welker, an air force veteran, who has a background in physics, and astronomy, adroitly suggested the following:

Step 1: *Imagine that you are Adam and you watch the stars around the North pole star each and every night.*

Each night you cut a notch in a stick to record one "day".

You ultimately see that the star you were watching, went all the way around the "center" and was pretty much back where it was a "year" ago.

So your stick-accounting has notches that like this:

|||||||||||||||||||||||||||||||||||||||||||||||||||||||||||||||||||||||||||||||||||||||||||||||||||||||||||||||||||||||||
(please imagine approx. 360 notches)

Step 2: *Similarly, you watch for the reappearance of the Moon after it was "eaten" by the Sun and you keep sticks of the number of days between the last time the moon was first seen and the next time it reappears after*

---

42 See Illustrations: Building the Wheel of Stars in Appendix.

being "eaten". You end up with many shorter sticks like this:

|||||||||||||||||||||||||||||||

(of 29, 30 and 31 notches)

Note: Some "moon stick groups" will have 29 notches, some 30 and a few—perhaps because you "goofed"—could have 31!

Step 3: *One day you lay your "moon sticks" next to your "sun sticks". A bit of trial and error and you discover that "12 moon sticks" fit next to "1 sun stick"! A bit more trial and error results in 12 moon sticks, each with the same number of notches which fit perfectly next to a sun stick with 360 notches. You then discard sun sticks with too many "notches". It might look something like this:*

(imagine 360 sun notches above and 12 sticks of 30 days below.)

Hopefully, you get the idea. Adam (or his descendant) ultimately sees that precisely 12 moon sticks line up on 1 "sun stick", and the 360-day year is born, with 12 "months" of 30 days – the only way it can fit.

Using this method, a 365-day year does not work, as 12 months of 30 days won't "fit". So, knowing nothing about math or orbital mechanics, you conclude it must "fit", and you soon see that if each "moon stick" has 30 ticks, and the "sun stick" has 360 "ticks" (though you really don't know what "360" is), then 12 moon sticks "fits" - exactly!

Thus, the 360-day, 12 month year is born. You don't learn until *much* later that something is wrong. Once you recognize that the stars not near the pole "reappear" on the horizon every 365 days, you see that your calendar is amiss. Then, you realize that the moon is not "reappearing" after 12 "sightings" exactly when it should if your "Sun stick & Moon stick Calendar" was correct. By then, everyone in the world was using a 360-day year, with 12 months. Great minds came along much later and "fixed" the problems by adding another "month." *The rest is history...*

How Do the Stars Keep Time?

And Elohim said: Let there be lights in the firmament of the heaven to divide the day from the night; and; and let them be for lights in the firmament of the heaven to give light upon the earth and *let them be for signs, and for seasons, and for days and years*. And it was so. And Elohim made the two great lights: the greater light to rule the day, and the lesser light to rule the night; *and the stars*. And Elohim set them in the firmament of the heaven to give light upon the earth, and to rule over the day and over the night, and to divide the light from the darkness; and Elohim saw that it was good. And there was evening and there was morning, the fourth day. Genesis 1:14-19 (Matara)

One question that precious few consider is this: What is the role of the stars in bringing about the seasons, as is clearly stated in the quotation above and here:

*"Can you bind the beautiful Pleiades? Can you loose the cords of Orion? Can you bring forth the **Wheel of Stars**[43] into its seasons and stand in the path of Ayish/Iyutha (Aldebaran) and her satellites (Hyades). Do you know the laws of the heavens and can you establish their rule over the earth?...Have you given wisdom to the Lance Star (Antares) or intelligence to the Bow Star?"* (Hebrew & Aramaic Job 38:31-33, 38, cross referenced to the translation of T.K. Cheyne: Journal of Biblical Literature, Vol. 17, No. 1 (1898), pp. 103-107)

Once again, it bears repeating: YHWH uses the constellations themselves to mark off the seasons, so, if at this early period, the moon is not marking the months, a point we visit later, there had to be another mechanism that spoke to how to count the days of a full 365.2422 day year that

---

43 The original translator writes "Zodiac", but this can be a confusing term. The NAS Old Testament Hebrew Lexicon defines the Hebrew word *mazzaroth*, "the 12 signs of the Zodiac and their 36 associated constellations." It is important that a clear distinction be made between the Zodiac/Wheel of Stars as an absolute marker for a region of the sky as opposed to the dwelling places of false deities.

would work side by side with the "practical" 360 day/year system to be described later.

Perhaps the best way to show this before giving the full explanation is to consider the calendar of ancient Egypt, which Moshe himself was familiar with. The Egyptians kept 12 months, 30 days each, and then the remaining 5+ days were considered "between the years". They also tracked the rising of what we call Sirius or the Dog Star to synchronize their sacred year, which ran on a different schedule than their civil year, much like the Jewish calendar does today. Then, once every 1,460 years the two main calendars would come back into synchronization and the result was a tremendously festive year for the Egyptians when magic seemed to return to the earth in force.

The use of constellations, along with the solar cycle, coordinating the rising and setting of the sun with a given star or group of stars was exactly the way Adam, Noah and Abraham also timed their planting and harvest seasons. The 360 day system would have never allowed seeding and harvest to get too far out of season before adjusting with a 30 day leap month at the end of 6 years. The stars and constellations would have provided the "double check." They would, for example, look for the sun to rise in Aries to know spring had begun. Even if they officially counted their months in 30 day increments, they would seed and plant crops according to the stars.

I call this parallel system: ***the Constellation Clock***, and its "months," I suspect you will already be familiar with:

Aries: March 21-April 20
Taurus: April 21-May 20
Gemini: May 21-June 20
Cancer: June 21-July 20
Leo: July 21-August 20
Virgo: August 21-September 20
Libra: September 21-October 20
Scorpio: October 21-November 20
Sagittarius: November 21-December 20

Capricorn: December 21-January 20
Aquarius: January 21-February 20
Pisces: February 21-March 20

Aries and Libra are highlighted because they are special times. These "star-months" begin precisely at the time of the vernal and autumnal equinoxes. Both Josephus and Philo mention this fact and tie the festivals of Pesach (Passover) and Sukkot (Feast of Tabernacles) not only to the full moons but to the full moons immediately after their respective equinoxes. What this means in simple terms is that while Pesach cannot start prior to the Vernal Equinox, its position in relation to that event will determine Sukkot's timing, which can be either before or after the Autumnal Equinox.

As a result, the constellations, full moon and the sun all had a role in setting these great feasts in ancient Israel! How the Israelites would have "seen" the equinox, has to do with two special stars that are directly opposite one another along the "ecliptic" which is an imaginary straight line across the visible sky with each of these "border stars"—Aldebaran and Antares—forming the dots that connect the line. Bill Welker explains how tracking these equinoxes with these stars was very easy for ancient Israel to do:

> In Moshe's time, when the sun *was* in Aries at the Vernal Equinox (VE), on March 21ˢᵗ, it was pretty close to Aldebaran (52 degrees, (also within about 25 degrees of the Pleiades). As the sun is making its annual trek toward VE, it is moving daily along the ecliptic closer and closer to Aldebaran. (Almost exactly 3 weeks after VE, the sun and Aldebaran have the same ecliptic longitude.) So, what I am saying is this: In Moshe's time, as the sun was approaching VE, each night just after sunset, one could watch Aldebaran and the Pleiades setting in the evening sky. Each night, the Pleiades and then Aldebaran set earlier and earlier, such that, at the time of VE, Aldebaran is just barely visible at Nautical Twilight, and the Pleiades is no longer visible at sunset! Thus, since one cannot see the stars "behind" the sun due to the sun's brightness, Aldebaran and the Pleiades are the last notable signs visible just before VE. The Pleiades, being an open cluster of fainter stars, disappears in

the glow of sunset first; then you start watching for Aldebaran. When, after sunset, just as the stars start becoming visible, you notice that Aldebaran is becoming very hard to spot, you know VE is near or has happened!

The same is true of the Autumnal Equinox. As the sun and Antares are setting in the evening sky (again in Moshe's time) the sun is getting ever so close to Antares. Finally, when Antares is either no longer visible just after sunset, or very, very difficult to spot just after sunset (what we would call today Nautical Twilight), then you know the Autumnal Equinox has happened or is about to happen.

As will be detailed later, all the other ancient nations around Israel could make these observations very easily and some of those same nations held Israel captive for long periods as well. Therefore, there is no reason to suggest that ancient Israel, or even Babylon, where Abraham was from, did not understand this and practice it for agricultural purposes. Missing the window of time for planting could have had dire consequences.

We will, however, also address calculations that the priests and Sanhedrin were privy to. Josephus and Philo tell us this plainly:

> [222] ***Moses puts down the beginning of the vernal equinox as the first month of the year***, attributing the chief honor, not as some persons do, to the periodical revolutions of the year in regard to time, but rather, to the graces and beauties of nature which it has caused to shine upon men; for it is through the bounty of nature that the seeds which are sown to produce the necessary food of mankind are brought to perfection. And the fruit of trees in their prime, which is second in importance only to the necessary crops, is engendered by the same power, and as being second in importance also ripens late; for we always find in nature that those things which are not very necessary are second to those which are indispensable.[44] (Philo, On Moses 2:222)

---

44 The fact that Philo says the **beginning** of the vernal equinox is the first month, rather than the VE happening mid-way through the lunar month of Abib, is highly significant. Here Philo is echoing Josephus' testimony about using not just Abib but that exact part

[16] And the sun, the ruler of the day, making two equinoxes every year, both in spring and autumn. *The spring equinox in the constellation of Aries, and the autumnal one in Libra, gives the most evident demonstration possible of the divine dignity of the number seven. For each of the equinoxes takes place in the seventh month*, at which time men are expressly commanded by law to celebrate the greatest *and most popular and comprehensive festivals; since it is owing to both these seasons, that all the fruits of the earth are engendered and brought to perfection; the fruit of corn, and all other things which are sown, being owing to the vernal equinox; and that of the vine, and of all the other plants which bear hard berries, of which there are great numbers, to the autumnal one*. (Philo, On Creation 1:116)

[184] and twelve is the perfect number, of which the *circle of the zodiac in the heaven is a witness*, studded as it is with such numbers of brilliant constellations. The periodical revolution of the sun is another witness, *for he accomplishes his circle in twelve months, and men also reckon the hours of the day and of the night as equal in number to the months of the year*, (Philo, On Flight and Finding 1:184)

[217] Now, the seven lamps signified the seven planets; for so many there were springing out of the lampstand. *Now, the twelve loaves that were upon the table signified the circle of the zodiac and the year*; [218] but the altar of incense, by its thirteen kinds of sweet smelling spices with which the sea replenished it, signified that God is the possessor of all things that are both in the uninhabitable and habitable parts of the earth, and that they are all to be dedicated to his use. (Josephus, The Jewish War 5:217-218)

---

of Abib where Aries makes its first appearance. The other huge insight that Philo brings on this matter is that it dovetails perfectly with other research putting Exodus day on the time of the VE, adjusted for the Hebrew day ending at sunset. What better reason could Moshe have to also adapt a stellar month schedule, than to know and pass on to the priests that followed, that this was the star-sign that returned on the day they were freed from bondage?

[186] *And for the twelve stones, whether we understand by them the months, or whether we understand the like number of the signs of that circle which the Greeks call the Zodiac, we shall not be mistaken in their meaning*. And for the mitre, which was of a blue color, it seems to me to mean heaven; [187] for how otherwise could the name of God be inscribed upon it? (Josephus, Antiquities 3:186-187)

[123] And the color of the stars is an additional evidence in favor of my view; for to the glance of the eye the appearance of the heaven does resemble an emerald; and it follows necessarily that six names are engraved on each of the stones, because each of the hemispheres cuts the zodiac in two parts, and in this way comprehends within itself six animals. [124] *Then the twelve stones on the breast[45], which are not like one another in color, and which are divided into four rows of three stones in each, what else can they be emblems of, except of the circle of the zodiac?* For that also is divided into four parts, each consisting of three animals, by which divisions it makes up the seasons of the year, spring, summer, autumn, and winter, distinguishing the four changes, the two solstices, and the two equinoxes, *each of which has its limit of three signs of this zodiac, by the revolutions of the sun, according to that unchangeable, and most lasting, and really divine ratio which exists in numbers*; [125] on which account they attached it to that which is with great propriety called the logeum. For all the changes of the year and the seasons are arranged by well-defined, and stated, and firm reason; and, though this seems a most extraordinary and incredible thing, by their seasonable changes they display their undeviating and everlasting permanence and durability. (Philo, On Moses 2:123-125)

What this also means is that the first spring constellation, which anciently was Aries but now is Pisces, was the final marker that set the year. When needed, the first spring constellation acts as a "tie-breaker". For example, in the year 30 when Y'shua died, the "normal" regulation of the month as the time of the lunar conjunction after sunset was suspended because of the return of Aries. The month of Adar normally would have had a 30th day added due to the general "bookend" rules that were in force in the first

---

45 That is, on the high priest's breast plate as becomes clear throughout the entire discussion.

century, but what would have normally been Adar 30 was the day of the Vernal Equinox instead. Josephus and Philo more than suggest in several places that such an instance requires the constellation sign (Aries-VE) to trump the addition of day 30 by the moon, though this is extremely rare. Only in that manner, do the rest of the historical sources make sense in unanimously pointing to the day of Y'shua's death being 15 Abib, a Thursday.[46] But the calculation of Aries was not disseminated to the general population of Israel for fear the Zodiac's role would encourage a lapse into paganism.

We will see those trends develop more clearly as we near the end of this book and also in my next publication entitled *Y'shua Year by Year*.

Introducing... the Real New Moon

This is one of several topics that we will introduce and return to several times in this book because it is so important and also because it can be very easily misunderstood. A reference book of this nature also sometimes gets read out of order, and I want to make very sure that potential misconceptions do not arise simply because I didn't reproduce the necessary clarifications in each relevant place as needed. So here is the first piece of new information that I need to emphasize:

I in *NO* way, shape or form denigrate the importance of sighting the crescent of the New Moon. Nor am I saying to ignore the crescent totally either. Rather, I am saying that all calendar mechanisms need to be put into proper historical context. The crescent, in conjunction with other YHWH-commanded criteria, is a Set-Apart ritual in Torah. I believe strongly, and will show the proof, from Scripture, that using the first sighted waxing crescent *alone* comes from pagan tradition. If we are honest, we should also be open to what the Scripture gives us in its original language and context. For those who don't see that as true yet, please know that I respect your viewpoint while I also invite you to examine and discuss what is and what is not in Scripture.

---

46 There is plenty of discussion as to whether Y'shua was crucified on a Wednesday, Thursday or Friday, I hold to the Thursday scenario.

What follows is a "short version", super brief and simplistic, of why using the crescent alone as a forward marker is un-Scriptural; but using the crescent sightings from both Old and New Moons in conjunction with the sun as YHWH also commands, is Scriptural. In other words, if you concur, you will still sight the crescent in connection with the new month as you do now. All that will change is how you view the functionality of the kind of "newness" that the crescent presents from Tanakh. Here is my main point for now. There will be plenty more evidence discussed later:

> [27] It came about the next day, *the second day of the new moon*, that David's place was empty; so Saul said to Jonathan his son, "Why has the son of Jesse not come to the meal, either yesterday or today?"…
> [34] Then Jonathan arose from the table in fierce anger, and did not eat food on *the second day of the new moon*, for he was grieved over David because his father had dishonored him. (1 Samuel 20:27, 34 NAU)

Here you see two references that *the New Moon is celebrated over a two day period*. Those who hold to a crescent-only system believe the crescent shows the *immediate forward direction* of the month. But if that is the case, *where is their second day*?

The only way you can get two days for the beginning of the month, is if day 1 starts in darkness and day 2 has the crescent sighted that evening. *The fact is I sight the moon more than crescent-only folks!* The reason I say that is because *I sight both the full moon* and the *last waning crescent of the old moon* as a marker. When ancient Israel couldn't see the moon the next day after that waning crescent, they knew from repeated observation that it had gone "into darkness" to be born again, that is, into astronomical newness.

However, since the sun rules over the moon and the earth, the moon can't do anything until the sun, under YHWH's permission, "approves" the month! How does that happen? Very simple: At sunset on the day of the conjunction, the next Hebrew day is the first day of the month. When you do that, the crescent may or may not appear on that same day. For practical reasons, it became normal to think of the month as having a two-day period of "newness." This would confuse some in later times as being the only way to call it new. That is why the writer of 1 Samuel 20 doesn't even bother mentioning the actual month at all since the two day proclamation system applied regardless!

The reason this must be true is that we worship an invisible Elohim, and He noticed the other nations bowing down to the lighted forms of the sun, moon and planets. Here's what He had to say about that:

> "And beware not to lift up your eyes to heaven and see the sun and the moon and the stars, all the host of heaven, and be drawn away and worship them and serve them, those which YHWH your Elohim has ordained for all the peoples under the whole heaven to share. Deuteronomy 4:19 (Matara)

In order to keep us from lapsing into paganism, the worship of both the sun and the moon was very strictly prohibited. This is, perhaps, another reason why the Hebrew day begins at sunset, literally with the absence of the sun, so people wouldn't turn astray. What happens to the day starting with darkness must logically extend to the month, so that the sighted moon might <u>not</u> be venerated either!

The only way to not "go pagan" and maintain the necessary solar day length of 24 hours for each day of each month, is to track those 24 hours from sunset to sunset. In fact, I believe that the number one confusion that the crescentists have is in thinking that the moment the old lunar month ends is the same moment that new lunar month begins. That is what is implicit in a crescent-only forward marker system. We never end days in the middle of the 24 hours. In the end, there are only three ways to keep the proper timing of a solar year:

1) With our modern precision: pick an arbitrary discrete minute and hour to track the day, in our case midnight to midnight. OR...

2) From ancient reckoning: pick solar marker #1 for a 24 hour day

measurement (sunrise to sunrise) as pagans did to venerate the sun as a god.

OR…

3) From ancient reckoning: only worship YHWH and not His creations by reckoning from solar marker #2 for a 24 hour day measurement, sunset to sunset, so that the day and the month begin in darkness.

A fair question is asked by the crescentists at this point:

"Aren't there references all over the Tanakh of days later in the *chodesh* that cannot be construed as relating the renewal of the moon but the month itself?"

The answer is: that is correct. When you have sacred feasts and fasts hitting the 10th, 14th, 15th or other occasions on other days, it clearly means "X days from the last new moon". Furthermore, I would not proclaim that Pesach would happen "the 14th day of the newness of the moon" but rather "the 14th day since the new moon." So, crescentists do have a valid point that "newness" can't be applied to every day from the *chodesh*.

However, this misses the point with respect to the special case of the start of the month:

> [4] Hear this, you who trample the needy, to do away with the humble of the land, [5] saying, "***When will the new moon be over***, So that we may sell grain, And the sabbath, that we may open the wheat *market*, To make the bushel smaller and the shekel bigger, And to cheat with dishonest scales, [6] So as to buy the helpless for money And the needy for a pair of sandals, And *that* we may sell the refuse of the wheat?" (Amos 8:4-6 NAU)

Now, why would they ask when the new moon would be over? Didn't they know? My answer: They were waiting for confirmation of the calculation of the conjunction with the appearance of the crescent a day later! The reason I can be sure that the moon is in newness for two days as opposed to it merely being the second day of the month is because of this:

> [5] So David said to Jonathan, "Behold, ***tomorrow is the new moon***, and I ought to sit down to eat with the king. But let me go, that I may hide myself in the field ***until the third evening***. [6] "If your father misses me at all, then say, 'David earnestly asked *leave* of me to run to Bethlehem his city, because it is the yearly sacrifice there for the whole family.' (1 Samuel 20:5-6 NAU)

Why does it say "until the third evening"?

Because the New Moon starts the following day, and it will need two more days to be completed! The entire feast is two days long because it takes that long between conjunction, the next sunset and the crescent to confirm the start of the month!

28th Old Month	29th Old Month Conjunction	1st New Month	2nd New Month	3rd New Month
Last sighting of waning crescent **1 Sam 20:5 David says tomorrow is the new moon**		1st Waxing crescent sighted after sunset.		

However, as is often the case with Scriptural debate, answering one question leads to another question: Getting back to the people in Amos 8, why would they not be sure about when the Shabbat ended in this verse? Since Shabbat is an absolute count and not tied to the moon, wouldn't this question be unnecessary?

The answer has to do with the observance of Shabbat as opposed to the real ending of Shabbat. It became traditional in Israel to use Saturday night after sunset for a havdilah meal, a time that was still counted as "resting" even though, technically, the work week had begun at sunset. This was because of the obvious tendencies in ancient and modern work schedules:

And Abraham rose early in the morning, and saddled his donkey, and took two of his young men with him, and Isaac his son. And he cleaved the wood for the burnt-offering, and rose up, and went to the place of which Elohim had told him. Genesis 22:3 (Matara)

[4] Now when Moses' father-in-law saw all that he was doing for the people, he said, "What is this thing that you are doing for the people? Why do you alone sit *as judge* and all the people stand about you *from morning until evening*?" (Exodus 18:14 NAU)

The merging of the morning labor with Shabbat itself, probably, began here:

[21] "You shall work six days, but on the seventh day you shall rest; *even* during plowing time and harvest you shall rest. (Exodus 34:21 NAU)

Naturally, people plow and work the fields from dawn to dusk! The question the greedy men asked was if the righteous Israelites would count transacting business as "work" that they would not do also until the following morning. We know that sometimes the wicked tried to separate commercial activities from menial work to the rebuke of the prophets (Nehemiah 10).

In New Testament times we find Rav Shaul (the apostle Paul) keeping a havdilah meal until nearly midnight (Acts 20:7). Clearly havdilah is meant to "separate" the Shabbat from the rest of the week, and it was customary, though not required, to wait until the following morning to resume one's work.

Now, keeping in mind, that the men in Amos 8 are described as dishonest and greedy, they, of course, want to resume making money immediately after sunset, but they will only work if there are sufficient customers willing to buy from them! In other words, if the rest of Israel is keeping havdilah, they are not going out to market on a Saturday night, so the merchants who cheat these customers are wondering if it is financially viable to do so then, or the next morning! In the end, what they are really asking is "when will their resting and their ceasing from business be over"?

Finally, I will relate another aspect of the crescentist-only position. I was confronted by an individual who had done his own Bible commentary with his crescentist-only viewpoint. He initially stuck to the idea that the New Moon ceremony could only be one day long. After having these facts carefully shown to him, however, he revised his position to suggest that a two-day New Moon ceremony only happened if the sky was cloudy on the 29th and the crescent couldn't be seen.

From there, it was rather easy to point to three key facts that torpedoed such an assertion:

> 1) 1 Samuel 20 nowhere mentions the weather conditions, rather it leaves the precise month un-named, making any further assumptions tenuous at best.

> 2) The most likely explanation for why the weather didn't come up is that it was normal for the occasion to last two days.

> 3) The incident in question takes place the day before the New Moon, meaning that David could not have seen the crescent to know that bad weather would have forced a second "extra" day from this theory's perspective. Instead, David already knew to hide out for three days, and says so twice. That advance knowledge is the strongest piece of evidence possible in showcasing that the New Moon ceremony always lasted two days, and it also explains why the Talmud continues to talk about a two-day period for setting the month even after certain other pieces of information about the process were lost or misunderstood.

However, as stated earlier, there is much more upcoming material about this.

When Did the Hebrew Day Begin?

According to Scripture, the day begins not at midnight nor at sunrise[47], but at sunset. This is purely ancient understanding, not later Rabbinical innovation and is supported in both Hebrew Tanakh and Aramaic Peshitta.

> "In the beginning Elohim created the heavens and the earth. Now the earth was formless and empty, darkness was over the surface of the deep, and the Spirit of Elohim was hovering over the waters. And Elohim said, "Let there be light," and there was light. Elohim saw that the light was good and he separated the light from the darkness. Elohim called the light (aur--אור) "day," (yom--יום) and the darkness (khoshekh--חשך) he called "night" (layil--ליל). And there was evening (ereb--ערב), and there was morning (boker--בקר)--the first day" Genesis 1:1-5 (Matara)

From these very famous passages in Torah, we glean many important facts. The plain (*pshat*) language tells us:

- In the beginning it was dark, and light (1. אור) emerged from that darkness through YHWH's will. As a result, light became separated from that darkness (חשך).

- Then YHWH gave the light another name, that of 2. *yom* (יום) or "day."

- Similarly, YHWH then called the darkness by its alternate title 3. *layil* (ליל) or "night."

- When there is evening (4. ערב) followed by morning (בקר), this constitutes a fuller version of *yom* which counts as the first day.

An extremely small minority of misguided "sunrise-sunrise" advocates suggest that Hebrew could read "and there was evening and *(then)* there was morning, one day." In other words, they postulate that Hebrew might allow an interpretation that the starting point of the first day is *boker*, or dawn. However, other passages in the Tanakh show that this as way off the mark.

---

47 See The Divisions of the Day in Appendix.

Furthermore, just because the co
read, "and *then* there was" does i
from the second. That would be
report *and then* there was weathe
and weather could not be part of
example sounds, it is even more
"and *then* there was" into a pure s
occasions where Genesis 1 uses tl
in the Tanakh:

> Shema Yisrael! YHWH Elc
> YHWH is your Elohim; YHWH is One. And you shall love YHWH
> your Elohim with all your innermost being and with all your life-
> passion and with all the force you can muster. And these Words,
> which I am commanding you this very day, are to reside within
> your innermost being, and you are to teach them with great care to
> your children. ***You are to discuss them thoroughly when you sit
> at home, when you are traveling on the road, when you lie down
> and when you rise up.*** Deuteronomy 6:4-7 (Matara)

There are two evening-morning cycles mentioned here. The order is
when you sit at home, which is usually at night, when you walk along
the road, which is usually in the morning, when you lie down in evening
and then when you get up in the morning again! This statement from the
Psalms is even stronger:

> But I call to Elohim and YHWH saves me. ***Evening, morning and
> noon I cry out in anguish and He hears my voice***.
> Psalm 55:16-17 (Matara)

> You must pay (a worker) his wages on the same day before sunset.
> Deuteronomy 24:15 (Matara)

The reason for this is that after sun sets the next day begins!

> Then I heard a Set-Apart one speaking, and another Set-Apart

one said to him: "How long will it take for the vision to be made manifest—*the vision concerning the daily sacrifice* and the transgression that causes desolation with the abandonment of the Set-Apart place and the army that will trample it underfoot?" He said to me: "*It will take 2,300 evenings and mornings until the place that was previously Set-Apart may be restored.* Daniel 8:13-14 (Matara)

"And the vision **of the evenings and mornings** which has been told is true, but keep the vision secret because it is meant to apply to many days in the future." Daniel 8:26 (Matara)

A Preview: The Most Unique Day in History

Now let's look at a "preview" of Bible math. Undoubtedly, the core message is that the number seven is the underlying pattern of YHWH's creation. This is hardly surprising to anyone who studies Scripture. However, the application of that rule of seven as it related to what I call "Deliverance Cycles" was so shocking in its beauty and grace that YHWH had to ease me very gradually into this truth. Over an extended period of time, I needed to experience many lesser revelations before I could approach this big one, which as you will see, forms the basis of much of this book.

When the "sevens" all align across all the calendars, YHWH's true salvation will come. Furthermore, these "seven cycles" happen only on the true day of the Exodus![48] And as much as I would rather not use the analogy I am about to give, I can't think of a better one: It's as if the Universe were like one Astronomically Massive Mega-Jackpot slot machine waiting for all the sevens to come up to "pay off", except instead of coins, "the currency" is justice, peace and freedom!

---

48 As can be seen in my book *Y'shua Year by Year*, the Deliverance cycle regarding Y'shua's birth is equally spectacular and unique. The signs proclaiming his birth begin in 7 BCE, precisely 4,000 years after Adam's creation, and the Prophetic and Solar Pre-Metonic calendars both balance on a 4,000 year main cycle. What's more, the appearance of the three conjunctions of Jupiter and Saturn are also tied to key occasions in the Hebrew calendar, and the combination of the rarity of the triple conjunction also coinciding on such dates reaches astronomical odds

The other main advantage of this system is that it is the only one I am aware of that totally explains the requirement of Genesis 1:14-19; where the sun, the moon *and the stars* all set the year. Until I completed my research for this book, I had not in 30 years of study come across the true role the stars or their constellations / Zodiac in Scripture, as well as in Job 38:31-34. I also trust that YHWH has given the simple things of the world to confound the wisest among us, and the idea of the balancing of seven seems so simple and so obvious that most people might never see the full pattern. I speak from experience and include myself in that number, because it took not only years of research, but a few dreams and plenty of disappointments before I could see it.

In the sections that follow, you will see how the very best astronomical and computer software tools have been utilized to fully and definitively recover the precise time of the historical Exodus. I promise to make that case fully and transparently as we go forward. For now, though, let me give you the conclusion first:

The one and only day of the true Exodus is March 22nd, 1447 BCE.

This is the only date in all of Scriptural based chronology where the sevens align across all systems. That alignment also has a direct bearing on understanding the unique cycles related to the signs that preceded Y'shua's birth and death. It is also the case, that not even this day would have had the sevens align properly if the crescent was used as a forward exclusive marker. Therefore, *if* what I am about to preview here and document later has spiritual resonance for you, I would also humbly ask that you contemplate the ramifications of a crescentist only model which would remove this incredible pattern from the view of man!

One of the things that first tipped me off was a particular observation from Josephus who wrote:

> [248] *In the month of Xanthikos, which is by us called Nisan, and is the beginning of our year, on the fourteenth day of the lunar month, when the sun is in Aries, (for in this month it was that we were delivered from bondage* under the Egyptians,) the law

ordained that we should every year slay that sacrifice which I before told you we slew when we came out of Egypt, and which was called the Passover; and so we do celebrate this passover in companies, leaving nothing of what we sacrifice till the day following. (Antiquities 3:248)

This is, probably, the single greatest clue that Josephus gives us from the secret priestly records he has access to, and I will be showing this quote a lot as we go through this study. Philo also mentions equinoxes tied to Aries and Libra respectively, so it is clear these two men are reading from the same source which is keyed to Moshe's time only, because the equinoxes had precessed into Pisces before the birth of both of these historians!

Something in the way Josephus expresses himself here led me to believe that there was a lot more going on than tying a constellation to spring. As I suggested earlier, this didn't make sense until the calculations for the Exodus were verified as scientific and mathematical fact when synched to Biblical math and data like 1 Kings 6:1.

So then, what is the real significance of this? To begin with, understand that per Exodus 12:1-2, YHWH switched the calendar from fall to spring. But, at the same time, He "fulfilled" the fall to fall calendar by ending it off with cycles of seven. To be more precise, He fulfilled it through the perfection of those cycles aligning all at once.

Since that particular Exodus year would have gone fall to fall but for this intervention, we need to first understand that spring was its seventh month, and that Aries was the seventh constellation of the year from when it began.
From there, what was shocking to me was that the calendar was in a way synched not to 1 Abib, but to when Abib went into the vernal equinox, the full moon and the Aries constellation at the same time!

Also March 22nd was a Friday, so late that afternoon the Israelites were freed from bondage as their Shabbat was approaching, and at sunset YHWH struck the firstborn of Egypt down. Furthermore, the instruction, as clarified later, was not just to kill the lamb at "twilight," but "between the evenings" on the 14th day. That time reference means about 3 PM at that time of year, 2 days after the Vernal Equinox. This roughly divided the day and night, in a type of re-enactment of Creation Day 1. Since "between the evenings" is three hours before sunset, it was 21 hours from the previous sunset. This was the very same hour that Y'shua himself would die on the stake! March 22nd is also, adjusting for the day beginning at sunset, the very first day that Aries is in line with the sun! So, it's not just that the constellation Aries was in the area, but that it had arrived *that very day* to bear witness!

Here are your sevens:

1) Seven months from Tishri (Abib).
2) The first day of the seventh constellation from the old year (Aries).
3) The 14th day of the lunar month (two sevens) with the Full Moon to guide them out at night!
4) At the 21st hour of the day (three sevens) deliverance begins.
5) Since the 21st hour is also Friday afternoon, the Israelites began preparations for their departure with YHWH striking down the first born hours later on the seventh day Shabbat. The fact that their 400+ years of work literally came to an end just before Shabbat adds another remembrance for them to observe and keep it.

As mentioned previously: On no other Biblical date do these sevens align in this manner. YHWH definitely knows how to work the math into His equations for deliverance!

Technical Specifications

Bill Welker, whom I mentioned earlier, and who has provided invaluable assistance as a technical and scientific consultant, also detailed our methodology of tracking and recovering ancient dates and overcoming calendrical challenges. We have applied the Torah principle of going with the word of two witnesses or more. Our witnesses in this case are electronic and computer based but no less valuable.

Once Bill Welker determined how to adapt my unique calendar criteria to the data, the rest was a matter of crunching and double checking the numbers.

Here is what Bill Welker had to say in his own words:

In all cases, when using software to determine astronomical events in ancient times, there are four things to verify:

1. How the software handles dates prior to 4 Oct. 1582, and after 4 Oct. 1582.
2. Whether or not the software uses a year "zero" when counting back from year 1 CE (or AD).
3. How the software presents the resulting computed date, i.e. in the Julian proleptic calendar or the Gregorian proleptic calendar.
4. Accuracy of the computed results.

Number 1 –how does the software handle these dates:

The Gregorian calendar was instituted (though not worldwide) on 4 Oct 1582. Four October was followed by 15 October, correcting a 10 day accumulated error in the Vernal Equinox by the poor implementation of leap years in the Julian calendar. (Note: The date changed, but not the day–of–week. 15 Oct, 1582 was a Friday. The day before was Thursday, 4 Oct, 1582. There is no evidence through all of recorded history, that the steady counting of the 7-day week has ever been altered.) Not all calendar software handles this transition well between the Julian and Gregorian calendars, and most do not indicate any problem. There was no "5 October 1582" for example in the Gregorian Calendar, nor was there a "5 October 1582" in the Julian Calendar! Additionally, when entering a date prior to 1582, almost all available software both assumes the user has entered a Julian Calendar date, and provides the output in the Julian Calendar – again, without warning.

Number 2 –does the software use year zero:

This can be a very difficult problem to deal with. Logically, there was no "year zero". However, mathematical computations don't care, and are far easier if "year zero" is used. Therefore in most astronomical calculations, counting backward from 1 in the Common Era, one simply passes through "0", "-1", "-2", etc. Therefore, 1 BCE = 0, 2 BCE = -1, etc. The problem is, the majority of available software provides absolutely no indication how the CE to BCE transition is handled! One cannot tell by simply visually inspecting the output! Year "-55" for example could be 56 BCE or it could be 55 BCE because the software did not use year zero, rather, simply uses a minus sign to indicate "BCE"! Furthermore, even though it is far more common for the software to use year zero, and present BCE years as a negative number, often the software will correct for the year in the output since it is a nearly universally accepted fact that in the Julian Calendar (which was in common use from 45 BCE, to 1582 CE) had no year zero! Therefore, even though the user might enter "-55" for 56 BCE, the output might correct for this difference and present the output, without warning, as "-56"!

Number 3 –Julian or Gregorian proleptic calendars:

The concern here is how the computations are made when either the Julian proleptic calendar or the Gregorian proleptic calendar is used and how leap years are handled. It is bewildering that nearly 100% of available software use, without warning, the Julian proleptic calendar for dates prior to 45 BCE, and use the erred Julian Calendar method of handling leap years. Therefore, as one goes further and further back in time, the date of the equinoxes become more and more out of sync, and the dates rapidly become meaningless. Nevertheless, this is the common practice. Here it is also a concern that, once it has been identified that the software is using the Julian Calendar, how the year is presented, i.e., was the year zero accounted for or not. (See number 2).

Number 4 –accuracy of the computed results:

"Anchor dates" are required to ensure the software is producing valid output. For modern dates, this is entirely possible as there are countless records for events which occurred, and the documented record is easily compared with the computed output from the chosen software. But for ancient dates this is nearly impossible. What event happened on "21 July, 1216 BCE"? Who knows? There was no "July" in 1216 BCE! And there was no such thing as "1216 BCE"! In the real, physical year which, counting backward, we *label* as "1216 BCE", that actual year was more likely known locally as "the Xth year of King so-and-so's reign". Thus, valid anchor points for ancient dates are terribly hard to come by. One viable option is to use modern computers and astronomical software. Since planetary orbital mechanics is fairly precise, computation of the positions of the sun, moon, and stars can be determined to great accuracy. Therefore, the position of the sun, for example, can be calculated using the Gregorian proleptic calendar, and compared with Biblical and other historical accounts. Similarly, lunar and solar eclipses can be calculated back in time and compared with historical accounts. The state of the art today is such that several highly accurate computations have been done by great centers of science, such as NASA, the Jet Propulsion Laboratory, the US Naval Observatory, and others worldwide, and their computations can be compared with the computations of commercial and public domain software used to determine historical dates.

The following is a list of software and/or INTERNET based (World Wide Web) calculators, which were compared for consistency of output, and trusted to produce uniform results. There is no "be all", "do all" software, so different sources are required for differing desired output:

Date conversions

BCE/CE

Fourmilab:

http://www.fourmilab.ch/documents/calendar/

Calendrica:

http://emr.cs.iit.edu/home/reingold/calendar-book/Calendrica.html

Project Pluto "Guide 8" Astronomical Software

Sunrise/Sunset

BCE/CE

Project Pluto "Guide 8" Astronomical SoftwareCalendrica:

http://emr.cs.iit.edu/home/reingold/calendar-book/Calendrica.html

CE

MultiYear Interactive Computer Almanac (MICA) 1800-2050 (US Naval Observatory software)

Equinoxes

BCE/CE

Project Pluto "Guide 8" Astronomical Software

Institut de Mécanique Céleste et de Calcul des Éphémérides

http://www.imcce.fr/en/grandpublic/temps/saisons.php?

CE

MultiYear Interactive Computer Almanac (MICA) 1800-2050 (US Naval Observatory software)

Lunar Phases

BCE/CE

NASA Phases of Moon and Eclipses to 2000 BCE:

http://eclipse.gsfc.nasa.gov/phase/phasecat.html

Project Pluto "Guide 8" Astronomical Software

Sky & Telescope Moon Phases:

http://www.skyandtelescope.com/observing/objects/javascript/moon_phases   (Does not provide a time, but is useful for a confirmation of date and phase)

CE

MultiYear Interactive Computer Almanac (MICA) 1800-2050 (US Naval Observatory software)

In addition to Bill Welker's comments, I would like to add that what we are doing comes down to this process:

1) Verify and confirm Julian dates (the time of day is the same) for fixed phenomena (lunar phases, sunset and equinox times, etc.).

2) Use reliable converter programs to convert the Julian date into Gregorian terms (the days of the week have never changed).

3) Convert the Gregorian time in Hebrew reckoning, with the day beginning at sunset.

Chapter 2

The Solar Pre-Metonic Calendar

HE COMMANDS THE SUN, AND IT FAILS TO RISE;
HE SHUTS UP THE STARS UNDER HIS SEAL.
HE ALONE SPREADS OUT THE SKY AND WALKS ON THE
WAVES IN THE SEA. HE MADE THE GREAT BEAR, ORION,
THE PLEIADES AND THE HIDDEN CONSTELLATIONS OF
THE SOUTH. HE DOES GREAT, UNSEARCHABLE THINGS,
WONDERS BEYOND COUNTING.
JOB 9:7-10

Noah's Solar Year

The water prevailed upon the earth one hundred and fifty days.
Genesis 7:24 (NAU)

Scripture also tells us the day the flood started, the 17th of the second month. That is the day Noah and his family also went into the ark (Genesis 17:11-13). The text then says:

13 In the selfsame day [the 17th] entered Noah, and Shem, and Ham, and Japheth, the sons of Noah, and Noah's wife, and the three wives of his sons with them, into the ark; 14 they, and every beast after its kind, and all the cattle after their kind, and every creeping thing that creep upon the earth after its kind, and every bird after its kind, every bird of every sort. 15 And they went in to Noah into the ark, two and two of all flesh wherein is the breath of life. 16 And they that went in, went in male and female of all flesh, as Elohim commanded him: and YHWH shut him in.
Genesis 7:13-16 (Matara)

From this point on, the grammar in the Hebrew says, *"and then the flood came for forty DAYS."* In other words, the skies opened and the waters of the deep were released on the 17th, but it officially became a "flood" after Noah and his family were shut inside the ark. Therefore, we mark the end of the 17th at sunset (the beginning of the 18th) as the start of the forty day count.

It is also important to point out that while Scripture tells us that the flood happened "in the second month of Noah's 600th year" that year is solar and not from Noah's birth. For that reason Josephus adds:

> [80] This calamity happened in the six hundredth year of Noah's government [age], in the second month, called by the Macedonians Dios, but by the Hebrews Marchesuan; for so did they order their year in Egypt; (Antiquities 1:80)

In this case, we see that Noah is on a Tishri to Tishri reckoning, because "Marchesuan", aka: "Heshvan", is the month after Tishri. This will be an important clue for later, when YHWH switches the reckoning of the months from fall to spring. Meanwhile, there is another surprising difference between Noah's calendar and Moshe's to look at.

As we investigate Noah's calendar, we come to a startling fact: *There is no way that we can have exactly 5 consecutive months equal 150 days in a lunar system. Therefore, this calendar has to be solar!* The lunar calendar has to have months alternating between 29 and 30 days in order to stay accurate, but in this case, we have 30 days months five times in a row:

18th day, 2nd month to the end of that month	13
All of the 3rd month	30
All of the 4th month	30
All of the 5th month	30
All of the 6th month	30
To the 17th day of the 7th month	17
Total Days	**150**

However, for those who might think Noah's situation is some kind of statistical fluke, other lines of evidence clearly prove otherwise.

Evidence from Esther

One of the key principles with this calendar is that the Israelites were commanded to switch to the Moedic reckoning for setting their sacred occasions throughout the year. However, other nations including Persia continued to use the older system, as we begin to see below:

> [12] Now every girl, when her turn came, had to go in to King Ahasuerus, after undergoing, for a space of *twelve months*, what was ordered by the law for the women (for this was the time necessary for making them clean, that is, *six months* with oil of myrrh and *six months* with sweet perfumes and such things as are needed for making women clean): (Esther 2:12 BBE)

> [3] In the third year of his rule he gave a feast to all his captains and his servants; and the captains of the army of Persia and Media, the great men and the rulers of the divisions of his kingdom, were present before him; [4] *And for a long time, even a hundred and eighty days, he let them see all the wealth and the glory of his kingdom and the great power and honour which were his.* (Esther 1:3-4 BBE)

The first passage shows a 12 month period, or a full year, passing while the women are purified. But the second passage describes "a long time" of 180 days right after his third year in power begins. In light of what we have seen with Noah, it is fair to ask: Could this be six months of 30 days each, especially when 6 month intervals and patterns are evident in this book?

Well, we certainly know the Persians were expert astronomers and very experienced with using the Zodiac to keep track of time:

> *Old Persian inscriptions and tablets indicate that early Iranians used a 360-day calendar based on the Babylonian system* and

modified for their beliefs and day names. Its months had two or three divisions depending on the phase of the moon. *Twelve months of 30 days were named for festivals* or activities of the pastoral year. *A 13th month was added every six years to keep the calendar synchronized with the seasons*…The first calendars based on Zoroastrian cosmology appeared in the later Achaemenid period (650 to 330 BCE). They evolved over the centuries, but month names changed little until now. The unified Achaemenid empire required a distinctive Iranian calendar, and one was devised in Egyptian tradition, with 12 months of 30 days, each dedicated to a yazata (Eyzad), and four divisions resembling the Semitic week.- Wikipedia

And:

Although the earliest evidence of Iranian calendrical traditions is from the second millennium BC, predating the appearance of the Iranian prophet Zoroaster, the first fully preserved calendar is that of the Achaemenids. Throughout recorded history, Persians have been keen on the idea and importance of having a calendar. *They were among the first cultures to use a solar calendar and have long favored a solar over lunar and lunisolar approaches.* The sun has always been a symbol in Iranian culture and is closely related to the folklore regarding Cyrus the Great-Panaino, Antonio (1990), "Pre-Islamic Calendars", *Encyclopaedia Iranica.*

Notice that both the Persians and the Babylonians (like the Egyptians who held Israel captive previously) all kept a 360 day calendar! Therefore, from the earliest part of Tanakh to the latest, we have very solid evidence of the basics of this calendar being used! More to the point, however, is the fact that the Persians are using the exact same mechanism for the 40 year cycle that I am about describe for the Solar Pre-Metonic calendar.

More Specific Calendar Information from the Scriptures

In Daniel 7, we are given the first vision of the Beast who will make war against the righteous in the Last Days:

> The ten horns are ten kings who will come from this kingdom. After them another king will arise, different from the earlier ones; he will subdue three kings. He will speak against the Most High and oppress his saints and try to change the set times and the laws. *The saints will be handed over to him for a time, times and half a time.* But the court will sit, and his power will be taken away and completely destroyed forever. Then the sovereignty, power and greatness of the kingdoms under the whole heaven will be handed over to the saints, the people of the Most High. His kingdom will be an everlasting kingdom, and all rulers will worship and obey Him. This is the end of the matter. I, Daniel, was deeply troubled by my thoughts, and my face turned pale, but I kept the matter to myself. (Daniel 7:24-28-NIV)

Even in conventional Judaism, this is understood to mean a period of 3 ½ years (a time, two times, plus half). However, Revelation also provides more assistance in clearly explaining the matter:

> And to the woman were given the two wings of the great eagle, that she might fly into the wilderness, to her place*; where she is nourished a time and times and half a time*, from the face of the serpent. Revelation 12:14 (AENT)

> But the court which is without the temple, leave out, and measure it not, *because it is given to the Gentiles; and they will tread down the Set Apart city forty and two months*. And I will give my two witnesses; *and they will prophesy a thousand and two hundred and sixty days*, clothed in sackcloth. Revelation 11:2 -3 (AENT)

> And there was given to him a mouth speaking great things, and blasphemies: *and authority was given him to operate forty and*

two months. Revelation 13:5 (AENT)

Here we see here clearly that "time, times and half a time" equals 1,260 days, which, in turn, equals 42 months. Therefore:

30 days per month x 42 = 1,260
360 (1 time) + 720 (2 times) + 180 (half a time) = 1,260

We even find confirmation from First Century priestly sources like Philo that this was the proper understanding:

> [60] They were also created to serve as measures of time; for it is by the appointed periodical revolutions of the sun and moon and other stars, that days and months and years are determined. Moreover it is owing to them that the most useful of all things, the nature of numbers exist, time having displayed it; for from one day comes the limit, and from two the number two, and from three, three, *and from the notion of a month is derived the number thirty, and from a year that number which is equal to the days of the twelve months*, and from infinite time comes the notion of infinite number. (On Creation 1:60)

> [14] Why did the rain of the deluge last forty days and an equal number of nights? [Genesis 7:4]. 14. In the first place, the word day is used in a double sense. The one meaning that time, which is from morning to evening, that is to say, from the first rising of the sun in the east to his sinking in the west. Therefore they who make definitions, say, *"That is day, as long as the sun shines on the earth." In another sense, the word day is used of the day and night together. And in this sense we say that a month consists of thirty days, combining together and computing the period of night in the same calculation.* (Questions and Answers on Genesis 2:14)

And in another key passage, Philo goes even further, linking the solar year directly to the most ancient biblical people:

> [84] Why the man [Enoch] who lives a life of repentance is said to

have lived three hundred and sixty-five years[1]? [Genesis 5:23].
84. In the first place, *the year contains three hundred and sixty-five days; therefore, by the symbol of the solar orbit,* the sacred historian here indicates the life of the repentant man. (Questions and Answers on Genesis 1:84)

And from Daniel:

> *"From the moment that the perpetual sacrifice is abolished and the disastrous abomination erected: 1,290 days. Blessed is he who stands firm and attains 1,335 days."* (Daniel 12:11-12-NIV)

So here we see the same time period mentioned but this time the 3½ year portion equals 1,290 days. The second set of 3½ years equals a total of 7 years, or a prophetic week.

But, this is also literally true in terms of the calendar as well. The combined message then is this: *Once every seven years, the divine calendar will add a 30-day solar leap month! This is the same system just described in the Persian system.* More specifically, this occurs after the completion of the sixth year, but before the commencement of the seventh, mirroring the Shabbat pattern exactly.

And so, looking at this by the numbers, this is what we have:

$(360 \times 6) + 30 = 2{,}190$ days
2,190 days divided by 6 = **365 days/year**

---

1 This is an extremely important reference, as the only man in the Torah recorded as living 365 years is Enoch, the seventh generation from Adam, and these two numbers tell the tale. The seventh generation, like the seventh day, is a symbol of perfection. Added to this we have 365 years in this perfect man's life, who was in fact so righteous that YHWH took him up bodily without having him die. This honor is extremely rare, with the only other Scriptural example being Elijah many centuries later. In any case, the other aspect is that if a day can equal a year (Ezekiel 4:4-6) then a year can equal a day, and that means that the perfect man is given a perfect life span, which represents a full solar year. If the "fullness" of the year was intended to be lunar, then Enoch would have lived 354 years. The final remez, or hint, is in Enoch's name, which actually is rendered *khanoke* (חנוך) in Hebrew, which means "to dedicate." It is from this word that we also get *Hanukkah*, which is in turn known as the Festival of Lights. That linkage not only attaches to Mashiyach in John 10:22, but also back to the pattern of Creation itself, "Let there be light!"

Even so, it is fair to point out that the real solar year is 6 hours longer, or 365.25 days. How do we account for that?

First of all, we must understand how the 40 year compensation mechanism works. Let's look to Scripture for background:

> "I hate, I despise your religious feasts; I cannot stand your assemblies. Even though you bring me burnt offerings and grain offerings, I will not accept them. Though you bring choice fellowship offerings, I will have no regard for them. Away with the noise of your songs! I will not listen to the music of your harps. But let justice roll on like a river, righteousness like a never-failing stream! *"Did you bring me sacrifices and offerings forty years in the desert, O house of Israel? You have lifted up the shrine of your king, the pedestal of your idols, the star of your god - which you made for yourselves.* Therefore I will send you into exile beyond Damascus."* (Amos 5:21-27-NIV)

So we begin with a remez of two different events relating the same problem of idolatry. In both cases, 40 years of isolation is the chosen penalty. However, there is a **kosher** version where we admired the stars as servants of YHWH, Who made them. So now think 40 years and stars, and let's go to the next step:

> And Elohim turned away and delivered them to serve the powers of heaven as it is written in the books of the prophets, *(Why) for forty years in the wilderness[2]* did you sons of Israel offer me a slain animal or a sacrifice? But you have taken the tabernacle of Moloch *and the star of the deity* of Rephan that you made images to be worshipped. I will remove you beyond Bavel. *Behold the tabernacle of the testimony of our fathers in the wilderness was as He commanded who spoke with Moshe to make it in the likeness that he showed him.* And this same tabernacle also indeed brought our fathers with Y'shua into the land that Elohim gave them (as) an inheritance from those nations that He cast out from before them. And it was carried until the days of Dawid, he who found mercy

---

2 Another 40 year generation/calendar pattern.

before Elohim and asked that he find a tabernacle for the Elohim of Ya'akov. But Shleemon built the House. And the most High does not dwell in the work of hands, as the prophet said, *'Heaven (is) my throne and the earth a footstool that is under my feet.* What is the House that you build for Me? Says the Master, or what is the place of My rest. Behold, did not My hand make all these (things)? Acts 7:42-50 (AENT)

Moshe saw a pattern in heaven, and, of course, heaven signs are superior to earth signs. What about the stars then? Here is an interesting mention of one particular star:

I see him, but not now; I behold him, but not near. *A star will come out of Jacob;* a scepter will rise out of Israel. He will crush the foreheads of Moab, the skulls of all the sons of Seth. (Numbers 24:17-NIV)

Leaving aside the metaphoric/Messianic imagery, the verse literally identifies a star with Jacob, also known as Israel. However, this verse, as well as Genesis 1:14-19, tells us that certain stars are somehow marking time!

Next, we add the time both writers are talking about. This is the second year after the Exodus, and therefore, the time the rebellious Israelites spend wandering in the Wilderness until the generation that worshipped the Golden Calf was consumed. Torah clearly says this is a 40 year period. Then, after this time, the generation is considered "cleansed" and they are permitted to enter into Promised Land.

Therefore, if the Sun can rest for a Shabbat by having the leap month added after six years, it also seems reasonable that the 40 year cycle of the Israelites on earth is also first reflected in heaven. In other words, this year points to the time that the 40 year cycle is also completed in heaven, when it would then reset for the next 40 years.

What that means is that a 2,190 day/6 year cycle that repeats six times brings us to 36 years. Then, instead of waiting for another six years before the next solar leap month, we simply complete the generation and do it after three years, meaning after year 39 but before the beginning of year 40. When we do this, the math changes accordingly:

2,190 days x 6	= 13,140 days in 36 years
(360 days x 4) + 30	= 1,470 days
(between years 37 through 40)	
13,140 + 1,470	= 14,610 days in 40 years
14,610 days divided by 40	= **365.25 days/year**

At this point, the numbers get more complicated.[3] In order to reach the accuracy of our current Gregorian system, it is necessary to omit the leap month in the 100th occurrence of the 40-year cycle, or once every 4,000 years. That slight change will yield a year equaling **365.2425** days. So if the sun simply follows Torah, on Shabbat and generational time, we arrive at the exact same interval predicted with our current Gregorian calendar!

On the other hand, while there is no direct Scriptural reference for dissecting the numbers this finely, the general principles of following the sun and moon signs we have discussed earlier imply that we should be at this level. Remarkably though, we can even get more accurate. Let us see the Scripture first,

> You shall not bow down to them or worship them; for I YHWH your Elohim am a jealous Elohim, punishing children for the sin of their parents, to the third and the fourth generation of those who reject Me, but showing enduring love to the ***thousandth generation*** of those who love Me and keep My Mitzvot (Commandments). Exodus 20:5-6 (Matara-also see Deut. 7:9, 1; Chronicles 16:15; Psalm 105:8)

---

3 Once again I want to extend a large amount of gratitude to the folks who maintain the excellent website: www.360calendar.com. They have assembled an impressive catalog of data. These notes, however, go into topics that they have not at the time of writing dealth with: such as the priestly service calendar and Scriptural proofs for the 40 year cycle. It is relatively easy to compile things up to this point (40 year generation cycles). However, in order to take the final steps, I needed to verify a 100,000 year cycle.

A thousand generations is quite a major piece of time. Furthermore, as Numbers 32:13 and many other Torah passages teach, an individual generation is usually 40 years long.

Other Torah passages show that a generation can also equal 100 years! Let's see why:

> Never again will there be in it an infant who lives but a few days, or an old man who does not live out his years; *he who dies at a hundred will be thought* a mere youth; he who fails to reach a hundred will be considered accursed. (Isaiah 65:20-NIV)

The reason a person who dies at a hundred years is considered "accursed" is because, by the standard of the Messianic Age, he would have just barely reached a generation when compared with how long others will live!

But let's also see an earlier reference to this:

> And (Elohim) said to Abram, Know for certain that your seed shall be sojourners in a land that is not theirs, and shall serve them. *And they shall afflict them four hundred years*. And also that nation, whom they will serve, will I judge. And afterward shall they come out with great substance. But you will go to your fathers in peace. You will be buried in a good old age. *And in the fourth generation they shall come here again*. For the sin of the Amorites is not yet at its fullest extent. Genesis 15:13-16 (Matara)

In Hebrew, we are told that "four *meah* (מאה) of years" passes and *meah* is the Hebrew number for 100. However, the exact same period of time is also referred to here as "four *dorot* (דור)", the same word used for 40 year "generations" elsewhere. Therefore, a generation can also equal 100 years, and this should be reflected in YHWH's calendar. As I alluded to just now, that manifests in a 100,000 year cycle (1,000 generations in the Scripture times the 100 year per generation reference).

By crunching the numbers then, we come to a very simple conclusion. In the last 40 year cycle of the 100,000 year period, the 6th and 7th interval solar leap months are omitted. That will bring us to an even more accurate calendar than the one we currently use, with a year now equaling the exact length of the solar year: **365.2422** days.

However, there is one important proviso: The reason this 360 day cycle does not continue after Moshe's time is because, in the distant future, just before the 100,000 year cycle balances, the previous "scheduled" Vernal Equinox day will be, by definition, nearly 60 days off. As a result, it is important to insert the right mechanisms into the right calendars. When we study *the Constellation Clock* at the end of this book, we will see that it surpasses both the Gregorian and Mayan systems in accuracy. Pertaining to this part of the calendar, we can't mix the mechanisms of one with the other.

Again, as mentioned earlier, I am indebted to the research by the folks at www.360calendar.com for some of these finer points. Their research goes into much greater detail, but, for our purposes, it is sufficient to show that biblical numbers reveal the perfect solar year. It is important that we understand that this has always been tracked in Scripture.[4] Later, we will see how the detailed relationship between the heavens and the Israelites unfolds with clear celestial references from Scripture.

---

4 I sympathize with those who may object that not every detail here came from Scripture. Some may suggest that Scripture could only bring us to Gregorian calendar levels and that further calculations become speculative. The Gregorian loses a day every 3,300 years, the Julian loses a day every 128 years. However, Moshe lived around 3,500 years ago, so to address this issue, my suggestion is to take the incidents in Joshua and Isaiah literally. In Joshua, the sun and the moon stay frozen for almost a day. In Isaiah, the prophet gives a sign to a king by causing the shadows cast by the sun to roll back. If both of these calibrations are added together, it turns out YHWH used these miracles to synchronize our solar system's clock to the rest of the galaxy. A "day patch" is added, to keep the Biblical and Gregorian calendars in perfect alignment. I will explain to what degree later in the main text. For now, sufficed to say, I believe that both solutions are Scriptural as well as perfect, but I fully understand why some would prefer this version over its more detailed numerically based counterpart.

Philo Explains the Hidden Role of the Equinoxes

Speaking generally, the "shortcut" to understanding the role of equinoxes is rather simple. These two occasions represent another sky sign that parallels the division of night and day in Genesis 1. When the days and nights are almost totally equal, that "greater yom," forms another creation pattern expressed by the Hebrew word **tequwphot** that has the following meanings and uses in Scripture:

> **8498** [8499] תְּקוּפָה (Hebrew) (page 880) (Strong 8622)
>
> [תְּקוּפָה]† n.f coming round, circuit;—cstr. תְּקוּפַת הַשָּׁנָה Ex 34:22 (JE), adv., at the circuit (completion) of the year, so 2 לְת׳ הַשָּׁנָה: Ch 24:33; = pl. cstr. 1 לִתְקֻפוֹת הַיָּמִים S 1:20; sg. sf. of finished circuit of sun Psalm 19:7 (opp. מוֹצָאוֹ; cf. of moon, בתקופתו Ecclus 43:7).
> –Brown Driver Briggs

> [22] You shall observe the Feast of Weeks, of the first fruits of the wheat harvest; and the Feast of Ingathering at the **turn** of the year. (Exodus 34:22 1985 JPS Tanakh)

This "turn" can only be the autumnal equinox! Now let's see if we can find the other "turn":

> Two expressions refer to the seasons of the year (the spring or fall equinox): t® qûpat_ hashsh¹nâ "the turning of the year (Exo 34:22 [fall]: 2Chr 24:23 [spring]), and t®_ shûbat hashsh¹nâ⁵, "the returning of the year" (2Sam 11:l; 1Kings 20:22, 26 [spring]). Bibliography: Bruce, F. F., "Calendar, " In NBD. Finegan, J. Light from the Ancient Past Princeton University, 1959, pp. 561-98. Lilley J., "Calendar, " in ZPEB. Smick, E. B., "Caledar, " in WBE. H.J.A.

> תְּשׁוּבָה. return (to a place) 1S 717: litšûbat hašš¹nâ in the return of the year = spring 2S 111 1K 2022•26 1C 201 2C 3610; — 2. pl. answers, responses Jb 2134 3436. † (pg 396)—Holladay Hebrew and Aramaic Lexicon of the OT:

---

5 This is the other phrase that references the equinox in places like 2 Samuel 11:1(.תְּשׁוּבַת הַשָּׁנָה)

[22] Afterward, the prophet came to the king of Israel and said, "Strengthen your position and see what must be done, because next spring (lit. "turn of the year": לִתְשׁוּבַת הַשָּׁנָה) the king of Aram will attack you again."... [26] The next spring Ben-Hadad mustered the Arameans and went up to Aphek to fight against Israel.
(1 Kings 20:22, 26 NIV)

Deuteronomy 16:1 could possibly read, "*Guard the month of spring, and make then the Pesach offering.*" Therefore, the Vernal Equinox, the universal ancient marker of spring, must happen prior to Pesach.

From this Scriptural foundation, we have various confirmations of the equinoxes fixing both the spring and fall festivals. Here is just one example:

[116] And the sun, the ruler of the day, making two equinoxes every year, both in spring and autumn. *The spring equinox in the constellation of Aries*[6], and the autumnal one in Libra, give the most evident demonstration possible of the divine dignity of the number seven. *For each of the equinoxes takes place in the seventh month, at which time men are expressly commanded by law to celebrate the greatest and most popular and comprehensive festivals;* since it is owing to both these seasons, that all the fruits of the earth are engendered and brought to perfection; the fruit of corn, and all other things which are sown, owing to the vernal equinox; and that of the vine, and of all the other plants which bear hard berries, of which there are great numbers, to the autumnal one.
(Philo, On the Creation of the World, 1:116)

This idea is also generally confirmed in the Aramaic Targum of Genesis 1:14 according to Jonathan Ha Qaton:[7]

---

6 But not at the time Philo is writing! The equinox moved out of Aries around 70 BCE, or fifty years before Philo was even born. Therefore, here is another witness to the freezing of the constellation of Aries as it appeared at the time of the Exodus!

7 As explained in my ongoing Tanakh project known as *Matara*, there are two men named Jonathan ben Uzziel who are credited with creating Aramaic interpretations of some of the Tanakh in the early centuries of the Common Era. The more important Jonathan is the one who did the Prophets, and his is the authorized Targum for that section of Scripture. The other Jonathan did

[14] And YHWH said, Let there be lights in the expanse of the heavens, to distinguish between the day and the night; and let them be for signs and for festival times, and for the numbering by them the account of days, and for the sanctifying of the beginning of months, and the beginning of years, the passing away of months, and the passing away of years, the revolutions of the sun, the birth of the moon, and the revolvings (of seasons). (Genesis 1:14 Pseudo Jonathan Targum by J.W. Etheridge)

The Jerusalem Targum adds:

[14] And let them be for signs, and for seasons, and for the sanctifying by them of the beginning of months and years. (Genesis 1:14 Jerusalem Targum by J.W. Etheridge)

No matter how many ancient versions we look at, they all say, essentially, the same thing: The sun, moon and stars set the years and seasons. Not the barley. Not the rise and fall of kings. Only YHWH sending His signs counts here.

Also, every ancient witness agrees that the purpose of these heavenly bodies is *to divide the day from the night.* This is an important clue that tells us: as the sun does that for the days, so too will it do so for the year by evenly dividing day and night with the vernal and autumnal equinoxes.[8]

Although, what I found most interesting, is that when Philo fixes the equinoxes in time, he does so by Zodiac-constellation months, not solar or lunar months!

---

a Targum on the Torah, and he is who I am quoting here. Historians have generally called him: "Pseudo Jonathan"—or Fake Jonathan—but, since it is very possible that this man had this very common name and could have been the son of another man named Uzziel, I have opted for the less strident title of "Jonathan Ha Qaton" or Jonathan the Less.

8 Or to be precise, more evenly dividing the time of day and night. Modern astronomers go to great lengths to point out that the day and night are most evenly divided on an equinox day than at any other time of year, but the differing lengths of day and night will vary slightly based on one's location on the earth.

The Gregorian Patch

We need to take a slight diversion to lay down the necessary foundation to that argument. All solar calendars intercalculate in some way, whether it is by leap months or leap days, because the solar year has about a six hour remainder after its 365th day that has to be dealt with.

After all the effort put towards the 360 Prophetic calendar we need not correlate the Priestly Calendar because at the end of the cycle, we eventually come to the same number of days either way. There is no need to convert the Hebrew dates to the 360, and then to Gregorian, when going directly to Gregorian will serve just fine. Besides, without a direct conversion into Gregorian, the dates laid down thus far, will be meaningless.

On the other hand, many calendar experts warn that taking Gregorian too far backwards from its creation in 1582 is a perilous undertaking. If those doing the assessment do not believe in the literal truth of the Bible, then they aren't likely to accept this treatment.

The fact is, our Gregorian calendar was meant to correct the long-standing losses of the Julian calendar, which lost a day every 128 years. Julian was thus corrected going backward by adding 11 days. Then, going forward, Gregorian instituted 97 leap days in a 400 year period, instead of the Julian's 100 leap days in the same time frame. As a result, instead of losing a day every 128 years, the new calendar was accurate to losing a day every 3,300 years!

We immediately see the problem: Moshe's day is more than 3,500 years in the past, so it would seem that Gregorian loses its accuracy when looking at that period in history. Thankfully, however, Scripture does give us an ancient answer to this seemingly scientifically sound obstacle:

> Joshua said to YHWH on the day that YHWH gave the Amorites over to Israel: "O sun, stand still of Gibeon! O moon, [stay] over

the Valley of Ayalon." *So the sun stood still and the moon stopped in its place* until the nation took full vengeance on its enemies as it is written in the Book of the Upright[9] *The sun then stopped in the middle of the sky and delayed going down for almost a full day*. There has never been a day like it before or since, a day when YHWH listened to a man. Surely YHWH was fighting for Israel! Joshua 10:12-14 (Matara)

Then the word of YHWH came to Isaiah: "Go and say to Hezekiah, 'This is what YHWH, the Elohim of your ancestor David, says: I have heard your prayer and seen your tears. Behold! I will add fifteen years to your life. And I will deliver you and this city from the hand of the king of Assyria. I will defend this city. This is YHWH's sign to you that YHWH will do what he has promised: *I will make the shadow cast by the sun go back the ten steps it has gone down on the stairway of Ahaz.'" So the sunlight went back the ten steps it had gone down.* Isaiah 38:4-8 (Matara)

If we take these verses literally, it is beyond dispute that the sun and moon were held still for a combined day - at the very least! Since the sun and the moon are marking the year then, their pausing for a day while the rest of our galaxy keeps moving would have synchronized our solar system to the galaxy - in effect patching Gregorian, so it did not lose that day from 6600 years in the past or 3300 days from 1582[10]. In practical terms, any range of dates from about 5018 BCE to 4882 CE can be accurately charted with the Gregorian system without losing a day.[11]

---

9 Yasher, or, as it is typically rendered in most translations, Jasher, is not a proper name. It is an adjective meaning "upright/righteous". Contrary to popular speculation, all purported versions of this work are apocryphal and/or of very late origin.

10 A fair question that sometimes comes up is this: If the sun and moon paused in their orbits over Israel, why didn't other cultures report such an incredible event? While the text is not absolutely clear, the literal nature of the overall reference certainly is. The best I can suggest is that this sign was meant exclusively for the encouragement of Israel and the demoralization of her enemies. There would be no spiritual reason to have people anywhere else on the planet experience this. By the time YHWH was finished, their calendars too would be in perfect synchronization as well. If pressed for an educated guess, my personal belief is, that for this one very special day YHWH froze the rest of the people of the world into a kind of suspended animation until all the calendars got back in synch with the Galaxy. This occuring not just for their times, but for the duration of the remaining human ages prior to Mashiyach coming back.

11 This is because we need to bear in mind that since Gregorian is patched in this manner, we

Therefore, as we convert the other times into Gregorian, there will be no such concern about losing any time. We must bear in mind that such a situation means we can now turn to Lunar/Gregorian tables with great accuracy and even determine when a biblical year would have a leap day on February 29th by our reckoning.

Finally, to preview features of the Constellation Clock and its accompanying data set at: WWW.WHEELOFSTARS.COM. We find that the tables still point to the VE day of Friday, March 21, 1469 BCE, ending in year 6900 CE even though this date is more than 8,000 years out from its start point. The most we might have to "add" would be two days even from that distant starting point. From the Constellation Clock's perspective, it is still the time of the Vernal Equinox and means that when Gregorian lags a little behind it is more likely to see that same day on March 19th, rather than March 20/21.

---

can double the amount of years backwards from 1582 CE and maintain accuracy, encompassing 6,600 years in the past from that time. This will put the synchronization back before Adam's time, which is all we need.

Chapter 3

The Prophetic Calendar

"NOW YOU—SON OF MAN—TAKE FOR YOURSELF A SLAB
OF CLAY AND PLACE IT IN FRONT OF YOU. INSCRIBE
UPON IT THE LIKENESS OF THE CITY OF YERUSHALAYIM.
PICTURE IT AS IF IT WERE UNDER SIEGE; CONSTRUCT
TOWERS AGAINST IT AND RAISE GREAT BATTERING-
RAMS AGAINST IT! THEN TAKE AN IRON PLATE AND
SECURE IT AS AN IRON BARRIER BETWEEN YOU AND THE
CITY—DO NOT TAKE YOUR EYES OFF IT! THE CITY IS
UNDER SIEGE AND YOU ARE ITS ATTACKER! THIS WILL
BE YOUR SIGN-BANNER FOR THE HOUSE OF ISRAEL...
"NEXT, YOU ARE TO LIE ON YOUR LEFT SIDE, AND HAVE
IT SUFFER ALL THE GUILT OF THE HOUSE OF ISRA'EL- FOR
AS MANY DAYS AS YOU LIE ON YOUR SIDE, YOU WILL
SUFFER THEIR GUILT. FOR I AM ASSIGNING YOU ONE
DAY FOR EACH YEAR OF THEIR GUILT; IN THIS WAY YOU
ARE TO ENDURE THE GUILT OF THE HOUSE OF ISRA'EL
FOR 390 DAYS. THEN, WHEN YOU HAVE FINISHED THAT,
YOU ARE TO LIE ON YOUR RIGHT SIDE AND SUFFER THE
GUILT OF THE HOUSE OF Y'HUDAH FOR FORTY DAYS,
EACH DAY CORRESPONDING TO A YEAR; THIS IS WHAT
I AM ASSIGNING YOU. YOU ARE TO KEEP YOUR EYES
CONSTANTLY ON THE SIEGE OF YERUSHALAYIM, AND,
WITH YOUR ARM STRIPPED BARE, PROPHESY AGAINST IT."
YECHEZKEL 4:1-7 (MATARA)

Section 1: The Basics
Same Mechanism - Different Purpose (from Pre-Metonic)

In terms of the beginning points (creation of Adam), length of the year (360 days), and the balancing mechanism of leap months already described, these two calendars seem nearly identical and in fact I also viewed them as such until fairly recently.

However, there are two very significant differences between them. First, the Solar Pre-Metonic is a practical calendar meant for man's use, whereas the Prophetic is purely meant to showcase YHWH's eternal nature and to better help us understand the answers to some difficult questions in the Biblical record.

Second, the Prophetic is meant to do justice to the one sacred number, probably better expressed as "sacred interval", which the Solar Pre-Metonic ignored. In other words, both calendars use systems based on "Scripture Math" numbers like 7, 40, 100, and so on.

The one special number that Pre-Metonic does not address is 50, or the Jubilee cycle. It's not that 50 isn't "understood" by that calendar. Rather, it is the case that 50 is used to measure prophetic trends that a practical calendar is just not suitable for. This becomes a key concept when, for example, we realize that Y'shua's first coming was tied to the Land Shabbat cycle, but not the Jubilee, as in Daniel 9. Therefore, the Solar Pre-Metonic, in effect, defers to the Prophetic to unlock the mystery of both Advents. It cannot and does not proceed from the base generation of 40 years to the Jubilee of 50 but, instead, goes on to higher numbers that both calendars share.

The reason the First Coming is tied to the Land Shabbat is because Y'shua fulfilled that timescale the first time, and the next marker to herald his return is the Jubilee that this calendar, the Prophetic, was created to unlock.

Proving a 50 Year Jubilee Cycle

But first, we need to absolutely establish that a Jubilee is 50 years and not 49. My experience on this matter is that people think it unlikely that there could be two Sabbatical years back to back, which would be the case with years 49 and 50 of the Jubilee cycle. My answer to that is simply to prove that exactly such a scenario happens at a lower level and therefore is not precluded for the higher one. For example, an Annual Shabbat like the first or last day of Sukkot could run Thurs-Fri and the weekly one would start Fri-Sat. Here, we simply have two separate sanctification processes.

From there, it just comes down to Scripture:

> "Count off seven Sabbaths of years -seven times seven years -*so that the seven Sabbaths of years amount to a period of forty-nine years. Then have the trumpet sounded everywhere on the tenth day of the seventh month[1]; on the Day of Atonement sound the trumpet throughout your land. Consecrate the fiftieth year and proclaim liberty throughout the land to all its inhabitants. It shall be a jubilee for you*; each one of you is to return to his family property and each to his own clan. *The fiftieth year shall be a jubilee for you*; do not sow and do not reap what grows of itself or harvest the untended vines. For it is a jubilee and is to be holy for you; eat only what is taken directly from the fields. In this Year of Jubilee everyone is to return to his own property"
> (Leviticus 25:8-13 NIV)

Of course, we have already seen in the opening section how 50 is linked to the Tabernacle, the omer count, and the value of land and barley. *There are no coincidences in Scripture!*

---

1 This is not only because it is the seventh month but also the halfway point of the Hebrew year as marked by the autumnal equinox.

Understanding Prophetic and Practical:
Sabbatical and Jubilee Years

As we saw in the previous quoting of Leviticus 25:8-13, the counts for the Sabbatical and Jubilee years that Israel were given were tied to the entry into Canaan, not to the Exodus that happened 40 years earlier. We will see a bit later on though how there may have been an earlier component to the Jubilee law that was not given to Israel.

For now, the main point is that YHWH did not intend for there to be a 40 year delay in this Israelite portion of His instruction starting in Canaan. The delay was caused by the Israelites worshipping the Golden Calf. Even as Israel was still wandering, YHWH gave this warning as a reminder for what would happen after they got to the Promised Land:

> *Do not defile yourselves in any of these ways, because this is how the nations that I am going to drive out before you became defiled.* Even the land was defiled; so I punished it for its sin, and the land vomited out its inhabitants. *But you must keep my decrees and my laws.* The native-born and the aliens living among you must not do any of these detestable things, for all these things were done by the people who lived in the land before you, and the land became defiled. *And if you defile the land, it will vomit you out as it vomited out the nations that were before you.* (Leviticus 18:24-28-NIV)

However, when almost 90 percent of the nation was taken into captivity by the Assyrians in 722 BCE, it seems a question arose among the remaining leadership: Do we keep the Sabbatical and Jubilee years when most of our nation are scattered? As history shows, their answer appeared to be no, and the lack of observance of these times may have extended even further back, dovetailing with the fact that not even Passover was observed until centuries later.

But YHWH had other ideas, and tried to tell them so:

> Then the land will enjoy its Sabbath years all the time that it lies desolate and you are in the country of your enemies; then the land

will rest and enjoy its Sabbaths. (Leviticus 26:34-NIV)

When they still did not listen, the prophecy became true:

"Furthermore, all the leaders of the Cohenim [priests] and the people became more and more unfaithful, following all the abominations of the Nations and defiling the temple of YHWH, which He had Set-Apart in Jerusalem. YHWH, the Elohim of their ancestors, sent word to them through his messengers again and again, because He had compassion on his people and on His dwelling place. *But they mocked Elohim's messengers, despised His words and scoffed at His prophets until the wrath of YHWH was aroused against His people and there was no remedy.* He brought up against them the king of the Babylonians, who killed their young men with the sword in the Set-Apart Place, and spared neither young man nor young woman, old man or aged. Elohim handed all of them over to Nebuchadnezzar. He carried to Babylon all the articles from the Temple of Elohim, both large and small, and the treasures of YHWH's Temple and the treasures of the king and his officials. They set fire to Elohim's Temple and broke down the wall of Jerusalem; they burned all the palaces and destroyed everything of value there. He carried into exile to Babylon the remnant, who escaped from the sword, and they became servants to him and his sons until the kingdom of Persia came to power. *The land enjoyed its Sabbath rests; all the time of its desolation it rested, until the seventy years were completed in fulfillment of the word of YHWH spoken by Jeremiah."* 2 Chronicles 36:14-21 (Matara)

We see then that YHWH intended Israel to forever vouchsafe her presence in the Land through continuously righteous behavior. But, when, after rebellion they were expelled, the Land took its Sabbaths anyway. Since the Jubilee is also based, at least partly, on the seven-year Sabbaths, it should not be surprising that there is a difference between the idealized Jubilee system YHWH instituted that knew no breaks, and the "practical" system that came about when rabbis began counting those same occasions from the time they returned to the Land.

It is for these reasons that the rabbinical Jubilee and Sabbatical year counting became flawed and at odds with the dates given to us by Torah. It seems that whatever the number of Jews that YHWH required to be in the Land to keep the Jubilees going was always much smaller than what the religious elite believed. It can also be shown that there was always a Jewish presence in the Land even during the Diaspora, meaning that from YHWH's perspective, that Jubilee Clock, once started in 1406 BCE, should never have stopped in the first place.

Why the Jewish leadership, including today's rabbinate and Sanhedrin, always seem to ignore this command is difficult to tell, however, the bad practice still continues. When Israel was re-born in 1948, the leading rabbis chose 1951 as the first Jubilee since the majority of Jewry returned to the Land. This has no foundation in Scripture.

That idea then leads to this final point on this subject:

> Therefore wait for Me, says YHWH, for the day I will stand up to testify. I have decided to assemble the Nations, to gather the kingdoms and to pour out my wrath on them - all my fierce anger. *The whole world will be consumed by the fire of my jealous rage. Then will I purify the lips of the peoples, that all of them may call on the name of YHWH and serve Him shoulder to shoulder.* From beyond the rivers of Cush my worshipers, my dispersed people, will bring me offerings. On that day you will not be put to shame for all the wrongs you have done to Me, because I will remove from this city those who revel in their pride. Never again will you be arrogant on My Set-Apart hill. But I will leave within you the meek and humble who trust in the name of YHWH. *The remnant of Israel will do no wrong; they will speak no lies, nor will deceit be found in their mouths. They will eat and lie down and no one will make them afraid.* Zephaniah 3:8-13 (Matara)

So clearly, in the "latter days" or the "end times", proper knowledge *will* be restored to Israel so that they may serve YHWH perfectly again.

Jubilee of Jubilees!
Can We Name the Time of Mashiyach's Return?

Perhaps the most surprising discovery is seeing how the Jubilee Pattern may point, at least in a general sense, to the Second Coming of Mashiyach Y'shua. Before explaining further, let's remember that Y'shua said that only Father YHWH knows for sure when this will happen,[2] and that we will not know the hour. However, YHWH also gave us clues that clearly point to the overall time, and almost all Jewish and Christian scholars agree the clock started ticking in 1948, when Israel became a state.

There have been numerous Christian prophetic debacles in history where folks like William Miller[3] misinterpreted Scripture and followed their own human reasoning. However, even he recovered from that disaster and went on to do other things that benefit people today. If that's the worst that can happen, it is better to risk than to remain silent on the most amazing Scriptural pattern that I have ever seen.

Like its rabbinic counterpart, the Solar Pre-Metonic / Prophetic systems insert a 30 day leap month at regular intervals to compensate for the lunar year being 11-12 days shorter than the solar. However, unlike the Rabbinic, these calendars synchronize this addition, not through a 19 year lunar cycle, but through the vernal and autumnal equinoxes. In simplest terms, 1 Abib would occur on the New Moon nearest to the Vernal Equinox, although the sign of that year is not the Equinox itself but something that only happens on that day.

This conclusion is confirmed through ten years of research done by www. torahcalendar.com, which was very helpful in clarifying the details of my argument. However, while I may have the same conclusion, I have a different mechanism and explanation of the same result. My first ancient clue came from this line in Philo, ***all emphases are my own***[4]:

---

2 See Matthew 24:35-36 and Acts 1:7.
3 William Miller was a Protestant minister who predicted the world would end in 1843 and then 1844. When neither apocalypse happened, it led to what is now known as "The Great Disappointment". However, he recovered his reputation somewhat and at least two mainline Protestant offshoots, including the Seventh Day Adventists, trace their origins back to him. See William Miller in Appendix.
4 All quotes from Philo, unless otherwise stated, are from *The Works of Philo Judaeus, the*

[204] The last of all the annual festivals is that which is called ***the feast of tabernacles, which is fixed for the season of the autumnal equinox***. And by this festival the lawgiver teaches two lessons, both that it is necessary to honor equality, the first principle and beginning of justice, the principle akin to unshadowed light; and that it is becoming also, after witnessing the perfection of all the fruits of the year, to give thanks to that Being who has made them perfect. (On the Special Laws, 2:204)

From there, it simply comes down to counting. If Sukkot was fixed to the Autumnal Equinox, then by definition Pesach had to be fixed to the Vernal Equinox. *As a result, Abib 1 could occur either before or after the Vernal Equinox but Pesach would always be after*, thus ensuring the barley would ripen on time in the spring.

Josephus also agrees with this system in two quotes that need to be taken together:

[167] But Herod deprived this Matthias of the high priesthood, and burnt the other Matthias, who had raised the sedition, with his companions, alive. ***And that very night there was an eclipse of the moon.*** (Antiquities 17:167)

[213] Now, upon the approach of that feast of unleavened bread, which the law of their fathers had appointed for the Jews at this time, which feast is called the Passover {a} and is a memorial of their deliverance out of Egypt, (when they offer sacrifices with great alacrity; and when they are required to slay more sacrifices in number than at any other festival; (Antiquities 17:213)

Even a cursory reading of Josephus' text between these two events easily reveal an interval of several weeks, meaning that this eclipse of the moon on March 11th, 4 BCE cannot be the same full moon under which Pesach arrived that year.

Then, when we turn to NASA tables, the only lunar eclipse that happened

---

Contemporary of Josephus, Translated from the Greek, C. D. Yonge, 4 vols., London: Henry G. Bohn, 1854-55.

at that time in 4 BCE was on March 11th. Since eclipses can only happen at the time of the full moon, Pesach had to be a month later, at the next full moon. The new moon would then be squarely between the two events of the eclipse and Pesach, and is the one nearest to the Vernal Equinox, on March 25th!

To further confirm this was true of both equinoxes and festivals, I researched Philo for more evidence and found a great amount of detailed confirmation:

> [161] But to the seventh day of the week he has assigned the greatest festivals, those of the longest duration, *at the periods of the equinox both vernal and autumnal in each year; appointing two festivals for these two epochs, each lasting seven days; the one which takes place in the spring being for the perfection of what is being sown, and the one which falls in autumn being a feast of thanksgiving* for the bringing home of all the fruits which the trees have produced. And seven days have very appropriately been appointed to the seventh month of each equinox, so that each month might receive an especial honor of one sacred day of festival, for the purpose of refreshing and cheering the mind with its holiday. (The Decalogue[5] 1:161)

The Israelite calendar, in Biblical times, used the Exodus to act as the Jewish equivalent of using "BC" and "AD" as a marker for the Church. Ultimately, the full Hebrew calendar attempted to also fix the creation of Adam at Year 1.

Meanwhile, we need to look at a very important confirmation of this overall evidence from Josephus:

> [248] *In the month of Xanthikos, which is by us called Nisan, and is the beginning of our year, on the fourteenth day of the lunar month, when the sun is in Aries, (for in this month it was that we were delivered from bondage* under the Egyptians,) the law ordained that we should every year slay that sacrifice which I before told you we slew when we came out of Egypt, and which

---

5 Literally in Greek "the Ten Words" or Ten Commandments given at Sinai.

was called the Passover; and so we do celebrate this Passover in companies, leaving nothing of what we sacrifice till the day following. (Antiquities 3:248)

That is why the sky of the Exodus is frozen in Israelite memory as it was, and not as it appeared in Josephus' time or our own; because, currently the constellation in ascendancy at the time of the Vernal Equinox is one month before Aries, or Pisces.

From there, the priests would forever be tracking the time based on the constellations, the sun/equinoxes and the moon; bringing things into season through what some would call: the Zodiac. In fact, Josephus even tells us how these phenomena were tracked by the priests themselves:

[186] And for the twelve stones, whether we understand by them the months, or whether we understand the like number of the signs of that circle which the Greeks call the Zodiac, we shall not be mistaken in their meaning. (Antiquities 3:186)

[217] Now, the seven lamps signified the seven planets; for so many there were springing out of the lampstand. *Now, the twelve loaves that were upon the table signified the circle of the zodiac and the year*; [218] but the altar of incense, by its thirteen kinds of sweet smelling spices with which the sea replenished it, signified that God is the possessor of all things that are both in the uninhabitable and habitable parts of the earth, and that they are all to be dedicated to his use. (Jewish War 5:217-218)

Philo confirms this ancient priestly understanding as well:

[184] *and twelve is the perfect number, of which the circle of the zodiac in the heaven is a witness*, studded as it is with such numbers of brilliant constellations. *The periodical revolution of the sun is another witness, for he accomplishes his circle in twelve months*, and men also reckon the hours of the day and of the night as equal in number to the months of the year, [185] *and the passages are not few in which Moshe celebrates this number, describing the twelve tribes of his nation, appointing by law the offering of the twelve cakes of shewbread, and ordering twelve stones, on which*

inscriptions are engraved, to be woven into the sacred robe of the garment, reaching down to the feet of the high-priest, on his oracular dress. (On Flight and Finding 1:184-185)

[87] *Then on his chest there are twelve precious stones of different colors*, arranged in four rows of three stones in each row, being fashioned so as an emblem of the zodiac. *For the zodiac also consists of twelve animals, and so divides the four seasons of the year*, allotting three animals to each season. (The Special Laws, 1:87)

Philo actually goes further still, linking the Wheel of Stars well before Moshe's time to Joseph's dream in Genesis:

[7] *And the other relates to the circle of the zodiac, and is, "They worshipped me as the sun and the moon and the eleven stars."* And the interpretation of the former one, which was delivered with great violence of reproof, is as follows, "Shall you be a king and reign over us? or shall you be a lord and lord it over us?" The interpretation of the second is again full of just indignation, "Shall I, and thy mother, and thy brethren come and fall down upon the ground and worship thee?" (On Dreams 2:7)[6]

The bottom line is that both equinoxes fix the sacred seasons. Philo makes a fairly poetic insight by explaining that both systems of keeping the Jewish year have an equinox and a great Festival happening in the seventh month, as a double confirmation of the perfection of that number. That is another very important reason why Pesach can never take place before the Vernal Equinox, but Abib 1 certainly can. The other key point is that all ancient civilizations seem to be using one equinox or the other to represent their New Year's Day and to synchronize their harvest festivals as well. Egypt, for example, began the year at the autumnal equinox and Babylon and Persia ordered their year at the other one in the spring.

---

6 This reproof that Philo records also tells us the difference between the Wheel of Stars declaring the glory of YHWH and the Greeks and others who bowed down to the signs of the Zodiac as gods.

The Straight Count

Let's look at two distinct methods for counting the Jubilees. The first one, as implied already, sets a starting point from 50 years after the Israelites enter Canaan counted continuously and without gaps, from then to now. Since the Israelites wandered in the Wilderness due to their worship of the Golden Calf, the year of the Exodus or 1447 BCE, would end the exile 1407 BCE. A final adjustment for their new spring to spring calendar would put the entry into Canaan in the early months of 1406, let's count:

1) 1405, **2**) 1404, **3**) 1403, **4**) 1402, **5**) 1401, **6**) 1400, **7**) 1399
8) 1398, **9**) 1397, **10**) 1396, **11**) 1395, **12**) 1394, **13**) 1393, **14**) 1392
15) 1391, **16**) 1390, **17**) 1389, **18**) 1388, **19**) 1387, **20**) 1386, **21**) 1385
22) 1384, **23**) 1383, **24**) 1382, **25**) 1381, **26**) 1380, **27**) 1379, **28**) 1378
29) 1377, **30**) 1376, **31**) 1375, **32**) 1374, **33**) 1373, **34**) 1372, **35**) 1371
36) 1370, **37**) 1369, **38**) 1368, **39**) 1367, **40**) 1366, **41**) 1365, **42**) 1364
43) 1363, **44**) 1362, **45**) 1361, **46**) 1360, **47**) 1359, **48**) 1358, **49**) 1357

This brings us to spring of 1357 BCE. At Yom Kippur in 1357 BCE would come the announcement that the spring of the next year would be the Jubilee:

> [8] 'You are also to count off seven sabbaths of years for yourself, seven times seven years, so that you have the time of the seven Sabbaths of years, *namely*, forty-nine years. [9] 'You shall then sound a ram's horn abroad on the tenth day of the seventh month; ***on the day of atonement you shall sound a horn all through your land.*** [10] *'You shall thus consecrate the fiftieth year* and proclaim a release through the land to all its inhabitants. (Leviticus 25:8-10 NAU)

So from 1 Abib in 1356 to the 29th of Adar in 1355 is the Jubilee year. The period between this first spring count in 1406 to the proclamation is actually 49 years and 6 months, but the "50th year" must technically start at the next Abib 1 when it "turns over". The Autumnal Equinox marks the half way point of the Hebrew year, which is why the announcement is made at Yom Kippur, which will always be near that event.

In other words, the "counting" of each year is spring to spring. Forty nine (49) springs must be completed, then add 6 months to announce that the next spring (in yet another 6 months) is the Jubilee.

1355 - 49 = 1306 BCE (announcement year)

Then we go here:

1305 (actual Jubilee year) – 49 = 1256 BCE (announcement year)

1255 (actual Jubilee year)

Then count to the next Jubilee:

1) 1254, 2) 1253, 3) 1252, 4) 1251, 5) 1250, 6) 1249, 7) 1248
8) 1247, 9) 1246, 10) 1245, 11) 1244, 12) 1243, 13) 1242, 14) 1241
15) 1240, 16) 1239, 17) 1238, 18) 1237, 19) 1236, 20) 1235, 21) 1234
22) 1233, 23) 1232, 24) 1231, 25) 1230, 26) 1229, 27) 1228, 28) 1227
29) 1226, 30) 1225, 31) 1224, 32) 1223, 33) 1222, 34) 1221, 35) 1220
36) 1219, 37) 1218, 38) 1217, 39) 1216, 40) 1215, 41) 1214, 42) 1213
43) 1212, 44) 1211, 45) 1210, 46) 1209, 47) 1208, 48) 1207, 49) 1206

To simplify things, let's do this for the next one:

1206 (announcement year)

1205 (actual Jubilee year)

Subtract 7 from 1205 for first Land Shabbat: 1198

Subtract intervals of 7s from there for the rest of the count: 1191, 1184, 1177, 1170, 1163 and 1156 (announcement year).

Jubilee is the following year, 1155.

I provide these multiple examples of the same process because counting backwards in BCE time can be a bit confusing at first. Also, this is too important a topic to leave to chance.

Here's the final shortcut before proceeding to the actual list. This is the real procedure in miniature whose rules have already been shown in detail:

1) Start in spring of 1406 BCE.

2) Have the next year of 1405 be your year 1 of the first Jubilee. Then 1404 is year 2, and so on.

3) Subtract 6 more years from year 1 to get to Land Shabbat 1: 1399

4) Count 6 more intervals of 7 from there, or 42 years to 1357 BCE or the announcement year.

5) Subtract (from BCE dates) 1 more year for the actual Jubilee (1356).

6) Subtract 50 years to the next announcement year (1306) and 50 years thereafter to get to all following announcement years.

Then, as we progress with two Jubilees each century, that is any year that ends in '06 or '56, we have the following list of Jubilees counted:

BCE 1) 1356, 2) 1306, 3) 1256, 4) 1206, 5) 1156, 6) 1106, 7) 1056, 8) 1006, 9) 956, 10) 906, 11) 856, 12) 806, 13) 756, 14) 706, 15) 656, 16) 606, 17) 556, 18) 506, 19) 456, 20) 406, 21) 356, 22) 306, 23) 256, 24) 206, 25) 156, 26) 106, 27) 56, **28) 06—6 BCE.**

For CE dates we must remember: there is no year 0. Then, starting from 6 BCE, subtract 6 years to get to 1 CE:

-5, -4, -3, -2, -1 (NO YEAR 0) +1

Now with 1 CE as the 6th year, add:

CE +2 (7th)
3 (8th), 4 (9th), 5 (10th), 6 (11th), 7 (12th), 8 (13th), 9 (14th)
10 (15th), 11 (16th), 12 (17th), 13 (18th), 14 (19th), 15 (20th)
16 (21st), 17 (22nd), 18 (23rd), 19 (24th), 20 (25th), 21 (26th), 22 (27th)
23 (28th), 24 (29th), 25 (30th), 26 (31st), 27 (32nd), 28 (33rd), 29 (34th)
30 (35th), 31 (36th), 32 (37th), 33 (38th), 34 (39th), 35 (40th), 36 (41st)
37 (42nd), 38 (43rd), 39 (44th), 40 (45th), 41 (46th), 42 (47th), 43 (48th)
44 (49th)! 45 (50th- Jubilee)!

The first Jubilee in CE time is year 45, the next 95, and so on. Here are those Jubilees:

CE 29) 45, 30) 95, 31) 145, 32) 195, 33) 245, 34) 295, 35) 345, 36)
395, 37) 445, 38) 495, 39) 545, 40) 595, 41) 645, 42) 695, 43) 745, 44)
795, 45) 845, 46) 895, 47) 945, 48) 995, 49) 1045, 50) 1095, 51) 1145,
52) 1295, 53) 1345, 54) 1395, 55) 1445, 56) 1495, 57) 1545, 58) 1595,
59) 1645, 60) 1695, 61) 1745, 62) 1795, 63) 1845, 64) 1895, 65) 1945,
66) 1995, 67) 2045, 68) 2095, 69) 2145, 70) 2195

*By this method, 1995 was the start of the 66ᵗʰ Jubilee since the Israelites
entered Canaan.*

It is my contention that, just as Daniel 9:24-27 will show that the Land
Shabbat cycle named the very year of Y'shua's public debut, so too will
the only remaining timescale, the Yovel/Jubilee, presage his return. This
was, in effect, William Miller's mistake. He didn't realize that all the
timescales in Scripture, just like the sacred festivals of ancient Israel, had
to be fulfilled in some way relating to Mashiyach's first coming, ministry,
death, resurrection, ascension or return. With the 7 year Shabbat cycle
clearly fulfilled to the very day of the crucifixion, 490 years from the
issuing of the decree to rebuild *all* Jerusalem and not just her Temple
(Ezra 7:1-26), the return had to be synchronized to the only cycle of time
left.

This makes even more sense when we realize the purpose of the Jubilee:

> [10] Consecrate the fiftieth year and proclaim liberty throughout the
> land to all its inhabitants. It shall be a jubilee for you; each one of
> you is to return to his family property and each to his own clan. [11]
> The fiftieth year shall be a jubilee for you; do not sow and do not
> reap what grows of itself or harvest the untended vines. [12] For it is
> a jubilee and is to be holy for you; eat only what is taken directly
> from the fields. [13] "'In this Year of Jubilee everyone is to return to
> his own property. [14] " 'If you sell land to one of your countrymen
> or buy any from him, do not take advantage of each other. [15] You
> are to buy from your countryman on the basis of the number of
> years since the Jubilee. And he is to sell to you on the basis of
> the number of years left for harvesting crops. (Leviticus 25:10-
> 15 NIV)

So let us be realistic and ask the critical question: Who ultimately is the real owner of the land if not YHWH Himself? If Mashiyach's return is synchronized to the only remaining timescale system and that system is the one with the most apocalyptic imagery (all things being restored as they should be, the world turning upside down, the first last, the last first and so on) then the number of these cycles must also be relevant to his return.

Therefore, if 70 prophetic weeks was the pattern of his first coming, 70 Jubilees, in some form, must be the pattern for the Second Coming! *For more information on this 70 week pattern in Daniel, please see: The Seventy Weeks of Daniel 9 in section 2 of this calendar. Also, stand by for the Constellation Clock's confirmation of the 70 cycle at the end of this book!*

By the Straight Count then, we have about 200 years before Y'shua can come back. I personally have no great eagerness to hasten the arrival of that date. That is, of course, unless other evidence forced me to, at least consider the possibility. That other evidence is what I call:

The Long Count

Ultimately the Jubilee/Yovel Pattern is this:

1) A group of people move into a particular part of land. It always begins and ends with more than one person.

2) These people become wicked.

3) When their wickedness gets too great, YHWH expels them from the land they defiled either by banishment or destruction.

4) If they don't sin, however, they could stay there forever.

Unlike the Absolute Yovel, these Jubilees are on *YHWH's time table*, which I will explain shortly. *So my question is, where have we seen these "Proto-Jubilees" before and how many of them happened prior to the time of Moshe?*

The first of these "Proto-Jubilees" would, most likely, have to be the expulsion of Adam and Eve from Paradise for disobeying YHWH's Torah! However, what wouldn't count, would be Cain's wandering into Nod, since that expulsion only affected him and he didn't "know his wife" or have children until after he left (Genesis 4:17-18). Plus, the expulsion of Cain was directly linked to the larger event of Adam and Eve being booted out of Eden.

The second Proto-Jubilee is even more obvious: almost all of humanity is wiped out by the Flood specifically because of their wickedness. That disaster is followed by Proto-Jubilee #3: the destruction of Sodom and Gomorrah, again, for the reasons as denoted previously.

And finally, the Canaanites are expelled from their land for "detestable practices" (like cutting out and offering the hearts of their young sons and daughters to the sun gods). The fact that YHWH uses their plight to warn the Israelites that the same fate may befall them if they disobey, is the strongest piece of evidence we have that the Jubilee Principle preceded the Israelite entry into Canaan.

In saying all this, a necessary question gets asked: Would the 50 year Jubilee cycle apply *backwards* from Moshe's day? My answer is no, because the interval is never mentioned in any place prior to the conquest of Canaan and this is what I mean by "on YHWH's time" i.e. not tracked by man counting a fixed amount of his human years. In saying this, I know some would disagree and want to apply 120 50 year cycles to the prophecy in Genesis 6:3. *For more information on how this alternate method still results in the same calculations, please see The Prophecy of Genesis 6:3 Explained.*

The other issue here is that nowhere is the timing for the *punishment* of disobedience mentioned in either system. Therefore, the best we can do is simply leave that matter to YHWH's own timing and judgment. To force an interval or outcome that isn't even hinted at in terms of its fruition is, in my view, the height of irresponsibility and disrespect to the Scripture.

Returning to the main point of this section, the Long Count would simply append the Proto-Jubilees to the other Jubilees, *resulting in 1995 being the 70*^{*th*} *Jubilee since the creation of Adam and Eve made the keeping of this clock necessary by YHWH.* Again, if Y'shua appeared the first time at the end of the previous 70 cycle, *chances are excellent he will return before the end of this 70 cycle, or somewhere between now and 2045.*

During that same interval in our century, the 2000th anniversary of the resurrection is, most probably, in the year 2030 and no later than 2033, making this range within the overall range especially significant. Here are some other facts to consider in assessing this paradigm:

Fact 1: The Various Meanings of Yovel/Jubilee also point to the bigger picture of the "rules"

Between the Great Flood and the death of Moshe is the clearest example of what I am talking about:

> And YHWH said to Moshe, "Go to the people and set them apart today and tomorrow. Have them wash their clothes and be ready by the third day, because on that day YHWH will come down on Mount Sinai in the sight of all the people. Place boundaries for the people around the mountain and tell them, *'Be careful that you do not go up the mountain or touch the foot of it. Whoever touches the mountain shall surely be put to death.* He will certainly be stoned or shot with arrows; not a hand is to be laid on him. Whether man or animal, he will not be allowed to live.' Only when the *ram's horn sounds* a sustained blast may they go up to the mountain." Exodus 19:10-13 (Matara)

Here we see that another sacred piece of real estate has been set aside. If they go up the mountain at the right time, all is well. But, if they go before the ram's horn blows, they are to die, a sure way to be separated or expelled out of the land!

Even more remarkably, the word used for "ram's horn" is the same word for "jubilee"—*yovel*! This is, once more, an exchange of property between YHWH and Israel.

Fact 2: Y'shua himself ties the Jubilee imagery to his Second Coming
There are a total of three places where Y'shua directly references different components of this Jubilee pattern, I will only show two for now. Here is the first:

> Then Keefa drew near to him and said, "My Master, how many times should I forgive my brother with me who is at fault. Should I forgive him up to seven times?" Y'shua said to him, "I do not say to you up to seven times, rather up to...***seven times seventy***." Matthew 18:21-22 (AENT)

This passage is important because of two words. The first is *zabnea*, rendered as "times" but also possessing two other key meanings of "period/cycle" or "seasons". The Jubilee pattern is clearly both 70 "seasons" for the longer cycle and 490 day/year cycles from Daniel to Y'shua's first coming.[7]

The next and last phrase, seven times seventy, also has relevance to the topic of forgiveness. Y'shua is hinting here that you should forgive during these seasons, because after them, forgiveness won't be available during the judgment. The second reference to the Jubilee pattern by Y'shua is here:

> (Y'shua said), "And he will send his Messengers with a large trumpet, and they will gather his chosen ones from the four winds and from one end of heaven to another." Matthew 24:31 (AENT)

If we follow this speech all the way to the end of the chapter, it is crystal clear that Y'shua is saying the blowing of a trumpet, actually the Aramaic word for "shofar", is linked to his return (Matthew 24:42). ***Another word for ram's horn is yovel (Jubilee).***

Fact 3: The Canaanites were warned that their disobedience would cause them to lose the right to live in Israel. This warning was echoed to the Israelites.

1406 BCE was a time that a Jubilee came due for the Canaanites. It was at this same time that the Israelites took possession of the land that was

---

7 For more information on this topic, please see *The Seventy Weeks of Daniel 9*.

sworn to Abraham. This reversion of the land to its official owners is the
essence of the Jubilee definition. Let's see what Scripture tells us:

> Who is like unto You among the (false) gods O YHWH?[8] You are
> majestic in Your Set-Apart Being and wondrous in glory in the
> working of miracles. You stretched forth Your right hand and the
> earth swallowed them whole. In your loving kindness You have
> led the people whom you have redeemed[9] and in Your might You
> will guide them to Your Set-Apart abode. The Nations will hear
> and tremble; anguish will take hold of the Philistine people. The
> rulers of Edom will be dumbstruck with fear. The leaders of Moab
> will likewise be gripped with trembling terror while the people of
> Canaan have melted away into nothingness. Terror and dread will
> fall on them! By the power of Your arm they will be still as stone
> until Your people pass by O YHWH! Until the people you have
> bought pass by! You will bring them in and place them upon the
> mountain of Your legacy. That place, O YHWH, is what You made
> for Your residence, the Set-Apart place O YHWH that Your hands
> placed on a firm foundation. YHWH will rule forever and ever!
> Exodus 15:11-18 (Matara)

These are all residents of what would later become Israel! Some more
explanation is given here:

> For Gaza will be abandoned and Askelon laid to waste. Ashdod will
> be emptied out by noon and Ekron will be uprooted. *Woe to you
> who dwell near the coast of the sea! O Kerethite people the word
> of YHWH is against you! O Canaan, land of the Philistines: "I
> will destroy you completely and leave none alive.*" The land near
> the sea, where the Kerethites live, will be the abode of shepherds
> and sheep pens. It will become a possession for the house of
> Yehudah, for there they will find pasture. In the evening they will
> sleep in the houses of Askelon. YHWH their Elohim will take care
> of them and restore their wealth. Zephaniah 2:4-7 (Matara)

So it was clearly written. So it was done!

8 This phrase "who is like unto You El" actually is micha mocha el in Hebrew, and is the source
for the name of Michael.
9 Or, "paid the price for". the same word used when Boaz redeemed Ruth.

Section 2: The Mechanics
Reviewing the Cycles

To start off this section, let me re-visit the calendar system laid out previously:

1) The Prophetic/Solar Pre-Metonic Calendar systems involve the sun, moon, and the constellations bringing the seasons into proper synchronization.

2) There is a descending pecking order of authorities which must approve the year and stay true to the command of Genesis 1:14-19.

3) That pecking order begins with the synchronization of main 4,000 year cycle which, at a macro level, manifests in not losing a day for 100,000 years. Longer time cycles, in the trillions of years, while not detailed here, are also shown from Scripture, making the calendar, essentially, eternal. For our purposes, consider the 4,000 year main cycle as that of the constellations' role in keeping the festivals on time. Other mechanisms, such as the Gregorian Patch, assist the calendar by making sure the Earth is in total harmony with the rest of our Milky Way Galaxy, which is the most precise timekeeping system currently known to Man.

4) From there the hierarchy gives ultimate annual authority to the signs of the sun. When the sun, under YHWH's guidance, of course, "approves" the year, it passes authority to the moon to regulate the months for the duration of that year (but never the week). The appointed time cycle is guaranteed to have the lunar months progress properly from Spring to Spring. (The time barley will be ripe.) This "ripeness" alone will never be used to set the year. The barley, our main earth sign, simply confirms the time of year after approval has been given it by the sun and moon.

5) When the days of the year run out, power returns to the sun to re-synchronize each year. In a pattern that echoes that of: *"and there was evening and there was morning day one"* the equinoxes evenly divide the day and night for the two sacred seasons of the year, Pesach and Sukkot. The Feast of Pesach (on the 14th day of the month) is synchronized so as to never occur prior to its accompanying equinox; but the Vernal Equinox can occur either before or after Abib 1.

Applying Details from the Big Picture

From these main points we turn to the Biblical data to see how certain recurring numbers relate to keeping the festivals in season:

6) Scripture tells us that a 42 month period is 1260 days and other times 1290 days.

7) Scripture also tells us that the overall count in a Biblical year are 12 months of 30 days each, existing side by side with the, more familiar, compound lunar-solar calendar that is used to regulate when Pesach and other Great Feasts occur in the year. Noah counted 5 months of 30 days each to come up with a total of 150 days. The constancy of the 30 day month is also recorded by other reliable ancient authorities.

8) In order for the 360 day calendar to harmonize with a 365.2422 day year, the data above, and previously discussed items, it must show that a common sense, intercalculary month system that existed at least a thousand years before the Metonic cycle was developed in Babylon and later adapted by the Rabbinic calendar. Genesis 1:14-19 says that the sun and moon must set the year together, as opposed to barley, the ascension of kings, or other similar ancient man-made schemes.

9) So the first cycle is a 360 day year x 6 years = 2,160 days. When we add a leap month, just before the commencement of the 7th year, the addition will bring our total to 2,190 days. 2,190/6 = 365 days.

10) Now, because our year is actually 365.25 days, we need another calibration to balance the "leap year". That tweak is that we will go through 6 of the aforementioned cycles (36 years), with a leap month added before the commencement of the 7th year. In order for this to coincide with the generation as 40 year model in Scripture, the 40th year also has a leap month added. Here's that math:

(2,190 day 6 year periods) x 6	= 13,140 days
Then ADD 4 360 day/years: 13,140 + (360 x 4)	= 1,440 days
Then ADD another leap month for the 40th year	= 30 days
TOTAL sum of days = 13,140 + 1,440 + 30	= 14,610 days
Then DIVIDE the total sum by 40 to get the year length: 14,610/40	= **365.25 days/year**

11) Technically, the year is just slightly shorter than 365.25 days with an actual length of 365.2425 days per our Gregorian system. In order to make sure that very small difference doesn't compound and error, we need to bring in the 100 year generation tool. This tool, like the 40 year mechanism introduced earlier, will be shown to match Scripture in an upcoming section. For now, I am trying to paint a solid general picture. In this case, the two generational timescales (40 and 100) combine for a total period of 4,000 years, after which, the leap month does not occur. So, every 4,000 years, the scheduled leap month would be **omitted**. It is, in essence, a 40 year generation cycled 100 times with the last cycle losing the extra month.

12) To understand why this is the case, let's remember that the 360 day calendar adds 7 leap months every 40 years, or **one leap month after the 6th, 12th, 18th, 24th, 30th, 36th and 39th years**. That gives us 14,610 days. Let's use the math to take it from here:

(14,610 days in 40 year periods x 100) – 30 days omitted in the 100th cycle = 1, 460,970 days in 4,000 years.

DIVIDE 1,460,970 days by 4,000 years = **365.2425 days/year**

Why Does this Work?

It works because YHWH is not the Author of confusion and because He has given us all of these mathematical formulas in Scripture, not just for the ancients to use, but for use in our own day as well. The heart of this calendar, and by far the most important fact regarding it, is the 40 year cycle, so let's see where that comes from.

YHWH said to Moshe and Aaron in Egypt, "This month is to be for you the first month, the first month of your year. Exodus 12:1-2 (Matara)

Many people know this passage extremely well, but few realize its total significance. YHWH says, "this is to be the first month" and previously, in Genesis 15:13-16, that Israel will be captive for 400 years (4 centuries, cycles of time, *dor* and *meah* in Hebrew). He is letting Moshe know that both the enslavement and deliverance are happening on His timetable that was set long ago. This is why we are told the following:

> [10] *I make known the end from the beginning, from ancient times, what is still to come*. I say: My purpose will stand, and I will do all that I please. [11] From the east I summon a bird of prey; from a far-off land, a man to fulfill my purpose. *What I have said, that will I bring about; what I have planned, that will I do*. [12] Listen to me, you stubborn-hearted, you who are far from righteousness. [13] *I am bringing my righteousness near, it is not far away; and my salvation will not be delayed. I will grant salvation to Zion, my splendor to Israel.* (Isaiah 46:10-1 NIV)

As alluded to previously, we have both 40 and 100 year cycles or "generations" in Scripture, the product of which adds up to a 4,000 year super-cycle. The reason we can be so certain of this, is that 40 year patterns begin directly after this time.

According to Deuteronomy 1:3, Israel entered Canaan precisely 40 years after the Exodus. At that time, their leader Moshe was exactly 80 years old and would live exactly 40 more years, the time a generation had to wander in the Wilderness for worshipping the Golden Calf. Moshe finally dies at 120, the precise ideal lifespan for man given by YHWH (Genesis 6:3). Before this time, Moshe had spent 40 years in Midian and a prior 40 years in Egypt (Acts 7:23-30).

The fact that the firmly dated Exodus occasion became the equivalent of "BC" and "AD" for the Christian world is evident in the actual records kept in Solomon's court. The Exodus ocurred 480 years before he began building the Temple (1 Kings 6:1). Four hundred and eighty years is of course 12 generations of 40 years each. This is our anchor. This is the start of YHWH's cycle told to us directly by YHWH Himself![10]

---

10 As the author of www.360calendar.com correctly observes: "Observe that an overlap of one month (30 days), therefore, occurs between the years 6 BC and AD 2555 (2560 years). This is because the 4000-calendar from the Exodus will not complete its first cycle until AD 2555 thereby being ahead of the Creation-calendar by one leap-month all during this 2560-year span. This means that currently, and for the next 560 years, there is a one-month gap between the two

Y'shua's Birth the Ultimate Time Marker!

We saw earlier how the Exodus day was unique, mathematically speaking, in the heavens with the alignment of all the possible sevens across all systems. Similar properties are also in evidence for the year that Y'shua's coming was announced in the heavens as well as the year he died and was resurrected.

Later, we will look at using the Patriarchal Ages from all the ancient Witnesses, employing a "majority rule" approach to affix the time of Adam's creation. That time frame is agreed upon by most scholars to be about 4,000 BCE. When I accept a date for an ancestor's age regarding the birth to their son as being factually established by two or more of these ancient witnesses, the date I come up with is for Adam's creation is precisely 4,000 BCE. It is, likely, closer to 4,007 BCE[11], because YHWH's pattern is to have all intervals evenly divisible by a factor of 10. This will bring us to an interval of 2,560 years between Adam and the Exodus, and exactly 4,000 years between Adam and the beginning of the Triple Conjunctions of Jupiter and Saturn that announced to the Magi Y'shua was about to be born in 7 BCE![12]

The 4,000 year cycle commencing with the Exodus, tells us that we have other 4,000 year intervals to explore:

> So also is it written: *"Adam, the first man, became a living soul;"* *the second Adam (became) a resurrecting spirit.* And the spiritual was not first; but the animal, and then the spiritual. *The first man was of dust from the earth; the second man was Master YHWH*

---

calendars." There are many other details about the intricacies of these calendars on the website that I feel are worth a separate read as opposed to my summarizing all of them. Sufficed to say, everything works, 100% of the time, as YHWH intended.

11 Because of the way my "majority rule" approach is set up, 4000 BCE, is in fact, the latest time that Adam could be born. For example, my adoption of the shorter 215 year interval for the sojourn into Egypt would, if incorrect, add two more centuries to the total amount of time between Adam and us. As a result, the minimal rounding to an even ten year period would have to be backwards from 4,000 BCE and not forwards. Such is my most educated guess from the available data.

12 For more information on why the Star of Bethlehem is actually the planet Jupiter, please consult my book, *Y'shua Year by Year*.

from heaven. As he was of the dust, so also those who are of the dust; and as was he who was from heaven, so also are the heavenly. And as we have worn the likeness of him from the dust, so will we wear the likeness of him from heaven.
1 Corinthians 15:45-49 (AENT)

This is a hugely important hint! The first Adam brought death, but the second (or last) Adam brings eternal life, right? *Well isn't it fair to say that he also brings about eternal time through both of his origins as the Word and our future?* That being the case, it cannot be a coincidence that 4,000 years is the interval between the birth of Adam and the announcement in the heavens of the imminent birth of Y'shua our Mashiyach; the last Adam.

Since Adam means "man", this may be another meaning of Genesis 6:3: that life will not abide in *man* forever. The second manifestation of this "*man*" brings eternal life during this exact interval of time! Therefore, 4,000 years is the heart of the "life count" for the whole calendar. Isn't it nice to know that YHWH, in His fashion, is also using the template from Adam to Y'shua as the measuring stick for the foundational unit of humanity? If that isn't preaching the Good News through His timings, I don't know what is!

Additional Intervals for the Wheel of Stars

The last interval I am going to address directly is the 100,000 year cycle. This is because it is the last interval that is easily and directly provable from Scripture *and* has a practical benefit for mankind during his observable past and foreseeable future on this planet. From this point, we get into a rarified and exceedingly abstract system that will essentially be eternal, balancing properly for trillions of years. I will leave that aspect to the folks at www.360calendar.com to fully elucidate. Perhaps if there is further interest, I may add additional elements for those that would request it. But, for now, it seems sufficient to focus on how Biblical data yields a calendar more accurate than our own and that it will continue into the exceedingly distant future long after everyone reading (and writing) this is gone.

The principal purpose of revealing this calendar is to demonstrate how, through its ancient characteristics, YHWH has preserved all our time and, from that time forward, show how Scriptural concepts lead us inexorably to the time of Mashiyach's return. Once Mashiyach comes back, all bets on the nature of time and space are off anyway.

And so, that brings us to the last interval directly deduced from Biblical numbers:

> You will not make for yourself an idol in the form of anything that exists in the heavens above or on the earth beneath or in the waters below. You will not bow down to them or worship them because I, YHWH, your Elohim, am a jealous Elohim, *punishing the children for the sins of their fathers to the third and fourth generation of those who hate me but showing love to a thousand generations of those who love Me* and keep My commandments. Exodus 20:4-6 (Matara. Also see Deuteronomy 5:10, 7:9; 1 Chronicles 16:15; Psalm 105:8)

The multiple witnesses of this interval admirably showcase its overall importance. From here, only two permutations are left. Forty thousand years (1,000 generations at 40 years each), is already covered in the other cycles mentioned previously. That leaves the only other number for generations: 100 years X 1,000 generations, or 100,000 years total.

All that we have seen before, tells us these numbers balance. Therefore, with the previous foundation laid squarely from Scripture, we must turn to the one remaining way 100,000 year cycles balance based on the previous equations.

Here's how it works:

> 40 year cycles are the foundation of the calendar and each of these consist of 7 intervals where an intercalculated month is added.
> 4,000 year cycles omit the leap month that would have occurred at that time, or the 100th leap occurrence does not happen, even though it does occur in the preceding 99.

The last 40 year cycle, of the last 4000 year cycle of 100,000 years, consists of the regular addition of a leap month every 6 years, except that the *6th leap month is omitted at the 36th year*, and the *7th leap month is omitted at the 40th year*. The omission of the last two intercalary months brings the total number of days in 100 millennia to **within hours** of the actual number of days in 100,000 tropical years.

Or, to put it another way:

100 cycles of 40 years = 4,000 years = (14,610 days per 40 years x 100) – 30 days omitted in 100th cycle = 1,460,970 days each 4,000 years

25 cycles of 4,000 years = **(1,460,970 days x 25) – 30 days** = 100,000 years

Therefore, 100,000 years = 36,524,220 days/100, 000 = **365.2422 days/ year**

That figure, 365.2422 days, is more accurate than our current Gregorian Calendar (365.2425 days) and extremely close to the tropical year as it is measured today at 365.2421897 or 365 days, 5 hours, 48 minutes, 45.19 seconds. This is how amazingly accurate we can get by simply following the blueprint YHWH our Creator laid out in His Word!

The Seventy Weeks in Daniel 9

Now let's review the other key 70 cycle, as explained by Daniel. Let's start with what YHWH tells him here:

> "Daniel, I have now come to give you insight and understanding. As soon as you began to pray, an answer was given, which I have come to tell you, for you are highly esteemed. Therefore, consider the message and understand the vision: Seventy 'sevens' are decreed for your people and your holy city to finish transgression, to put an end to sin, to atone for wickedness, to bring in everlasting righteousness, to seal up vision and prophecy and to anoint the most

holy. Know and understand this: From the issuing of the decree to restore and rebuild Jerusalem until the Anointed One, the ruler, comes, there will be seven 'sevens,' and sixty-two 'sevens.' It will be rebuilt with streets and a trench, but in times of trouble. After the sixty-two 'sevens,' the Anointed One will be cut off and will have nothing. The people of the ruler who will come will destroy the city and the sanctuary. The end will come like a flood: War will continue until the end, and desolations have been decreed. *He will confirm a covenant with many for one 'seven.' In the middle of the 'seven' he will put an end to sacrifice and offering.* And on a wing of the temple he will set up an abomination that causes desolation[13], until the end that is decreed is poured out on him." (Daniel 9:22-27-NIV)

The majority of the time verses 24-27 (from the first mention of "seventy sevens") are what draws most of the attention. I have also written about how Daniel's Mashiyach clock starts in the year 457 BCE, the seventh year of Xerxes. The reason was simple: Of the three decrees that Jews received to return and rebuild, the last one was the only one that specifically allowed the entire city of Jerusalem, not just the Temple, to be restored.

Following the day = year pattern outlined in Ezekiel 4:4-6, 69 weeks equals 483 years, bringing us to 27 CE, the time of the Baptism. The "he will confirm a covenant with many for one seven, but in the middle of the seven, will put an end to sacrifice and offering" passage would refer to the 70th week, or the three and a half year ministry of Y'shua. Other translations are even clearer saying he is "cut off" at this time, a sure metaphor for death (Isaiah 53:8).

Daniel hits the very day of the crucifixion on the nose from 500 years out, as Y'shua dies in the middle of the week after three and a half years are completed (if we follow John's chronology of multiple Passovers and other Great Feasts, including Tabernacles and Hanukkah).

---

13 As mentioned in Andrew Gabriel Roth's *Ruach Qadim*, this prophecy was fulfilled when the Romans put their pagan ensigns on the burnt remnants of the destroyed Temple, as was recorded by Josephus. This also explains the shadow and type of Anti-Mashiyach that is referred to by Rav Shaul in his letters.

Some argue that the 70th week in Daniel will not be fulfilled until we are close to Mashiyach's return. I was equally convinced at one time, however, that the 70th week followed right on the heels of the end of the 69th, which coincided with the Baptism. Now it seems, both assertions may be right. This part of Daniel represents a multi-layered embedded prophecy speaking to two different covenants on two different time scales.[14] In previous study, I refer to the "sealing up" metaphors in Daniel as marking the boundaries between the long and short term prophetic branches. Similar language is found when the messenger Gabriel responds to Daniel's prayer and brings him wisdom and understanding, as we saw above.

Additionally, the prayer Daniel gives specifically harkens back to the time of Moshe and provides us a vital hint:

> *And now, YHWH[15] our Elohim, Who brought Your people out of Egypt with a mighty hand and Who made for Yourself a Name that has lasted to this very day, we have sinned* and we have done evil, O YHWH, according to all Your righteous deeds, turn back from Your anger and wrath away from Jerusalem Your city and Your Set-Apart hill. Our sins and the sins of our ancestors have made Jerusalem and Your people an object of scorn to everyone around us. Now, our Elohim, hear the prayers and petitions of Your servant. For Your sake, O YHWH, look with favor on Your desolated Set-Apart place. Incline Your ear to us, O Elohim and hear us. Open Your eyes and see the desolation of the city that bears Your Name. We do not entreat you because we are righteous but because You have great mercy. O, YHWH hear us! O YHWH, forgive us! O YHWH, hear and act in our behalf! For your sake, O my Elohim do not be hindered, because Your city and Your people bear Your Name. Daniel 9:15-19 (Matara)

So, with Daniel linking the more recent sins to the original time of the Exodus, it is possible to see two strands of "70 weeks". The first strand

14 For a full analysis of how embedded prophecies work with respect to the virgin birth and Isaiah 7:14, please consult the appendix of the AENT. (see WWW.AENT.ORG)
15 Everywhere "YHWH" appears in 9:15-18 was replaced with "Adonai" by the Masoretes. YHWH is therefore restored here.

is on "Jubilee" time and is referring to the total working out of salvation from either the creation of Adam or the entry into Canaan, (depending on the counting method) until the return of the Mashiyach. Alternatively, the second strand is much smaller; showing the time from the decree to rebuild Jerusalem to Mashiyach's first coming. In both cases, we are dealing with 70 sevens!

Furthermore, this ordering makes perfect sense, since you must be in the Land before you can build (and rebuild) the Temple. There is also good reason to believe that the Temple was built on Mt. Moriah where Abraham was about to sacrifice his son Isaac, which confirmed the covenant with Abraham's seed in the first place!

The Prophecy of Genesis 6:3 Explained

The reader should note that the following abbreviations for versions of Scripture are used throughout this section:

MT = Masoretic Text, or the standardized version of the Hebrew Bible completed by the Masoretes in about the 11th century, but based on many ancient versions and readings that were adopted in the long history of the Hebrew people.

LXX = Septuagint (or "Seventy"), the Greek translation of the Tanakh ("Old" Testament)

Sam/Samaritan/SP = The Samaritan version of the first five books of the Bible ("Pentateuch"), oldest manuscript known, dated at about 128 BCE.

DSS = Dead Sea Scrolls. Other references are for parts of this collection. So, for example 4QExod means "found in Qumran Cave 4, a version of the book of Exodus".

Problems with Previous Chronology Systems

The following appears in Easton's Bible Dictionary under "Chronology":

> To show, at a glance, the different ideas of the date of the creation,

it may be interesting to note the following: **From Creation to 1894**. According to Ussher, 5,898; Hales, 7,305; Zunz (Hebrew reckoning), 5,882; Septuagint (Perowne), 7,305; Rabbinical, 5,654; Panodorus, 7,387; Anianus, 7,395; Constantinopolitan, 7,403; Eusebius, 7,093; Scaliger, 5,844; Dionysius (from whom we take our Christian era), 7,388; Maximus, 7,395; Syncellus and Theophanes, 7,395; Julius Africanus, 7,395; Jackson, 7,320.

So, whether we are talking ancient versions of Scripture or modern interpretations of it, the data is such that multiple interpretations are possible and firm dates elusive. That is why I sought to use a model that relied on more fixed phenomena. But, it's also clear that for many, proper prophecy is tied to the dates of the Patriarchal Age.

In addition, knowing how these ancient versions read, I have yet to see anyone really deal systematically with the variants between the Masoretic, LXX, Samaritan Pentateuch and Josephus. Many tend to pick one wholesale chronology over another and, as we will soon see, oversimplify the matter.

Here's one example from Josephus:

> [80] This calamity happened in the six hundredth year of Noah's government [age], in the second month, {d} called by the Macedonians Dios, but by the Hebrews Marchesuan ; for so did they order their year in Egypt; [81] but Moshe appointed that Nisan [April], which is the same with Xanthikos, should be the first month for their festivals, because he brought them out of Egypt in that month: so that this month began the year as to all the solemnities they observed to the honour of God, although he preserved the original order of the months as to selling and buying, and other ordinary affairs. Now he says that this flood began on the twenty-seventh [seventeenth] day of the before mentioned month; [82] ***and this was two thousand six hundred and fifty-six [one thousand six hundred and fifty-six] years from Adam, the first man***; and the time is written down in our sacred books, those who then lived having noted down, {e} with great accuracy, both the births and deaths of illustrious men. (Antiquities 1:80-82)

Notice the copy of Josephus says 2,656 years between Adam's creation and the Flood. But the translator William Whiston put 1,656 years in parentheses. The question is: Why? Let's see:

Josephus' chronology (Antiquities 1.34) is as follows:

> For indeed Seth was born when Adam was **230**...Seth begat Enos in his **205th** year [Enos] delivered the government to Cainan his son, whom he had in his **190th** year... Cainan had his son Malaleel, who was born in his **170th** year... This Malaleel...died, leaving his son Jared, whom he begat when he was in his **165th** year...Then his son Enoch succeeded him, who was born when his father was **162** years old. ... Now Mathusela, the son of Enoch, who was born to him when he was **165** years old, had Lamech for his son when he was **187** years of age Now Lamech... appointed Noah, his son, to be ruler of the people, who was born to Lamech when he was **182** years old.

So let's add it up...

> 230 + 205 + 190 + 170 + 165 + 162 + 165 + 187 + 182 + 600
> (Noah at flood) = 2,256 years

Here Josephus says 2,656 years between Adam and the Flood, but the translator put 1,656, the sum of years less Noah's time, agreeing with the Hebrew text. This scribal error skews the mss total by 1,000 years!

Generally speaking, many such discrepancies happen because some of these traditions only have a single written witness and two or three fragments at best. Since the letters in Hebrew and Greek are also numbers, a scribal error there could throw off the entire chronology! So, the best we can do is look for multiple agreement between sources as our best shot at maintaining accuracy. ***Let's see how this works:***

1) The first 5 generations, from Adam to Malaleel, have total agreement from the Masoretic and Samaritan Pentateuch.

2) The 6th generation, Jared, has total agreement between the Masoretic and the LXX.

3) The 7th generation, Enoch, has perfect agreement between the Masoretic and the Samaritan versions.

4) The 8th generation, Mathusela has agreement between the Masoretic and the LXX.

5) Only Lamech doesn't have an exact match, but it's close: Between 182 (MT) and 188 (Samaritan).

6) All versions agree that Mathusela lived to be 969 years and that the flood happened in Noah's 600th year.

7) The major discrepancies, such as the Samaritan saying Lamech was only 53 when he had a son or the first 2 generations in the LXX being 230 and 205 at their son's births rather than 130 and 105 respectively in the others, are best explained by scribal errors.

8) So while unanimous verdicts are not possible for the patriarchal ages in the ancient records, it is very easy to get a "majority" opinion based on at least two witnesses agreeing, just as Torah requires!

Therefore, I have no issue proclaiming 1,656 years from Adam to the Flood! But now we need to understand the greatest "split decision" the ancient scriptures have ever known!

The Ancient Split Decision Problem

Now the time that the children of Israel dwelt in the land of Egypt was 430 years.—Exodus 12:40 (Masoretic Text/Dead Sea Scrolls reading)

The Septuagint, the Samaritan Pentateuch, and, apparently, the apostle Paul in Galatians 3:17 understood the 430 years of Exodus 12:40 to include the three generations from Abraham to Jacob. The Masoretic Text and [Dead Sea Scrolls manuscript} 4QExod confine the period to the time of Egypt alone. The debate evident in these ancient texts continues to this day. The Dead Sea Scrolls Bible (Abegg, Flint and Ulrich), p. 45.

I should also add that Josephus, going along with the understanding of the Samaritan and the LXX, renders the 430 years "In Egypt and in Canaan". This is significant because Josephus is an eyewitness to the actual pre-Masoretic Hebrew text that is now lost, or, at least, how that text was understood in his day.

So if one group is right, 430 years includes 3 generations of Israelites before being enslaved, 430 years being the total they were in both Canaan and Egypt. But if the so-called "traditional" interpretation of the Masoretic text is correct, those 430 years were only spent in Egypt. Therefore, the total for the alleged Masoretic version is 645 years in Egypt and Canaan but only 430 years for the same events in the other parts of the ancient record.

This is no small discrepancy! Trying to decide who is right and who is wrong leaves 215 years hanging in the balance. If we go the way of "traditional" Masoretic interpretation, we have 215 years in Canaan and an additional 430 years in Egypt, some 645 years in all. If it's the other way, however, the total from Canaan and Egypt equals only 430 years.

So, if I defend Josephus and the apostle Paul, it seems I will deny the traditional text's reliability. I do not believe this is the case. *This is a false choice!*

There are only two ways to deal with this issue:

> 1) Declare the issue un-resolvable and split the difference between the accounts to minimize the discrepancy (i.e. add 108 years to the 430 minimum, that all sources agree on, and accept that as the minimum range: $430 + 108 = 538$ years.)

> 2) Pick the most plausible interpretation. *I have chosen the second path.*

My first task is to strip away previous assumptions and start from scratch. One of these assumptions that needs to be eliminated, we have already seen:

"The Masoretic Text and 4QExod confine the period to the time of

Egypt alone. The debate evident in these ancient texts continues to this day."—The Dead Sea Scrolls Bible (Abegg, Flint and Ulrich), p. 45.

The reason I question this assumption is because of a clarifying statement in the Tanakh:

> And (Elohim) said to Abram, Know for certain that your seed shall be sojourners in a land that is not theirs, and shall serve them. ***And they shall afflict them four hundred years***. And also that nation, whom they will serve, will I judge. And afterward shall they come out with great substance. But you will go to your fathers in peace. You will be buried at a good old age. ***And in the fourth generation they shall come here again***. For the sin of the Amorites is not yet at its fullest extent. Genesis 15:13-16 (Matara)

This passage tells us:

1) The first part of the prophecy can go with either 430 years from Abraham's time or 430 (roughly 400) years from when Abraham's family began sojourning in Egypt.

2) But the second part clarifies the first:

"In the fourth generation your descendants will come back here."

The Hebrew word "dor" can mean "generation" but also can correspond to a period of 100 years as exemplified in the line "mistreated 400 years". Abraham had his mistreatment too, including the taking of his wife by Pharaoh. Notice that if the normal generation of father to son was meant, we are at the third generation by Joseph's day and many more after that, albeit, before the Exodus! ***And then there's this clue:***

"...for the sin of the Amorites has not yet reached its full measure."

So let's see when this happened...

> *"We utterly destroyed them, as we did to Sihon king of Heshbon, utterly destroying the men, women and children of every city. But all the animals and the spoil of the cities we took as our booty.*

"Thus we took the land at that time from the hand of the two kings of the Amorites who were beyond the Jordan...".
(Deuteronomy 3:6-8 NAS)

So, even leaving the Exodus 12:40 quote alone, we find other details in the Masoretic text supporting the more specific understanding of 430 years total in Egypt and in Canaan. We have two methods for marking the time (counting the 100 year generations and the destruction of the Amorites as a historical marker).

It is my conclusion that the intended interpretation of the Masoretic reading has always been calculated and understood as the more specific rendering in the LXX and the Samaritan Pentateuch. That understanding doesn't contradict the vague wording, but points more to its original meaning. This was passed down through the ages to the greatest Jewish scholars in the world, including Josephus, the scholars who did the LXX, and the great Rabbi Gamaliel, who taught the truth to Rav Shaul! We still need a firm historical date for all the related dates to totally make sense.

Scripture gives us, <u>beyond any doubt</u>, the precise year of the Exodus...

> "In the four hundred and eightieth year after the Israelites had come out of Egypt, in the fourth year of Solomon's reign over Israel, in the month of Ziv, the second month, he began to build the temple of YHWH." -1 Kings 6:1 (Matara)

So, what we need to look at is the following data:

1) Liberal scholars who believe in a late Exodus under Rameses II in about 1290 BCE, rashly assume that 1 Kings 6:1 is a "rough estimate" of 12 generations of 40 years each.

2) The same priestly chroniclers record the years, months and exact days that their kings served, so why play fast and loose with the far more important Exodus?

3) It is almost universally accepted, thanks to the works of Thiele and

others, that Solomon's 4th year is 967 BCE[16].

Therefore:

1) 480 years before 967 BCE brings us to **1447 BCE** for the year of the Exodus.

Next question: How many years from the Flood to Abraham's birth? Using our multiple witness process, this is what we found:

1) The Dead Sea Scrolls have not preserved the key text, Genesis 11.

2) But we do have the Masoretic, LXX, Peshitta (Aramaic Tanakh) and Samaritan versions to compare.

3) The MT and the PT have 95% agreement, the sole exception being that Terah is 70 when he begets Abraham in the MT and 75 in the PT.

4) The LXX, following the pattern we saw before, generally agrees with the other two. But when it occasionally disagrees, it's another scribal error adding 100 years.

5) The Samaritan has similar scribal errors but mostly agrees with the others.

6) So, in this instance, the most accurate process is to adopt the Masoretic convention. Even if the last generation is five years off, there is no reason to go against MT in light of the textual evidence.

So now let's count:

---

16 For more information on this, please consult Old Testament Survey, p. 260, 292-297. There are certain key dates that are referenced in Scripture and in Egyptian and Assyrian records such as the invasion of Pharaoh Shishak (or Sheshonk) in 926 BCE and counting backwards to Solomon's 4th year. Other clarity is retrieved by understanding various methods for counting times that each kingdom used, i.e. accession or non-accession year systems and confirming them through extra-biblical sources. This cross checking forms the basis of other key resources such as E.R. Thiele's The Mysterious Numbers of the Hebrew Kings.

Shem is 100 years old (2 years after Flood) when he fathers
Arphaxad. From the Flood to Arphaxad: 102 years.
Arphaxad to Shelah: 35 years.
Shelah to Eber: 30 years.
Eber to Peleg: 34 years.
Peleg to Reu: 30 years.
Reu to Serug: 32 years.
Serug to Nahor: 30 years.
Nahor to Terah: 29 years.
<u>Terah to Abraham:</u>   <u>70 years.</u>
TOTAL: **392 years.**

Now let's review what we know:

1) From the birth of Adam until the Flood in Noah's 600th year, we
   have an interval of 1,656 years.

2) From the Flood to Abraham's birth: 392 years.

3) From the prophecy given to Abraham in Genesis 15:13-16 until the
   day of the Exodus is precisely 430 years.

4) The Exodus is firmly dated at 1447 BCE.

Now we only need one more piece: The time from Abraham's birth until
the prophecy kicks in.

My first observation is that the reason for 400 vs. 430 years is that it took
at least 25 years from the time YHWH first appeared to Abraham to when
his "official generation" with Isaac was born. YHWH said in Genesis
17:21 that the covenant began manifesting (as opposed to when it is
issued) with Isaac, and it's 30 years exactly to the time Isaac is weaned.
Regardless of whether this idea is accepted or not, there are actually three
places where Abraham is promised the land of Canaan.

The first is in Genesis 12 where we are told he was 75, and coincides
with his leaving Haran (12:4). More details are unveiled relating to his
progeny (Genesis 15) and the covenantal descent through Isaac (Genesis
17). Though the details take many years to unfold, ***the timing is fixed to***

Abraham's 75th year!

Now let's check the score…

1) From the birth of Adam until the Flood in Noah's 600th year is an interval of 1,656 years.

2) From the Flood to Abraham's birth: 392 years.

3) From Abraham's birth to the prophecy: 75 years

4) From the prophecy given to Abraham in Genesis 15:13-16 until the day of the Exodus is precisely 430 years.

5) The Exodus is firmly dated to 1447 BCE.

Therefore: From Adam's creation to the Exodus in 1447 BCE: 2,553 years, which then means:

   1) Adam's creation is (1447 +2553) in 4,000 BCE.

   2) The Flood is 1,656 years later, in 2,344 BCE.

   3) Abraham is born 392 years later, in 1,952 BCE.

   4) YHWH's prophecy is given 75 years later, in 1,877 BCE.

From here, we proceed to the Big Show:

Every number that we have crunched so far has brought us precisely to this point:

> Then YHWH said, "My Spirit shall not strive with man forever, because he also is flesh ; nevertheless his days shall be one hundred and twenty years." (Genesis 6:3 NAS)

Many prophecy advocates insist that this is the real Jubilee cycle. What is generally done is to apply the 49/50 year cycle backwards to the birth of Adam, and then count 120 of those intervals forward to the time of the Last Days. Before explaining further, let me point one thing out: *If the 49 year Jubilee interval was correct then the time of Mashiyach's return would have been from 1880 to 1929, and this, obviously, didn't happen. So from here on out, we assume a 50 year Jubilee.*

This brings us to why I didn't delve into this prophecy in Genesis 6:3 previously:

1) First, as we have seen, there are certain difficulties in firmly fixing time across all the ancient versions. My approach has been a best attempt, rather than a final answer.

2) There is no mention of any fixed Jubilee cycle, 49 or 50, being applied pre-Moshe. As a result, I would prefer not to make an assumption.

For those who disagree, I should point out that the vast majority of scholars have already concluded that 4,000 BCE is the best approximate date for Adam's creation. This is especially true if all the ancient witnesses are married to a firm 1447 BCE date for the Exodus.

But even if the critics are correct about Genesis 6:3, notice what happens:

120 Jubilees x 50 years each = 6,000 years

6,000 years from 4,000 BCE brings us to the year 2,000 for their last Jubilee.

My last (70th) Jubilee by the Long Count begins only 5 years earlier: in 1995.

And most importantly, the Last Jubilees, by both systems, will include the 2000th anniversary of the resurrection! *No matter how you parse the time, since Y'shua did not return prior to the completion of Genesis 6:3's 120th cycle. We must be looking at this same period of time for his likely return*, unless we do the Straight Count only from the entry into Canaan!

Conclusions to this Section

While certain difficulties in all chronological systems of the patriarchs exist, there is a way to use "majority rule" to get to a highly accurate consensus position. However, because of these same problems, I sought to bypass this method in favor of what I explained here.

Even if my critics are correct, the fact that Y'shua didn't return before the year 2000 strongly suggests that both methods are looking at the same Final Cycle, which crosses the 2000th anniversary of the resurrection. This idea raises one more important question that needs answering:

Is it a plausible scenario that the last Jubilee has happened and we are now in the 121st cycle?

The short answer: No. That's one reason why I don't subscribe to the Genesis 6:3 interpretation in the first place.

Another issue is that the ambiguity in the ancient sources also makes it possible to believe that Adam could have been born decades or even centuries later, meaning that the 120th Jubilee still isn't completed. If that is the case, then their system and mine would roughly match with the Straight Count, both crossing the Rabbinical Year 6000. Therefore, the best I can do is to show all the evidence and leave the conclusions to the reader.

A Wider Model Emerges for Noah's Flood Timing

This system described above is a very literal and conservative one that assumes no gaps, and that a majority agreement is always correct. Over the long haul, this is the best approach to use when dealing with a situation that demands a reliable consensus.

However, there are other factors involved that may, in one instance, elevate a minority voice over that of its majority brethren:

1) YHWH always balances on base 10.

This is my observation after years of detailed research and analysis. YHWH's math always seems to center on overall structures of base 10 and internal measures within that structure of base 7. The product of these two numbers is 70, which, as The Wheel of Stars demonstrated, is the main mechanism associated with Mashiyach's first and second advents.

Furthermore, we find two concurrent 490 year periods in the major prophetic stream. Israel is propelled into Captivity because she didn't keep the Land Shabbats every 7 years. The Captivity was 70 years long so the land could get those Shabbats back. This means that if they had kept the Land Shabbat as they were commanded to, we would have had a full interval of 70 x 7 = 490 years.

After the 70 years of Captivity are up, the Jews return to Israel and another 490 year clock starts from the issuing of the decree to rebuild the entire city of Jerusalem (Ezra 7:1-26, Daniel 9:24-27). Other indices are that both short (40 years) and long (100 years) generation counts are divisible by 10, as are the omer and Jubilee counts (both 50).

2) Prophetic calendar balances on a period of 4,000 years.

To sum up the matter briefly, leap months are added at certain intervals to 360 day years to keep them synchronized. The two generation markers, 40 and 100, when multiplied, add up to 4,000 years, as the main balancing mechanism of this calendar kicks in. The fact is that even a rough conservative count from Y'shua's birth back towards Adam's creation comes to within 8 years of that 4,000[th] anniversary. This was significant and so I had to wonder: Is it possible that the 4,000 year balancing ran from 4007 BCE for Adam's time to 7 BCE, the year when Y'shua's birth is announced by the triple conjunction of Jupiter and Saturn?

3) 4006 BCE a "Jubilee year"?

Another consideration had to do with the following year, 4006 BCE. As detailed in Wheel of Stars, YHWH had an absolute count of the Jubilee from the time the Israelites entered into Canaan, making Jubilee 1 50 years after that. A quick bit of math reveals the following with a 1447 BCE Exodus:

- The commencement of the 40 years of wandering in the wilderness begins in the following year, 1446 BCE.
- The wandering period ends 40 years later, in 1406 BCE.
- The first Jubilee is 50 years later, in 1356 BCE.

Therefore, every BCE year that ends in -56 or -06 is when YHWH intended the Jubilee to be, as opposed to when Israel wanted it to be, and as a result, they never celebrated it properly.

My point is a simple one: 6 BCE, the year before Y'shua's birth, was YHWH's Jubilee and He came to "proclaim the release of the captives and the year of YHWH's favor" in Luke 4!

The problem is that we can't reliably apply the 50 year Jubilee interval backwards from Moshe. It was never mentioned pre-Moshe. Instead, what is mentioned, is that the basic rules of the Jubilee, less the 50 year counting method, have been in force as long as YHWH has kicked people out of their land or destroyed them in that land for disobedience, which would include Adam and Eve, the Flood, and so on. That is why I hesitate to label 4006 BCE a Jubilee year, even though it would have been if the Moshe-period rules had been applied.

Instead, I suggest starting that 4,000 year Prophetic cycle in 4007 BCE, which then becomes "fulfilled" in this manner near the time of Mashiyach's birth:

- 7 BCE (the 49th year of the previous Jubilee) when Israel was supposed to announce the following spring as a Jubilee. Instead, YHWH announces the birth of His Son in the heavens for them!

- 6 BCE, the Jubilee year, the birth of Yochanan the Immerser, forerunner of Mashiyach and symbolizing Elijah's return to announce Mashiyach. It is the forerunner's job to "prepare the way for YHWH, make straight paths for Him" and the Jubilee year confirms that symbolism by having the land return to its original owner, namely YHWH Himself.

  - 5 BCE: Year 1 of the new deliverance cycle, the Savior is born.

4) The Samaritans have the missing piece?

The last factor to discuss here is that it is possible to reconstruct the exact year of 4007 BCE from the ancient records. Again, if we apply "majority rule" to picking the ages of the patriarchs, that brings us to 4000 BCE.

However, Samaritan Pentateuch says the following as I demonstrated previously:

> ***Only Lamech doesn't have an exact match, but it's close between 182 (MT) and 188 (Samaritan).***

So what if we, in this one instance, take the Samaritan's word over the MT, but leave everything else intact? That 6 year play puts us squarely back to 4007 BCE! The reason I say this is in Noah's time the calendar ran Tishri-Tishri, or fall to fall. The flood comes "in Noah's 600th year, in the second month" (Heshvan) and Noah himself was born in Tishri, the same month that Adam was created. So, counting backwards 6 years in BCE time is really 7 years inclusive, hence 4007 BCE.

Let us add those 6 years to the 1,656 years we established from Creation to the Flood by the more conservative method and we get 1,662 years. This working model then leads to the obvious equation:

4007 - 1662 = 2345 BCE (year of the Flood)

We also know the month and year Noah was born:

2345 + 600 = 2945 BCE (in the month of Tishri)

Finding reliable lunar tables this far back is quite a challenge. The best resource I know of, NASA, actually only goes back to 2,000 BCE. Thankfully, Noah is not using a lunar calendar! He is using a 360 day calendar of 12 months of 30 days each. We know that Noah and *company* spent five consecutive 30 day months in the ark from two direct scriptural references.

The Kosher Zodiac is calibrated from Moshe's time in terms of what constellations appeared at given periods in the sky. Because the constellations shift about 1 degree every 100 years[17], a 30 degree slice where a constellation appears will be out of that "house" about every 3000 years. So when Noah was born, the first constellation of spring is what we would now refer to as Taurus. By Moshe's time it had shifted backwards to Aries. Then, in about 90 BCE, it shifted again, this time to its current position with Pisces as the first sign of spring.

However, by freezing the sky as it appeared on the night of the Exodus, all concerns about the precession of the equinoxes are null and void as the year will seamlessly progress from whatever constellation appears first in the spring to whenever that same constellation appears the next spring. This occurs regardless of what others would have called that group of stars. It is also important to point out that by the time of the Flood, 600 years later, the first constellation of spring had moved on to Aries, which is the same that Abraham, Moshe, David and everyone in the Tanakh knew.

In any case, the sign of the Flood would have been the constellation after the autumnal equinox, because, at this period of history, equinox days were the first days of the stellar months. The fact is that these were "new year's days" for nearly every ancient culture that has left records behind.

So, in order to proceed more deeply into the calendar of the Flood, we need to stop thinking lunar or solar and think in terms of "constellation time". In this system, "months" correspond to the time of the signs of the Zodiac and are a separate and parallel system with the lunar months that are intercalculated as needed, to synchronize once at the end of every 6 year period. This is required to balance the generational interval of 40 years by having a leap month at the end of the 39th year. The lengths of each "constellation month" are the same as we have for the current Zodiac as expressed through our Gregorian calendar. In later times, great

---

17 The precession of the equinoxes was discovered by the great Greek astronomer Hipparchus in 128 BCE. Hipparchus' work, along with the more famous *Almagest* by Ptolemy, would have been required reading for an historian like Philo, who lived in the city which had the greatest library the ancient world had ever known: Alexandria, Egypt. It is to Philo that we owe a lot of special information on the calendar that was otherwise kept secret. He was the only one who could correlate the secret priestly information passed down to him from his family with the best astronomical records that were housed in his local library!

sages like Moshe will use coordinates from both constellation and lunar years to firmly fix dates.

The autumnal equinox is day 1, month 1, roughly corresponding to our September 21st and, it is with this last piece, that we can build our calendar grid for this year. Notice that Noah is shut in the ark on the 17th day, that's Shabbat! The Hebrew months references are approximate and not meant to be taken literally since they are not yet regulated by the lunar cycles. Please note that the Zodiac month names are used only for convenience. We will see later how all traces of paganism were purged from the sacred and secret Constellation Calendar of ancient Israel.

Noah's Constellation Year

Begin Thursday, September 21st, in AE {Gregorian} time.[18] According to Gregorian rules, this year would have had a February 29th leap day, which means the following year cannot.

Next constellation month begins: October 21st.

-2345	S	M	T	W	T	F	S	Sign
TIS/HES	27	28	29	30	1	2	3	LIBRA-SCORPIO
	4	5	6	7	8	9	10	17th (flood day)
	11	12	13	14	15	16	17	= Oct 16
	18	19	20	21	22	23	24	

18 There are detailed methodologies discussed here in Wheel of Stars that explain how to extrapolate reliable days this far back in time. For now, let me give two websites that assisted me. The first, http://www.imcce.fr/en/grandpublic/temps/saisons.php is for recovering the day of the AE in Julian time. The second http://fourmilab.ch/documents/calendar/ is for converting that Julian date into our Gregorian reckoning, but either way, the day of the week is the same. Also the ancients tracked the equinoxes by their matching constellation and not by sight. In this case Libra, after which the AE happens within the next 24 hours.

-2345	S	M	T	W	T	F	S	Sign
HES/KIS	25	26	27	28	29	30	1	SCORPIO
	2	3	4	5	6	7	8	
	9	10	11	12	13	14	15	
	16	17	18	19	20	21	22	

Next constellation month begins: November 21st

-2345	S	M	T	W	T	F	S	Sign
KIS/SHE	23	24	25	26	27	28	29	SAG
	30	1	2	3	4	5	6	
	7	8	9	10	11	12	13	
	14	15	16	17	18	19	20	

Next constellation month begins: December 21st

-2345/4	S	M	T	W	T	F	S	Sign
SHE/TEV	21	22	23	24	25	26	27	SAG/CAP
	28	29	30	1	2	3	4	4th is Jan 1
	5	6	7	8	9	10	11	
	12	13	14	15	16	17	18	

Next constellation month begins: January 21st

-2344	S	M	T	W	T	F	S	Sign
TEV/ADA	19	20	21	22	23	24	25	CAP/AQU
	26	27	28	29	30	1	2	
	3	4	5	6	7	8	9	
	10	11	12	13	14	15	16	

Next constellation month begins: February 21st

-2344	S	M	T	W	T	F	S	Sign
ADA/2 ADA	17	18	19	20	21	22	23	AQU/PIS
	24	25	26	27	28	29	30	
	1	2	3	4	5	6	7	
	8	9	10	11	12	13	14	

Note: Scripture tells us the ark rests on the mountains of Ararat in the seventh month, which means this year clearly has a leap month![19]

Next constellation month begins: March 21st

-2344	S	M	T	W	T	F	S	Sign
2ADA/ ABI	15	16	17	18	19	20	21	PIS/ARI
	22	23	24	25	26	27	28	**10 is 17th of 1st month**
	29	30	1	2	3	4	5	= Apr 7
	6	7	8	9	**10**	11	12	

Our April 7th is the day that Noah is saved and the flood waters recede enough to let the ark rest. Something else of great importance also happened on April 7th: the resurrection of our Master Y'shua! We need to continue with some more months to fill out the Constellation Year. Three more months will bring us to the next milestone:

---

19 This is because the seventh month has always been Abib in the ancient system, and this system is in accord with that of Babylon and Persia that always intercalculated the year in the spring, regardless of which equinox represented their new year's day. So, even when the elect like Noah were counting fall-fall, the leap months of the Prophetic and Solar Pre-Metonic were always added in the spring.

Next constellation month begins: April 21st

-2344	S	M	T	W	T	F	S	Sign
ABI/IYA	13	14	15	16	17	18	19	ARI/TAU
	20	21	22	23	24	25	26	
	27	28	29	30	1	2	3	
	4	5	6	7	8	9	10	

Next constellation month begins: May 21st

-2344	S	M	T	W	T	F	S	Sign
IYA/SIV	11	12	13	14	15	16	17	TAU/GEM
	18	19	20	21	22	23	24	
	25	26	27	28	29	30	1	
	2	3	4	5	6	7	8	

Next constellation month begins: June 21st

-2344	S	M	T	W	T	F	S	Sign
SIV/TAM	9	10	11	12	13	14	15	TAU/GEM
	16	17	18	19	20	21	22	
	23	24	25	26	27	28	29	**1 = 10th month**
	30	1	2	3	4	5	6	

From the tenth month, Scripture tells us plainly how to track this period:

> 5 *The water decreased steadily until the tenth month; in the tenth month, on the first day of the month, the tops of the mountains became visible.* 6 *Then it came about at the end of forty days, that Noah opened the window of the ark which he had made;* 7 *and he sent out a raven, and it flew here and there until the water was dried up from the earth.* 8 Then he sent out a dove from him, to see if the water was abated from the face of the land; 9 but the dove found no resting place for the sole of her foot, so she returned to

him into the ark, for the water was on the surface of all the earth. Then he put out his hand and took her, and brought her into the ark to himself. *¹⁰ So he waited yet another seven days; and again he sent out the dove from the ark. ¹¹ The dove came to him toward evening, and behold, in her beak was a freshly picked olive leaf. So Noah knew that the water was abated from the earth. ¹² Then he waited yet another seven days, and sent out the dove; but she did not return to him again.* (Genesis 8:5-12 NAU)

Breaking the chronology down, it works out this way:

- 10th month, day 1: tops of mountains become visible.
- 40 days later [11th month, day 11]: Noah sends out a raven and a dove.
- 7 days later [11th month, day 18]: sends out the dove a second time.
- Towards evening on that same day: the dove brings back the olive leaf.
- On the 25th: dove sent out and doesn't return.

Now let's plot this on the grids:

Next constellation month begins: July 21st

-2344	S	M	T	W	T	F	S	Sign
SIV/TAM	7	8	9	10	11	12	13	GEM/CAN
	14	15	16	17	**18**	19	20	18 = Dove brings leaf
	21	22	23	<u>24</u>	25	26	27	
	28	**29**	30	1	2	3	4	

Next constellation month begins: August 21st

-2344	S	M	T	W	T	F	S	Sign
AB/ELUL	5	6	7	8	9	10	11	CAN/LEO
	12	13	14	15	16	17	18	
	19	20	21	22	23	24	<u>25</u>	
	26	27	28	29	30	1	2	

Next constellation month begins: September 21st

-2344	S	M	T	W	T	F	S	Sign
ELUL	3	4	5	6	7	8	9	LEO/VIR
	10	11	12	13	14	15	16	
	17	18	19	20	21	22	23	
	24	**25**	<u>26</u>	27	28	29	30	
TISHRI	1	2	3	4	5	6	7	**LIBRA**

So, in terms of the Constellation Cycle, the year has run out after sunset on September 20th but 4 days before the end of the Solar Pre-Metonic 30 day month. There is still more we can track:

> [13] *Now it came about in the six hundred and first year, in the first month, on the first of the month, the water was dried up from the earth.* Then Noah removed the covering of the ark, and looked, and behold, the surface of the ground was dried up. [14] *In the second month, on the twenty-seventh day of the month, the earth was dry.* (Genesis 8:13-14 NAU)

Next constellation month begins: October 21st

-2344	S	M	T	W	T	F	S	Sign
TIS/HES	8	9	10	11	12	13	14	LIB/SCO
	15	16	17	18	19	20	21	
	22	23	24	25	26	**27**	28	27 = earth dry
	29	30	1	2	3	4	5	

What all this means is simple: By preserving the days of the flood, ancient Israel could track the exact length of the tropical year by remembering what signs were in the sky throughout the year of Noah's flood. The fact that Noah and Moshe would both have tracked with Aries as the first constellation of spring would make this very easy for them to maintain. Even after their calendar shifted from spring to spring, this system would still work perfectly for them. However, as we will see later, it is possible that this Kosher Zodiac had, at least, one spring to spring variant that worked just as well.

Chapter 4

The Equinox Pre-Metonic (Moedic) Calendar

THE HEAVENS DECLARE THE GLORY OF ELOHIM;
THE SKIES PROCLAIM THE WORK OF HIS HANDS...
IN THE HEAVENS HE HAS PITCHED A TENT FOR THE SUN,
WHICH IS LIKE A BRIDEGROOM COMING OUT FROM HIS
PAVILION, LIKE A MIGHTY MAN REJOICING TO RUN HIS
COURSE. IT RISES AT ONE END OF THE HEAVENS AND
MAKES ITS RETURN CIRCLE/CIRCUIT TO THE OTHER;
NOTHING IS HIDDEN FROM ITS HEAT.
PSALM 19:1, 5-6 (MATARA)

Counting from the Exodus as Year One

The two previous calendars focused on the time of the creation of Adam as "year one" and synched to the solar year for the general benefit of mankind. These last two calendars, starting with this one, have another origin point in mind.

In order to understand why, we must put ourselves back in the mindset of the ancient Israelites. For centuries they had been oppressed in Egypt, crying out in bondage and pain for YHWH to send His deliverer Moshe. YHWH told Moshe from the Burning Bush that the cries of their afflictions had reached Him and now He has chosen the time of their emancipation.

What is true of Moshe is also true of Y'shua. Both births were foreshadowed with great tumult and a slaughtering of the innocents. Both men were destined to bring freedom and righteousness to Israel through great miracles and wonders: "with a mighty hand and an outstretched arm, with signs and portents." These men both calmed the waters and fed multitudes where no food existed. They climbed mountains to be transformed by the light of YHWH's love and judgments. They stood up for what was right even when their people and members of their own family lost faith and were divided. It was just as Y'shua said, "two against three and three against two". Finally, both men, for different reasons, stood as the indispensible persons of the true faith. Nothing wonderful could ever happen later without them. Moshe, because he interceded and prevented Israel's destruction in the first place ("or blot me out of the book you are writing") and Y'shua, without whose sacrifice and resurrection our faith and obedience would be worthless today.

Is it any wonder that Christendom would mark their calendar BC and AD? I don't think so. I may prefer BCE and CE to be sure, but I definitely understand the impulse since I know the ancient Israelites did for the Exodus what Christianity did for their majority, albeit wrong opinion, on the time of Y'shua's birth. Like those Christians, we in the West have forgotten the original roots and connections that ancient Israel lived by. Thankfully, that path has been in the Scripture all along, waiting for us to search out and find. What I will show is exactly how those Scriptural trends were realized in history.

The Final Sky Sign: What Really Set the Year?

Throughout this study, the Vernal Equinox has been referenced as the presumptive time for starting the year. While the Vernal and Autumnal Equinoxes are a key clue to help in setting the general seasonal time, they are not the final sky signs that officially kick off the year. There are two main components required to understand this fact. The first is showing how a kosher version of the Zodiac was used by ancient Israel to track the solar year. The second is explaining what that ultimate "year sign" really is, and what it is not.

As stated earlier, both Josephus and Philo descended from families of priests.[1] They were eyewitnesses to the intricacies of Temple practice[2]

---

1 Josephus was of Hasmonean blood which would allow him access to privileged materials. See autobiography entitled "Life" in the William Whiston translation, by Hendrickson Press. For information on Philo's lineage please see: The Works of Philo, Translated from the Greek, C. D. Yonge, 4 vols., London: Henry G. Bohn, 1854-55, (1995: Hendrickson edition) p. xix.

2 Although we only know of one trip to Jerusalem undertaken by Philo, there has never been

and were very educated men who had access to oral and written traditions that have since been lost. As long as general agreement can be maintained between these men and Torah teaching and practice, it is the closest we can come to those original sources.

Let us see how Josephus and Philo describe how their ancestors regarded the Equinoxes,[3] sun, moon and stars for the timing of festivals:

> [204] The last of all the annual festivals is that which is called the feast of tabernacles, which is fixed for the season of the autumnal equinox. (The Special Laws 2:204)

> On the fourth day He adorned the heaven with the sun, the moon, and the other stars; and appointed them their motions and courses, that the changes of the seasons might be clearly signified. (Antiquities 1:31)

> [244] Upon the fifteenth day of the same month, ***when the season of the year is changing to winter, the law enjoins us to pitch tabernacles in everyone of our houses, so that we preserve ourselves from the cold of that time of the year;*** [245] as also that when we should arrive at our own country, and come to that city which we should have then for our metropolis, because of the temple therein to be built, and keep a festival for eight days... (Antiquities 3:244-245)

Going a step further, both Josephus and Philo show us how the priests were tracking the solar year and Zodiac cycle, right down to the memories enshrined in their garments:

> But in the void place of this garment there was inserted a piece of the bigness of a span, embroidered with gold, and the other colors of the ephod, and was called Essen...On these were engraved the names of the sons of Jacob, in our own country letters, and in our own tongue, six on each of the stones, on either side; and the elder

---

any proof that he went up before or since that particular occasion. At a minimum, Philo has access to priestly documentation that has been lost since the destruction of the Temple, and it is a pretty safe bet that Josephus is reading from those same sources, given how the two men agree so closely on the contents of this extra material.

3 In addition to the Aries-Passover connection Josephus provided us in Antiquities 3.10.5.

sons' names were on the right shoulder. Twelve stones also there were upon the breast-plate, extraordinary in largeness and beauty... Now the names of all those sons of Jacob were engraved in these stones, whom we esteem the heads of our tribes, each stone having the honor of a name, in the order according to which they were born...*And for the twelve stones, whether we understand by them the months, or whether we understand them like number of the signs of that circle which the Greeks call the Zodiac, we shall not be mistaken in their meaning.* (Josephus: Antiquities 3.163-169; 186)

[87] Then on his chest there are twelve precious stones of different colors, arranged in four rows of three stones in each row, being fashioned so as an emblem of the zodiac. For the zodiac also consists of twelve animals, and so divides the four seasons of the year, allotting three animals to each season.
(Philo: The Special Laws 1:87)

In both cases, the linkage to the Zodiac specifically designates a solar year. It was the most accurate measure of a solar year available to the ancients. Only the measuring of the year from the center of our galaxy, which was not in use prior to the 19th century, is more accurate. We must separate fable from fact with respect to the Zodiac as an astronomical system. Here is additional background from Wikipedia, an online encyclopedia:

For any spherical celestial coordinate system, one needs to define an equatorial plane and designate an origin for longitude. From these definitions, longitudinal meridians perpendicular to the equatorial plane meet at the north and south poles of the celestial sphere and one can precisely specify a unique position on the sphere.

First, the zodiac coordinate system designates the ecliptic as the equatorial plane. One should not confuse the zodiac's equatorial plane with the Earth's equator which is so named because it serves as the equatorial plane for our terrestrial coordinate system. Instead, the ecliptic is aligned with the Earth's orbital plane with the Sun. The Earth tilts at an angle of approximately 23° with respect to the orbital plane. This tilt is partly due to the Earth's precession as it gyrates and rotates on its axis. It contributes to the divergence between a tropical year and a sidereal year and, thus, contributes to the precession of the equinoxes which marks the difference between tropical and sidereal celestial coordinate systems.

Secondly, a system of coordinates must normally specify an origin (0° point) for longitude. However, the zodiac system names twelve equal regions (called signs) and technically any sign can serve as the beginning or the end of the sphere's precession. The system further divides each sign into thirty degree units. One reason this system of coordinates was particularly useful in antiquity is that writing large numbers was difficult before the introduction of Arabic numerals. The zodiac system of coordinates kept every number below ninety (the highest value for zodiac latitudes). Since the constellations along the ecliptic varied in size, defining 12 equal signs of 30° each did require an arbitrary assignment of boundaries roughly corresponding to the ecliptic constellations.

It is believed that many of the classical astronomers specified zodiac signs using two bright stars near the ecliptic and opposite each other to serve as equatorial nodes or poles (not longitudinal poles): Aldebaran and Antares in the constellations Taurus and Scorpius respectively. These stars served rather well because not only were they on opposites sides of the ecliptic, but they also fell very near the center of their constellations and were designated as Taurus 15 and Scorpius 15, meaning the middle 15° points within those signs. From these two stars, the remaining equatorial boundaries of the 12 signs of the zodiac follow).[4]

These ideas bring us back to the reading in Job that was referenced earlier:

"Can you bind the beautiful Pleiades? Can you loose the cords of Orion? Can you bring forth the Wheel of Stars into its seasons and stand in the path of Ayish/Iyutha (Aldebaran) and her satellites

---

4 Also see, Powell, Robert (2004). The Definition of the Babylonian Zodiac: (online at: www. astrologer.com/ aanet/pub/ transit/ jan2005/ babylonian.htm) PhD thesis entitled "The Definition of the Babylonian Zodiac and the Influence of Babylonian Astronomy on the Subsequent Defining of the Zodiac".

(Hyades). Do you know the laws of the heavens and can you establish their rule over the earth?...Have you given wisdom to the Lance Star (Antares) or intelligence to the Bow Star?" (Hebrew & Aramaic Job 38:31-33, 38, cross referenced to the translation of T.K. Cheyne: Journal of Biblical Literature, Vol. 17, No. 1 (1898), pp. 103-107)

According to NAS Old Testament Hebrew Lexicon, the word *mazzaroth* means "the twelve signs of the Zodiac and their thirty-six associated constellations". If this is what is being brought into season by YHWH, then it is extremely powerful proof that the Tanakh itself is harkening back to the solar and celestial synchronization that keeps the lunar based holidays in season.

What's more, the other stars mentioned in this passage of Job, according to the Aramaic traditions of the Tanakh and the 4th century Syrian Saint Mar Ephraim, are clearly the two points that determine the line that makes the Zodiac itself!

In Moshe's time there was a phenomenon visible at sunset of the sun approaching Aldebaran before the Vernal Equinox and Antares before the Autumnal Equinox. This is different from the Vernal or the Autumnal Equinoxes themselves because these are **signs**, whereas the equinoxes themselves are **not visible**. Also, this event of the visibility of Aldebaran clearly coincides with Josephus' description of the sign of Aries in the time of Moshe! And so, the return of the sun to this region of sky, when Aldebaran is the sign, only happens at the Vernal Equinox.

Finally, all of this data again harmonizes with Tanakh in terms of its definition that an annual event is also required to set the year:

> Afterward, the prophet came to the king of Israel and said, "Strengthen your position and see what must be done, *because next spring/turn of the year the king of Aram will attack you again."* (1 Kings 20:22-NIV)

The literal reading in Hebrew is *b'teshuwbah hayah shaneh* referring to the time after the year was expired, or in the spring of the year, depending on the translation.

Let us see this concept more clearly in the Strong's entry for *teshuwbah*:

> 8666. teshuwbah, tesh-oo-baw'; or teshubah, tesh-oo-baw'; from 7725; a recurrence (of time or place); a reply (as returned):-- answer, be expired, return. The same word is used four other times in reference to the Spring as the "turn of the year" (2 Samuel 11:1; 1 Kings 20:26; 1 Chronicles 20:1; 2 Chronicles 36:10).

The other Hebrew word used to describe the same idea is *tequwphot*:

> "And you shall observe the feast of weeks, of the first fruits of wheat harvest, and the feast of ingathering at the **year's end** (*tequwphot*)." (Exodus 34:22-NIV)

> The heavens declare the glory of Elohim; the skies proclaim the work of His hands. ..In the heavens he has pitched a tent for the sun, which is like a bridegroom coming out from his pavilion, like a mighty man rejoicing to run his course. **It rises at one end of the heavens and makes its return circle/circuit** (tequwphot) **to the other; nothing is hidden from its heat."**
> (Psalm 19:1, 5-6- Matara)

> Now it came about at the **turn of the year** (*tequwphot*)[5] that the army of the Arameans came up against him; and they came to Yehudah and Jerusalem, destroyed all the rulers of the people from among the people, and sent all their plunder to the king of Damascus. (2 Chronicles 24:23)

Strong's defines the word officially this way: 8622. *tequwfaw*. Coming round, circuit of time or space, a turning, circuit.

Therefore, Tanakh, Josephus and Philo are all linking spring to an

---

5 This time the word refers to spring. In the first verse, however, it was fall. This word is tracking the agricultural growing season, driven by the solar cycle.

annual event, the return orbit of the sun to the zero degree marker.
While it is true that practical considerations made the Vernal Equinox a
far easier mechanism to identify, *the technical occasion remained the
time when the sun returned to Aries, as viewed by ancient Israel at the
time of the Exodus when Aldebaran was consumed by the dusk.*

Another Take on the "Signs" of Genesis 1:14-19

At this point we need to revisit the root mechanism of all four calendars
once more-signs, seasons, days and years—in that order. Actually, to be
precise, this tiny section really only deals with the first two terms.

As we saw earlier, the Invisible Elohim ordained that we don't worship
the sun or the moon like the pagans did. That is why He has ordained the
day start at sunset and the month with the moon in darkness, as this is the
literal opposite of "glorying" (1 Corinthians 15:41).

However, in a recent discussion a Crescentist had an interesting question:
Wouldn't the sign/banner referenced by Genesis 1:14 refer to the visual
sighting of the crescent new moon?

My answer of course was no, it would not, but I wanted to discuss my
reasoning a little bit here. First of all a sky sign or banner is meant to
be big—even up to the size of the Universe itself in Creation. While
the moon is admittedly large, its appearance at crescent state is hardly
impressive and would therefore not be a suitable banner.

The other reason I say no has to do with the next term: *moed* (seasons).
As we also saw earlier this means "appointed times" and in Psalm 81:3
the word usually translated as "full moon" actually has this meaning
according to the Talmud:

> And they answered: He has already appointed a time for repenting,
> as it reads [Prov. 7.19]: "By the day of **kesa** only will he return,"
> **and the term kesa means "an appointed time,"** as it reads [Ps.
> 81.4]: "Blow on the new moon, the cornet at the time appointed

(kesa) on the day of our feast." –Rodkinson, Babylonian Talmud (Vol. 8), Sanhedrin, p. 301.

Later we will see how, whether this term also means "full moon" or not, it still favors the interpretation of the crescent as a backwards marker. For now though, even assuming it does mean "full moon", it is acting as a synonym for *moed*. That being the case, the first *moed* is also the first Feast of the year that happens to take place at the full moon—Pesach! So, no matter how you parse it the necessity of the "season" following the "sign" ensures that the sign is clarified by the full moon, and never the crescent moon.

Calculation vs. Sighted: Who is right?

The Karaite sect of Judaism insists that the New Moon crescent is to be observed (or calculated according to a potential observation if weather does not permit an actual sighting) by reliable witnesses in and around Jerusalem or the month cannot begin. To be fair though, this is also the claim of many Rabbinics, as well.

In looking at the Talmud we find multiple references to the Sanhedrin hearing from reliable witnesses that the crescent had been sighted. In return, the Sanhedrin would then give these men a fine meal and lodging for their troubles. Then they would light the lamps that were to signal Israel that the beginning of the month had happened. However, some of the problems of this story are even mentioned in the same source, in that enemies of Israel would also light fires to confuse the rest of the nation!

[2] Formerly bonfires were lighted (to announce the appearance of the new moon); but when the Cutheans practised their deceit, it was ordained that messengers should be sent out. How were these bonfires lighted? They brought long staves of cedar wood, canes, and branches of the olive tree, and bundles of tow which were tied on top of them with twine; with these they went to the top of a mountain, and lighted them, and kept waving them to and fro, upward and downward, till they could perceive the same repeated

by another person on the next mountain, and thus, on the third mountain, etc. Whence did these bonfires commence? From the Mount of Olives to Sartabha, from Sartabha to Grophinah, from Grophinah to Hoveran, from Hoveran to Beth Baltin; they did not cease waving the burning torches at Beth Baltin, to and fro, upward and downward, until the whole country of the captivity appeared like a blazing fire. (Rodkinson, Babylonian Talmud, Rosh Hashanna 2:2)

Therefore, there had to be a way to silence all controversy in this matter, if for no other reason that national security literally depended on it. And so there are a few ways of approaching this:

- The procedure of hearing from witnesses of the New Moon sighting was a community awareness service that is not necessarily enshrined in Scripture. There are no such Biblical examples of such process. Nor is there a single reference in Tanakh to sighting the New Moon, but only about what to do when the New Moon occurs.

- The purpose of this procedure was to reassure the people that they did not have to worry about enemy deception. If they did not go up to tell the Sanhedrin about the new month, they could have confidence that one of their fellow countrymen would.
- If the witnesses did not agree or if none came forward, however, there had to be a final judge that gave a clear decision in a timely manner and this was the calculated lunar month that we will examine later. For now though, the main thing to understand is that since the New Moon to New Moon cycle averages 29.53 days[6].

In dovetailing with the last point, it should also be understood that the two ideas of sighting versus calculation are not necessarily mutually exclusive. First of all, the lunar calculation is clearly based on many centuries of careful sightings at every stage of a lunar month. This is, as I mentioned earlier, the essence of the meaning of *shomer*, referring to taking into account the supply of a given item, whether it be with

---

6 Or, to be more precise: 29 days, 12 hours, 44 minutes, 2.8 seconds.

regards to monetary wealth or days. Here are just a few examples of this meaning of *shomer* clearly being intended in Scripture[7]:

> You will not **add** to the word which I am commanding you, nor take away from it, that you may **keep and do** (שמר) the Mitzvot (Commandments) of YHWH your Elohim which I command you. Deuteronomy 4:2 (Matara)

> And as the king passed by, he cried to the king and said, "Your servant went out into the midst of the battle; and behold, a man turned aside and brought a man to me and said, '**Guard** (שמר) this man; if for any reason he is missing, then your life shall be for his life, or else you shall pay a talent of silver. (1 Kings 20:39-NIV)

> And when the Cohenim (priests) came forth from the Set-Apart place, for all the priests who were present had set made themselves Set-Apart without **regard** (שמר) to divisions.[8] 2 Chronicles 5:11 (Matara)

As we saw earlier from 1 Samuel 20, David and Jonathan know with absolute certainty that the New Moon is the following day. They are not waiting for it to be sighted by witnesses or have it validated by a court process. Instead, David and Jonathan know their calculations are accurate. They also know that the king's court will rely on the same information they have, which can only be counting the Synodic cycles of the moon, exactly the sense of *shomer* that we have been talking about. From here a leading 19th century Talmud expert adds the following:

> And this brings up yet another difficulty. The Jews calculated the month according to the phases of the moon, each month consisting of either twenty-nine or thirty days, and beginning with the appearance of the new moon. But this opened a fresh field of uncertainty. **It is quite true that every one might observe for**

---

7 In fact, in the vast majority of places where שמר appears, it is with respect to YHWH's commandments being carried out. That being the case "observing" a mitzvah has nothing to do with visually seeing that commandment itself!
8 And notice here that since the priests would be dressed the same way, with nothing to visually distinguish one division from another, there is nothing to "observe" in the visual sense.

himself the appearance of a new moon. But this would again partly depend on the state of the weather. Besides, it left an authoritative declaration of the commencement of a month unsupplied. And yet not only was the first of every month to be observed as 'New Moon's Day,' but the feasts took place on the 10th, 15th, or other day of the month, which could not be accurately determined without a certain knowledge of its beginning. To supply this want the Sanhedrim sat in the 'Hall of Polished Stones' to receive the testimony of credible witnesses that they had seen the new moon. Alfred Edersheim, *The Temple: Its Ministry and Services,* Chapter 10[9]

And finally, these factors above may also explain why Philo in other places wishes to harmonize the fixed 30 day solar months with the approximate 30 day lunar month:

[257] And the expression "from," has a double sense. ***One, that by which the starting point from which it begins is included;*** the other that by which it is excluded. ***For when we say that from morning to evening there are twelve hours, or from the new moon to the end of the month there are thirty days, we are including in our enumeration both the first hour and the day of the new moon.*** And when any one says that such and such a field is three or four furlongs distant from the city, he clearly means to leave the city itself out of that measurement. (On Dreams 2:257)

When Did the Hebrew Month Begin?

In order to begin to understand this issue, we need to look at original word definitions and Scriptural examples. As shown previously, Noah kept a 12 month, 30 day calendar, or 360 day year which can be synchronized to the actual 365.25 day year by genuine astronomy married to Biblical data. We know this chiefly because Scripture tells us that 5 months

---

9 It is interesting to note that while Edersheim here talks about the "appearance of the new moon" he also references compelling reasons why it was unreliable and requiring "certain knowledge of its beginning".

to the day the Flood started equals 150 days, which is impossible in a strictly lunar system. The reason why this is impossible is because Scripture's definition of "month" is "from new moon to new moon" which astronomers today call *the Synodic Cycle*. The average time it takes the moon to complete its full cycle is 29.530589 days or in real terms, 29 days, 12 hours, 44 minutes and 2.8 seconds. The full range of time involved is strictly between 29.27 and 29.83 days, or a maximum variance of 13.44 hours per month.

Because of this most of us have seen the moon sometimes rise in the daytime as well as night. It also means that any lunar calendar must alternate between 29 and 30 days throughout the year. If we do that, then the moon will be New on time 100% of the time and that occasion will be the start of the month, or *rosh chodesh*. This brings us to the two Hebrew words that refer to "month":

2858 [2859] (Hebrew) **חֹדֶשׁ** (page 294) (Strong 2320) I. 282:חֹדֶשׁ n.m.:Gn 7:11 (f. MT 38:24 but m. Sam Di) (newness), new moon, month. –Brown Driver Briggs Pinches: BOR Aug. 1888, 207; Eth. *warhé: moon, month;* cf. sub חַרֵי)—abs. חַרֵי_Gn 37:9 + 25 t.; sf. חֲחָרֶיו Is 60:20:—*moon,* usually named with sun Jos 10:12, 10:13 (poem in JE), Psalm 72:5 ם-שֶׁע (89:38) (מֶשׁ וְלִפְנֵי יָרֵחַ) in these two, a symbol of permanence 121:6 , (Is ,60:19 Hb ,3:11 **Jo. 3:4; obj. of idolatrous worship Jb 31:26 (+ sun); in same sense also + sun and stars Dt 4:19, 17:3, 2 K 23:5, Je 8:2; as determiner of feast-times Psalm 104:19 (|| sun); + stars, as shining** by night Psalm 136:9 (|| sun, by day), so חֲרֵי תֵקֶה Je 31:35; (|| *id.*); elsewh. + sun and stars Gn 37:9 (E), Is 13:10, Ez 32:7, Jo 2:10, 4:15, Psalm 148:3, Ec 12:2; + stars Psalm 8:4, Jb 25:5; with neither sun nor stars only חֲרֵי יֶלְד-בַע_Psalm 72:7. –Brown Driver Briggs

This second word, *yarakh* also means "moon" (e.g. Genesis 37:9) but notice applications of this very ancient term can apply to either the sun or moon in a time marking capacity? This is a hint about how the sun and the moon work together in determining the Hebrew month.

But something rather odd begins to happen when we track the full moon in Scripture. It starts out rather clearly:

> And the light of the **moon** will be like the light of the sun, and the light of the sun will be brighter by seven-fold, as the light of seven days, the day when YHWH puts on the oil on the wounds of his people and heals them from the blows they have suffered.
> Isaiah 30:26 (Matara)

> [10] Who is she, **looking down as the morning light**, fair as the **moon**, clear as the sun, who is to be feared like an army with flags? (Song of Songs 6:10 BBE)

Here's the word for "moon":

> I. הַגְּבַל **(lebanaw) n.f.** moon, poet. (NH *id.*);—לְ Is 24:23 + 2 t.; shall pale before יהוה Is 24:23 (‖הַמָּה); shall become like sun (הַמָּה) in day of יהוה's redemption 30:26 (יְלָה רְאו); sim. of woman's beauty, הָפָי כַלְ Ct 6:10 (‖הַמָּה).-Brown Driver Briggs

> **Definition** 1. moon (as white) </TD< TR> **NAS Word Usage -** **Total:** 3 full moon 1, moon 2

In other words, this describes a white, full moon, brimming with light. But it seems another word translated as "full moon" means the opposite in Hebrew. Let's see the verse in question as it is normally translated:

> [3] Sound the ram's horn at the **New Moon**, and when the **moon is full**, on the day of our Feast. (Psalm 81:3 NIV)

Now we've seen this verse before. As pointed out earlier, it doesn't say to *see* the New Moon, only to blow the shofar *at* the New Moon. In this case though I wanted to show diversity in the way this is translated:

> Blow the trumpets in the new moon, **in the time appointed**, on our solemn feast days. (Psalm 81:3-Lamsa, from the Aramaic Tanakh)

Notice there is no "full moon" for Lamsa at all. That's because in the

Aramaic version of the Tanakh, Lamsa perceived that another Hebrew/ Aramaic meaning might be intended:

> And they answered: He has already appointed a time for repenting, as it reads [Prov. 7.19]: "By the day of **kesa** only will he return," **and the term kesa means "an appointed time,"** as it reads [Ps. 81.4]: "Blow on the new moon, the cornet at the time appointed (kesa) on the day of our feast." –Rodkinson, Babylonian Talmud (Vol. 8), Sanhedrin, p. 301.

This affinity between the sources should not be surprising, since the same group of Jews is responsible for compiling both the Peshitta Tanakh and later the Talmud itself! These Jewish scholars, perhaps more than any other group on earth, understood that "full moon" may not belong here.

There is another group of very important Jewish scholars that should be mentioned: Those who lived in Alexandria Egypt and compiled to Septuagint translation for its king. Let's see how they deal with this word from Hebrew/Aramaic sources as well:

> [3] Blow the trumpet at the new moon, in the glorious day of your feast. (Psalm 81:3, Brenton, The Septuagint with Apocrypha)

Therefore none of these ancient witnesses see a full moon here! It also doesn't make sense contextually since there is a better word for this in Hebrew that makes it totally clear and the fact is "full moon" is covered implicitly anyway since many Feasts like Pesach and Sukkot happen when the moon is full!

As a result, this is a hint, that perhaps "appointed time" is referencing a fixed counting method rather than a sighted one. But if that is not strong enough, another meaning of this same word may be:

> **3847** כסה כסה **qal**: pt. הָסֹכ, pass. cs. יסֻנכ: **cover**: — 1. **forgive** (sin); k®sûy μa‰¹°â whose sin is forgiven Ps 321 — 2. **keep s.thg hidden** Pr 1216•23. **nif.**: pf. הָתָסְכנ; inf. תֹסֻנכה: **be covered** Je 5142 Ez 248. –*Holladay, Hebrew and Aramaic Lexicon for the Old Testament*

Now here is where our search may appear to get downright bizarre. How is it that one word for full moon means "full of light" and the other potential synonym means the opposite: cover over in darkness? It's even a metaphor for forgiving sin, or making it disappear! Let's dig deeper:

a. (Qal) conceal, covered (participle)
b. (Niphal) to be covered
c. (Piel)
    1. to cover, clothe
    2. to cover, conceal
    3. to cover (for protection)
    4. to cover over, spread over
    5. to cover, overwhelm
d. (Pual)
    1. to be covered
    2. to be clothed
e. (Hithpael) to cover oneself, clothe oneself

</TD< TR> **NAS Word Usage - Total:** 151
closed 2, clothed 1, conceal 1, conceals 8, cover 50, covered 51, covering 4, covers 20, engulfed 3, forgive 1, hidden 1, hide 2, keep 1, made a covering 1, overwhelm 2, overwhelmed 2, take refuge 1

4558 כֶּסֶא [4559] (Hebrew) (page 490) (Strong 3677)

† כֶּסֶ Pr 7:20, כֶּסֶה Psalm 81:4 **n.[m.]** full moon (cf. Aram. *kesÀoÀ*; orig. dubious, cf. Lag:Symn. i. 93; perh. As. loan-word; cf. **As. *kusêu, headdress* or *cap,*** = *agú, id.,* and also *full moon* (as tiara of moon-god?), Dl:HWB, sub *kusêu, kubšu, agú*; yet v. Brock)—לְיוֹם הַכֵּ׳ Pr 7:20; as a feast-day, בַּכֵּ׳ Psalm 81:4 (opp. בַּחֹדֶשׁ, *at the new moon*).

So we see here that one of the meanings could be "headdress or cap" which would conceal an object, not by light, but in darkness.[10] This also

---

10 Also notice how hard the dictionary is straining to explain "full moon" as a possible meaning? The best it can do is suggest a crown for a moon deity is meant, and even then uncertainty forces them to add a question mark. For me then it is clear why: There is no way one can directly infer "full moon" from this word. Job 26:9 is a great case in point as it reads: "He obscures the face of the *kesa* moon." Well if it is obscured, that main meaning of *kesa* is expressed by a synonym and Hebrew often amplifies images through doubling of concepts and verbs. For example, it is

hints to me as to what state the moon is really in when it is "new". But in trying to reconcile these meanings with other sources like the Talmud I discovered a totally new possibility for the verse. First the Talmud:

> [4] The chief of the Beth Din then said: "It (the new moon) is consecrated," and all the people repeated after him: "It is consecrated; it is consecrated." Whether the new moon was seen at its proper time (after twenty-nine days) or not, they used to consecrate it. R. Elazar b. Zadok said: *If it had not been seen at its proper time it was not consecrated, because it had already been consecrated in heaven (i.e., of itself).* (Rodkinson- Babylonian Talmud, Rosh Hashanna 2.4)

So it seems that the Sanhedrin viewed the New Moon as consecrated in heaven even if it was not seen and then separately confirmed / consecrated on earth with the sliver being seen over Israel. When we plug the alternate meanings into the verse in question we come up with a shocking reading:

> Sound the ram's horn at the **New Moon**, when the *moon is covered*, on the day of our Feast. (Psalm 81:3)[11]

In this scenario the word *chodesh* means "sighted new moon" and the other term refers to an unseen new moon that nevertheless requires the shofar to be blown during the other meaning of this same word: *at the appointed time!* Such an idea may also explain this poetry in Hosea:

> *They have dealt treacherously against YHWH. They have given birth to illegitimate children. Now the new moon will devour them* with their land. *Blow the shofar* in Gibea and the trumpet in Ramah! Raise up a shot at Beth-aven! Behind you, Benjamin! Hosea 5:7-8 (Matara)

---

very common to say, "and he opened up his mouth to speak and he said" rather than "he spoke". As a result this sentence best reads, "He obscures the face of the covered moon". The only other place this word appears other than Psalm 81:3 and Job 26:9 is in Proverbs 7:20 where a seductress tells a man, "my husband will return at the *kesa* moon". Well, with no other time clues extant, couldn't this mean the new moon? Wouldn't it make sense that if he is away on a long journey that it's for the whole month?

11 The Psalms Targum: An English Translation, as translated by Edward Cook, has a very interesting reading for 81:3: "Blow the horn in the month *of Tishri, in the month in which* the day of our festivals *is concealed.*"

As we can easily see, the birth of a child is compared to the birth of the New Moon and the blowing of the shofar at that time. Children, it need hardly be pointed out, are formed in darkness and come into the light of life, as must the moon!

In this way all sources, Hebrew and Aramaic, Tanakh and extra-biblical, seem to harmonize. But there is one final proof we need to explore regarding the possibility that the New Moon is born in darkness and not the sliver of light that emerges from that darkness some time later:

> *Adar* , רֲדָא **n.pr.[m.]** 12th (Babylonian) month = Feb.-Mar. (late Heb. loan-word, = Bab. *A(d)-daru* v. Dl:Wp. 188, cf. Al 3 93, meaning dub. **perh.*adâru, be darkened, eclipsed***, but v. Dl:W p. 190) Est 3:7, 3:12, 8:12, 9:1, 9:15, 9:17, 9:19, 9:21; cf. Palm. Nab. אדר Vog:8 Eut:Nab 24. –Bible Works 8

Just like the following month, Abib, is descriptive of the ripening of Spring, so too is the last month of the year given a title for what is supposed to happen during its time: to be darkened, eclipsed, which is its original ancient Aramaic meaning. The only possible "eclipse" that would always happen in the 12th month and never any other time of year must be that last darkening of the moon that ends the year, from which the new year immediately springs without a gap in time. So in the 12th month, that Adar/eclipse leads to darkness, from which the light of the first month of the New Year begins!

And finally, we need to look at the word most often used for "month" in Scripture:

> **chodesh / שֵׁדֹח שְׁדָ֫ח** (μ¹dash) **renew, repair.** (ASV and RSV also restore.) (613a) שְׁדָ֫ח (μ¹d¹sh) **new, new thing, fresh.**

When *chodesh* refers only to the beginning of the month, it is naturally translated "new moon," which was a feast day. It is one of the "appointed feasts" and is listed with the Sabbath and the pilgrim feasts as involving burnt offerings (2Chr 8:13 et al.), and is also characterized by the blowing of trumpets (Psa 81:3 [H 4];

Num 10:10). Since it was a feast, David's absence from Saul's table at the new moon was especially noticeable (1Sam 20:5ff). – Theological Workbook of the Old Testament.

While Modern Hebrew provides different pointings for these meanings, the root and the word remain the same. What gets a little odd is that while many Hebrew dictionaries make the assumption this relates to crescent-sighting, the Scriptural proof for that assertion ranges from scant (Psalm 81:3, discussed elsewhere) to non-existent. But the fact remains nevertheless that there is not one Biblical example of sighting the crescent as a forward looking marker of "newness". Instead, when we look at one of the main meanings "new" above, we find clear evidence that its state begins in darkness:

> You have heard; look at all this. And you, will you not make it known? *I proclaim to you new* (חָדָשׁ) *things from this time, even hidden things which you have not known.* They are created now and not long ago; and before today you have not heard them, So that you will not say, Behold, I knew them. Isaiah 48:6-7 (Matara)

So here we see clearly that "new" means "hidden, unknown things". If we then see evidence of it, like a crescent sliver, then it isn't "new" anymore! Here's another example:

> Behold, the previous things have come to pass. *Now I declare new* (חָדָשׁ) *things. Before they spring forth* I declare them to you. Isaiah 42:9 (Matara)

Now we have two additional details: First, something is "new" *before it springs forth*. Again, wouldn't a crescent then be the precise form of "springing forth" that indicates a lack of newness? Second, it says the old things, "have come to pass" which in Hebrew really means, "gone away". This is why the lunar month really ends with the conjunction, at the time that it has literally "gone away"! For that reason Isaiah can't help believing that the same applies to the whole cosmos:

> For behold, *I create new* (חָדָשׁ) *heavens and a new* (חָדָשׁ) *earth and the previous things will not be remembered* or come to mind. Isaiah 65:17 (Matara)

The reason why the former things are not remembered is again, because they are gone. Even here though Isaiah is not finished with defining "new" and linking it across the board:

> *For just as the new* (חָדָשׁ) *heavens and the new* (חָדָשׁ) *earth* which I make will endure before Me, declares YHWH, So your offspring and your name will endure. And it shall be from *new moon* (חֹדֶשׁ) *to new moon* (חֹדֶשׁ) and from sabbath to sabbath that all mankind will come to bow down before Me," says YHWH. Isaiah 66:22-23 (Matara)

I think the imagery could not be clearer. When dealing with a brand new month, the new heavens and earth follow the same pattern as the "new things", starting from before they spring forth into the physical world! At a minimum this "strong suggestion" demands that said definition be taken into serious consideration rather than just cast aside for some "crescent rolls"!

A Poetic Defense

In response to this clear fact of linguistics, the leading Crescentist among the Karaites in Israel has decided to attempt through "poetry" (trickery), what cannot be done from the plain meaning of ancient Hebrew. The idea is that different Hebrew vowel pointing is used to elicit poetic trends. The problem of course is the pointing standardization is an invention of the Middle Ages. Ancient Hebrew and Aramaic had no full vowels, so the whole matter of making assumptions that such can be projected backwards is misguided at best and deceptive. Nevertheless, let's be generous, let's take the Karaite theory for what it is and prove that, even if they are right, they are still very wrong.

As it relates to Psalm 81:3 the "New Moon" represents one poetic opposite and the *kisa/keceh* moon represents the other. So, to put the matter succinctly, the opposite of *kisa/keceh* is the "New Moon" which means *kisa/keceh* must mean "full moon" after all, even though not a single other place the word is used means that. As I said, let's be generous.

But here's the problem that the Karaite theory cannot solve: If kisa/keceh is the opposite of the New Moon and therefore means "Full Moon", *how can that opposite (of New) be the Crescent?* I ask this because, astronomically speaking, the opposite of the Full Moon is the Conjunction in Darkness and not the Crescent which features some light!

In all fairness, if the Full Moon symbolizes the peak of the moon's luminosity, what must the New Moon—its poetic opposite—symbolize other than its complete darkness or concealment? And that is why Philo says:

> [140] Following the order which we have adopted, we proceed to speak of the third festival, that of the new moon. First of all, **because it is the beginning of the month,** and the beginning, whether of number or of time, is honorable. **Secondly, because at this time there is nothing in the whole of heaven destitute of light.** [141] Thirdly, because at that period the more powerful and important body gives a portion of necessary assistance to the less important and weaker body; **for, at the time of the new moon, the sun begins to illuminate the moon with a light which is visible to the outward senses, and then she displays her own beauty to the beholders.** And this is, as it seems, an evident lesson of kindness and humanity to men, to teach them that they should never grudge to impart their own good things to others, but, imitating the heavenly bodies, should drive envy away and banish it from the soul. (The Special Laws 2:140-141)

The beginning is "destitute of light" the opposite—poetically and scientifically—of the Full Moon! Poetic justice indeed!

Rising Crescent Rolls

[41] Now there are ten festivals in number, as the law sets them down. The first is that which any one will perhaps be astonished to hear called a festival. This festival is every day. The second festival is the seventh day, which the Hebrews in their native language call the sabbath. **The third is that which comes after the conjunction[12], which happens on the day of the new moon in each month. The fourth is that of the Passover which is called the Pascha.** The fifth is the first fruits of the corn-- the sacred sheaf. The sixth is the feast of unleavened bread, after which that festival is celebrated, which is really the seventh day of seventh days. **The eighth is the festival of the sacred moon, or the feast of trumpets.** The ninth is the fast. The tenth is the feast of tabernacles, which is the last of all the annual festivals, ending so as to make the perfect number of ten. We must now begin with the first festival. (Philo: The Special Laws 2:41)

One of the recurring themes in this book is that I endeavor to take the best elements of all the calendar theories and see how they might fit together in one over-arching process and methodology. I am therefore keenly aware how the moon-sighting versus moon counting debate stir up passions on both sides.

In talking with many like-minded people over the long gestation of this project, the one thing that seems to incense them is how their opponents— almost without exception—completely ignore the conjunction as a non-event in spite of first hand accounts that such a happening was tracked easily by the ancients and modern scientific confirmation that the conjunction and not the crescent is when the moon is astronomically new.

But if ignoring the conjunction to the exclusion of the crescent is wrong

---

12 This phrase "after the conjunction" is key in that Philo is not saying it starts with crescent, but in other places simply refers to the "growing crescent" as the first visible form of the lunar cycle. But if we go to the moment of the conjunction then the months will not alternate between 29 and 30 days in a regular manner and this will cause other chaos in Israel wit h a 2 day period from conjunction to crescent. It will also result in Pesach and Sukkot not starting on the first days of the full moon in their respective seasons, which was clearly unacceptable in ancient Israel.

so too is the opposite extreme of ignoring the crescent! There can be no denying whatsoever that ancient Israel sighted the crescent as part of their ceremony to set the month in motion. It is also an undeniable fact that in Hebrew as in English "moon" and "month" are derived from the same exact word. As a linguist and a historian, I cannot ignore that evidence even if I disagree with the conclusions that arise from that evidence.

What draws myself and most others away from crescentist traditions, is how they (the Karaites for example) do not align the full moons with the Feast dates. For example, in 2010 the moon became full over Israel at 4:25 AM on March 30th, yet for Crescentists the 14th of Abib was on March 31st. Their "Pesach window" added at least 18 additional hours. Scripture and ancient historical records are unanimous in that the Full Moon has a more distinguished role than Crescentist tradition affords it. For Tishri (the 7th month) 2010, Crescentists established September 11th as the first day of their month which put their Feast of Tabernacles celebration forward to September 25. Regrettably, the Full Moon occurred on September 23rd at 11:17 AM, missing the mark by two days.

By contrast, time after time and year after year, the ancient and Scriptural "Bookend" system synchronizes all the Great Feasts, starting with the occurrence of the Full Moon (14th or 15th of their respective months). I call this; *the Rule of the 15th*, which is why Philo tells us the following:

> 189 *On the fifteenth day, at full moon*, the feast which is called "the feast of booths" is celebrated for which the supplies of the sacrifices are more numerous. (The Special Laws, 1:189)

> 169 For some of them are offered up every day, and some on the days of the new moon, *and at the festivals of the full moon*; others on days of fasting; and others at three different occasions of festival. Accordingly, it is commanded that every day the priests should offer up two lambs, one at the dawn of day, and the other in the evening; each of them being a sacrifice of thanksgiving; the one for the kindnesses which have been bestowed during the day, and the other for the mercies which have been vouchsafed in the

night, which God is incessantly and uninterruptedly pouring upon the race of men. (The Special Laws, 1:169)

149 *And this universal sacrifice of the whole people is celebrated on the fourteenth day of the month, which consists of two periods of seven, in order that nothing which is accounted worthy of honor may be separated from the number seven. But this number is the beginning of brilliancy and dignity to everything.* 150 And there is another festival combined with the feast of the passover, having a use of food different from the usual one, and not customary; the use, namely, of unleavened bread, from which it derives its name. And there are two accounts given of this festival, the one peculiar to the nation, on account of the migration already described; the other a common one, in accordance with conformity to nature and with the harmony of the whole world. And we must consider how accurate the hypothesis is. This month, being the seventh both in number and order, according to the revolutions of the sun, is the first in power. (The Special Laws, 2:149-150)

We also have the same tradition reflected in the Apocrypha:

[156] Speak to all the people, that I say this month, [157] *at fullness of the moon, to sacrifice a Paschal lamb to God,* [158] *and touch the doors with blood before the fall of night,* [159] so that the awful angel might pass by the sign. [160] And you must feast that night on roasted meat. (Ezekiel the Tragedian, 1:156-160, from *The Pseudepigrapha* (English), Translated by Craig E. Evans, assisted by Danny Zacharias, Matt Walsh, and Scott Kohler. Copyright © 2008 Craig A. Evans.)

[2] When these men gave explanations for questions about the Exodus, the said that it is equally necessary for everyone to offer Passover sacrifices after the Vernal Equinox, in the middle of the first month. This takes place (during) the first segment of the sun, or --as some have said --while the sun is passing through the circle of the Zodiac. *And Aristobulus adds how on the Passover festival it is necessary not only that the sun should be in the equinoctial*

segment, but that the moon should be, as well. [3] *For, since there are two equinoctial segments --the Vernal and the Autumnal --and since they are equal to one another, and since the Passover is appointed to be on the fourteenth ay of the month, after sundown, the moon will be in position across from and opposite to the position of the sun, just as it possible to see it at the times of a full moon.* The one --the sun --will be in the Vernal equinoctial segment, while the other --the moon --must necessarily be in the Autumnal equinoctial (segment). (Fragments of Aristobulus 1:2-3, from *The Pseudepigrapha* (English), Translated by Craig E. Evans, assisted by Danny Zacharias, Matt Walsh, and Scott Kohler. Copyright © 2008 Craig A. Evans.)

On the side whence the light of the moon comes forth, there again she wanes till all the light vanishes and all the days of the month are at an end, and her circumference is empty, void of light.-Apocryphal Book of Enoch,.78:14, from *The Apocrypha and Pseudepigrapha of the Old Testament in English,* RH Charles, Clarendon Press (Oxford), 1913.

Furthermore, the day is divided by darkness and then light so it made sense the month would be as well, especially owing to the fact that the Aramaic name for the last month of the year means, "darken, eclipse" which strongly implies the new year comes out of the darkness seamlessly and into the next period of ripening, which is the meaning of the next month, Abib.

But there is another reason why I put this last calibration towards the end rather than in a calendar section per se: This goes back to where we started with the roots of all these timekeeping systems, *signs, seasons, days and years in that order.* When we were last doing that analysis, every single detail of major sacred observances on earth had a heavenly component that kicked it off. So YHWH resting on Shabbat after Creation made Creation the sky sign and man's keeping the Shabbat the same way YHWH did without the sun or the moon was the earth sign. And the fact is, you can go through all the Scriptural feasts in Torah and even major regular commands like circumcision and find the "sky sign/ earth sign" symmetry.

As said at the outset: ***There are no coincidences or meaningless details in the Hebrew Scriptures.*** So as we broaden our vision out from the specifics and into the general once more, let's look at the one thing that we know is true about Pesach that isn't true of any other Feast throughout the Hebrew year:

> You shall keep (the lamb) until the fourteenth day of the same month, then the ***whole assembly of the congregation of Israel is to kill it between the evenings (beyn ha eruvim--*** בין הערבים*)*. Then they are to take some of the blood and put it on the sides and tops of the doorframes of the houses where they eat the lambs. ***That same night*** they are to eat the meat roasted over the fire, along with bitter herbs, and bread made without yeast. Do not eat the meat raw or cooked in water, but roast it over the fire-head, legs and inner parts. Do not leave any of it till morning; if some is left till morning, you must burn it. (Exodus 12:6-10-NIV)

Once again we see this is ***beyn ha eruvim***—plural—with a literal meaning of "between the evenings". The word used more often in English, "twilight", doesn't really do the Hebrew term justice. There are two evenings in the Hebrew day. The first is from late afternoon (Jeremiah 6:4) to the beginning of the sun going down. The second is from the sun setting to absolute darkness (2 Chronicles 18:34). The whole concept of the English word "evening" is that the light and dark are evenly proportioned with the shadows lengthening, the exact meaning of *erev* that we saw earlier.

Nor is this the only place in Tanakh that tells us about the importance of this time of day:

> You shall command the sons of Israel, that they bring you pure oil of beaten olives for the light, ***to make a lamp burn continually***. In the tent of meeting, outside the veil which is before the testimony, ***Aaron and his sons shall keep it in order from evening to morning before YHWH; it shall be a perpetual statute throughout their generations for the sons of Israel***. Exodus 27:20-21 (Matara)

Here the light of the lamp is provided in the late afternoon, thus showing the transfer of light from the sun to the priests on earth tending the Tabernacle. It is a deep hint that, just as YHWH has the moon with no light of its own but can only get it from the sun, so too can the priests only have their light on earth by YHWH's command.

And finally, there is Pesach's "mirror" in the fall, at the other end of the Hebrew year:

> On exactly the tenth day of this seventh month is Yom Kippur (Day of Atonement); it will be a Set-Apart convocation for you, and you will humble your souls and present an offering by fire to YHWH. You will not do any work on this same day, for it is a day of atonement, to make atonement on your behalf before YHWH your Elohim. If there is any person who will not humble himself on this same day, he shall be cut off from his people. As for any person who does any work on this same day, that person I will destroy from among his people. You will do no work at all. It is to be a perpetual statute throughout your generations in all your dwelling places. It is to be an Absolute Shabbat of complete rest to you, and you will humble your souls; *on the ninth of the month at evening, from evening until evening you will keep your Shabbat.* Leviticus 23:27-32 (Matara)

Isn't it interesting then that, right around the time of the autumnal equinox, we have the only other occasion that begins and ends *before sunset*? Furthermore, it also appears we have a confirming witness about the nature of marking both the week and the month through varying mechanisms:

> [4] Hear this, you who trample the needy, to do away with the humble of the land, [5] saying, *"When will the new moon be over, So that we may sell grain, And the sabbath, that we may open the wheat market,* To make the bushel smaller and the shekel bigger, And to cheat with dishonest scales, [6] So as to buy the helpless for money And the needy for a pair of sandals, And *that* we may sell the refuse of the wheat?" (Amos 8:4-6 NAU)

In the case of the "new moon" this line clearly speaks volumes that more than the crescent alone determines the starting and ending points of the month. *"When will the Shabbat be over?"* undoubtedly fixes the end of Shabbat at sunset, regardless as to how someone chooses to mark it. But the point is, by the rules that have been laid down, occasionally the day may end "at evening" instead of sunset. Scripture is clear at letting us know when the "exceptions" are and that they occur often enough so as to be covered by the prophetic rebuke. And finally, the prophecy opens in the summer time, symbolized by a "summer basket of fruit", or the precise mid-point between the two equinoxes that divide up the overall year.[13]

Therefore, for the first and seventh months of the year, any New Moon appearing "between the evenings" but before darkness—or from about 3 PM to 6 PM—would have counted the New Moon to the following Hebrew day to minimize the discrepancy between conjunction and crescent. That is the only way to literally see the heavenly counterpart of slaughtering the lamb also "between the evenings" on the 14th. Pesach is the only time in the entire year where a festival begins not at sunset from when the previous day ended but from the late afternoon period after that sunset. And then, on the most sacred day in the entire Torah—the Day of Atonement itself—we begin symbolic expiation of our sins through fasting also evening to evening. *As in heaven so on earth!* When we do that calibration, the whole system keeps time perfectly throughout the year.

Synchronizing Lunar and Solar Days: Making "The Leap"

The next little piece is to realize that lunar month days and solar month days are not precisely the same thing. The "assumption" that most folks have is that within seconds of the New Moon being proclaimed—by any method they choose—the end of the "day" seamlessly follows with the beginning of the next. However, this is not exactly true.

---

13 In fact there are a number of seasonal time markers used by Amos in this section. 7:1 starts out with the locusts that swarm in early spring and 8:8 talks of the Nile flooding its banks and later subsiding, which happened every July. Y'shua also uses time clues from agriculture as well, talking of figs being a sign of summer. (Luke 21:29-30).

The reason has to do with the **.53** day remainder on the last day of the lunar month. Recalling our earlier discussion on how power / judgment resides with the sun, the days are also directly determined by the length of the solar year and the length of the solar day of 24 hours. In other words, each and every day of the solar year—and therefore the month— must be 24 hours long.

So what happens then with the "extra" 12+ hours on the solar "day" that the moon needs before it recycles? This is, perhaps, the single greatest confusion in all calendar studies, but it is also an opportunity to show how gracefully and hand-in-glove sighted and counted systems can work in tandem.

The problem is, crescent-only systems neglect of the lunar conjunction and act as if there is no gap between lunar days in a given month and solar days throughout a year that transcend the month. Again, these signs are constantly handing off control to one another, like a relay runner passing the baton to his teammate, but there must be one overall schema for tracking the time.

Before I give my answer to this "baton-passing" system, let us review again the words of Philo:

> [60] They were also created to serve as measures of time; for it is by the appointed periodical revolutions of the sun and moon and other stars, that days and months and years are determined. And moreover it is owing to them that the most useful of all things, the nature of number exists, time having displayed it; for from one day comes the limit, and from two the number two, and from three, three, *and from the notion of a month is derived the number thirty, and from a year that number which is equal to the days of the twelve months*, and from infinite time comes the notion of infinite number. (On Creation 1:60)

Of course we also saw other indications of consecutive 30-day months from Scripture earlier. My point though is this was done as a way to deal with that extra time on the 30th day, regardless as to the lunar month was counted as 29 or 30 days.

A good way to think of this in laymen's terms is to recall our current leap-day system with Gregorian. We must have February 29th about every 4 years because the solar year is 365 days and about 6 hours long. Over 4 years, 6 x 4 = 24 hours, an extra day, but the days remain 24 hours in length. Otherwise, we might go without leap days and if year 1 ended at midnight, year 2 would end 6 hours later, a 6AM, year 3, noon and so on, and then each day would run from variable time to variable time, not midnight to midnight.

Obviously that is too chaotic a system for us humans to use. That is why the right method for all proper solar calendar systems is to defer to the solar day length at the end of the cycle and make sure it comes out evenly to "balance". That balancing method is always to the nearest 24 hour period and what I am saying here is the same thing must happen to deal with the varying lengths between lunar and solar cycles.

Specifically the lunar day ends and begins with the conjunction at the end of its cycle, but the solar day is not dependent on that and cannot end synchronized to that cycle. As a result, if you try to get the solar day to "end" when the moon is New, that day will only be about 12 hours long! Or, to put it another way, if the lunar conjunction happens on say April 5th at 2 PM, then that solar day would only be from midnight to 2 PM—14 hours instead of the required 24. That would then throw off calculations for the rest of the year. Such is the real problem with using the crescent without any other data, but ironically we can still set the month accurately by sighting the moon! Here's how:

> 1) Starting after the Full Moon, track the moon by its appearance through its last quarter/waning crescent. That lunar appearance will intensify starting around day 24 (please see illustrations online at www.wheelofstars.com).

> 2) By day 28, you will be observing the last day of the waning crescent making note of when it rises. (Remember the Hebrew day begins at sunset.)

> 3) The very next day—24 hours from that waning crescent on day 28/29—the moon will be astronomically New.

4) Have others "confirm" the month by the sighting of the new crescent up to a day later, but understand that the crescent tells us when the month began the day before, not the day it happens.

5) For that first month, enjoy Pesach coming precisely 14 days later. Then enjoy the rest of the year being perfectly on time!

An Alternate Method That Does the Same Thing

However there is an easier way to the same thing. The days are solar, the moon may have control over the Hebrew month, but the days in the month, as we have seen, must be 24 hours in length and not synched to the rising, falling and subsequent re-rising of the moon, regardless as to its actual phase on a given day. As far as I am concerned, Scripture is crystal clear that the sun rules over the moon and rules over the length of the days since it also rules over the year, and I will not re-visit that as a discussion point.

Having said that, I also understand that relying on the exact moment on the day of the conjunction is also an extreme position, as is the idea of taking the previous sunset of a calculated conjunction. The reason is, again, the festivals of the full moon (Pesach and Sukkot) must take place on the right Hebrew day that must itself be the first day (14th or 15th) of the Full Moon. No earlier and no later. So that is why, taking the Scripture literally again, I have arrived at the only possible way to make sure those festivals happen on time:

The new month begins always after the Conjunction and is set to the day after the sunset that immediately follows it!

So if the moon is calculated to be in conjunction the last watch before sunset, say about 3 PM (precisely X number of hours from the last time we saw the Old Moon's waning crescent), sunset will "confirm" it for the following Hebrew day, which explains why Jewish debate over more than three thousand years has never expanded to a three day discrepancy of when the month begins, only two. Astronomy tells us plainly that the New Moon can be obscured in the brightness of the sun—and thus appear dark to us on earth—for up to 38 hours and definitely not less than 14 hours.

The reason I say this is because of simple math. If the moon begins conjunction an hour before sunset, which it does enough times to be a huge problem, this is what happens:

Day 1- Conjunction near sunset.
Day 2 -24 hours from that sunset to the next sunset.
Day 3-An "extra' half a day.

In other words, an hour before sunset means that more than 35 hours remain, for which the second day can only account for 24 of those hours. The remaining hours, up to 13 of them, are stuck on day 3, and then we have to see when sunset sets the next Hebrew day. But in the system I am describing, we not only can guarantee that Pesach and Sukkot hit their respective days accurately 100% of the time, this also explains why there are no arguments in Talmudic tradition of these being more than a two day events!

This is the only way all the sources harmonize and it is so simple that it is easy to miss in the passionate minefield that calendar research represents to the community of the faithful.

As Philo said, it is "after the conjunction" the new moon begins, but how soon after depends on where you live. Because again the sun is in charge of the days—not the moon—the sun will give its "permission" for the new month to begin. Then with that permission the moon will "confirm" the judgment by showing the crescent, once again validating Genesis 1:14-19, *signs, seasons, days and years—in that order!* When you do this, again, all festivals occur at their intended time 100% of the time, which not only gives validity for those who used to sight the crescent, but also those who sighted the full moon in relationship to the crescent! This is a boon for sighted and calculation people alike!

The Truth About the Crescent

This may be the most difficult passage of "Wheel of Stars" that I have to write, not because of technical aspects but because of my concerns that what I am about to say will be misunderstood.

I want to say this at the outset as I did at the beginning of this book:

> *I love, cherish and respect everyone who believes that sighting the crescent is a service to YHWH and who do so because they sincerely believe this is what Torah commands. It is also true that excesses exist on both sides of the argument, which is to say that the Cresentists have a right to be upset about certain aspects of the rabbinic calendar. When it comes to going totally to a calculated system that ignores the moon completely, this is wrong too.*

Jewish sources tell us of the lengths that one Rabbi, Saadia Gaon[14] (c. 892- 942) went to in his defense of the Hillel Calendar:

> "...Rejecting the fixed calendar as a heretic innovation, the Karaites held that by law of Scripture the beginning of the months must be determined by the appearance of the new crescent and no other means, and that this had been the practice of ancient Israel at all times. Rabbanite refutation of this extreme assertion found its most outspoken exponent in Saadia Gaon, who went to the opposite extreme in 'demonstrating' that the fixed calendar, computation of molad and tekufah, has the force of a Mosaic-Sinaitic law that had been followed at all ages of the past [like some in the CoGs proclaim], while observation of the new crescent was merely a passing episode in the history of the Jews, introduced at the time of the Sadducees to show that it confirmed the correctness of the prescribed calendaric regulation by calculation. Although this contention could easily be refuted by the Karaites as fanciful to the point of ridicule, Saadia's prestige was so great that his theory was

14 Saadia Gaon vigorously refuted Karaites for their threats against the Jewish community, he witnessed the early beginnings of Karaitism in Iraq in the 9th Century.

accepted even by leading scholars.....Maimonides [12th century A.D] is one of the few medieval Rabbanite authorities known to have taken issue with Saadia's and his followers' contention, and his refutation amounts to unmitigated reproach, indeed to expression of intellectual as well as religious indignation. [Maimonides commented:] 'I am truly astonished over a personage who rejects clear evidence, **asserting that the religion of Israel was based, not on observation of the new moon, but on calculation alone– and yet he [Saadia] affirms the authority of all these (just mentioned) Talmudic passages!** I think indeed that he did not believe his own assertions, but he merely wished to repel his [Karaite] adversary by any notion that just occurred to him, be it true or false, when he had found himself unable to escape the force of (his adversary's) argument.'" (The Code of Maimonides, book II, treatise 8, translated by Solomon Gandz, Yale Judaica Series, Volume XI, pp.lii-liii)

I have plenty disagreements as I said with Karaites, but in this case, we are in agreement. My main opposition to the rabbinic calendar though is historical. Again, the Metonic cycle on which it is based was unknown until a thousand years after Moshe died. For me, the fact that history proves it isn't scriptural, is enough to doubt the rabbis here, but that doesn't mean that while the Karaites are right about the problem that they are equally accurate about their proposed solutions to that problem. Those are two separate discussions.

But getting back to the main point, it is this: *For those in the Torah observant community who set their months to the crescent because that's the best you know, my rebuke here does not come upon you. But, like you, I too wish to follow Torah and do what it says to the best of my ability. As a result, it is incumbent on me to point out to you a very inconvenient truth: Crescent observation comes from paganism. If you permit, I will prove this wth humility and respect for your Torah zealousness.*

My obedience demands that I celebrate Pesach and Sukkot on the right days, the first days of the full moon in their respective months. Crescent observations will most certainly throw this off at least some of the time, and that is the heart of the problem with the Crescentist only system. But beyond this as well, as all the other linguistic information we have already covered, the fact is we worship an Invisible Elohim who began Creation in darkness and the day in darkness. This Elohim also gave us information that His treasures and secrets are also in darkness (Isaiah 45). So if we are going to talk then about the calendar Moshe used, why not look at what the Scripture from the period says about how that compares to what the nations around Israel did:

> [2] "If there is found in your midst, in any of your towns, which YHWH your Elohim is giving you, a man or a woman who does what is evil in the sight of the YHWH your Elohim, by going around His covenant, [3] *and has gone and served other gods and worshiped them, or the sun or the moon or any of the heavenly host, which I have not commanded*, [4] and if it is told you and you have heard of it, then you shall investigate the matter with great care. Behold, if it is true and the thing certain that this detestable thing has been done in Israel, [5] then you shall bring out that man or that woman who has done this evil deed to your gates, *that is*, the man or the woman, and you shall stone them to death. Deuteronomy 17:2-5 (Matara)

How did they worship the moon? They did so by "sanctifying" the crescent! The truth of the matter is, nowhere does Scripture link the crescent moon to the new moon because the word for "crescent moon" is almost non-existent in the Tanakh. In fact, here is *one* place it appears:

> [18] On that day *Adonai* will take away their finery- their anklets, medallions *and crescents*, (שַׂהֲרֹן) [19] their pendants, bracelets and veils; [20] their headbands, armlets, sashes, perfume bottles, amulets, [21] rings and nose-jewels; [22] their fine dresses, wraps, shawls, handbags, [23] gauze scarves, linen underclothes, turbans and capes. Isaiah 3:18-23 (Matara)

YHWH will remove the crescents! Just to be clear though, here is the official dictionary definition:

† [שַׁהֲרוֹן] **n.** [**m.**] moon, or crescent;—only pl. הַשַּׂהֲרֹנִים of (non-Israel.) ornaments of camels Ju 8:21, kings v:26, women Is 3:18, LXX μηνίσκοι Vulgate (Is 3:18) *lunulae;* on crescent as ornament v. Dozy:ii. 760 Lane:Egypt. ii. 314 Perles:Anal. 79, cf. Frä:58. –Brown Drivers Briggs

Now look at this same word in Judges:

> [19] Gid'on replied, "They were my brothers, my mother's sons. As surely as *ADONAI* is alive, I swear that if you had spared them, I would not kill you." [20] Then he ordered his oldest son, Yeter, "Get up, and kill them!" But the boy didn't draw his sword; being still a boy, he was afraid. [21] Then Zevach and Tzalmuna said, "You, do it. You, kill us. Let a grown man do what takes a grown man's strength.*" So Gid'on got up and killed Zevach and Tzalmuna; then he took the ornamental crescents from around their camels' necks. [22] The men of Isra'el said to Gid'on:* "Rule over us, you, your son and your grandson, because you saved us from the power of Midyan. *[23] Gid'on replied, "Neither I nor my son will rule over you; ADONAI will rule over you.*"[15] [24] Then he added, "But I have this request to make of you, that each of you would give me the earrings from the booty you have taken." For the enemy soldiers had worn gold earrings, like all the other tribes descended from Yishma'el. [25] They replied, "We're glad to give them to you." They spread out a robe, and each man threw in the earrings from his booty. *[26] The gold earrings he requested weighed more than forty-two pounds; and this doesn't include the crescents, pendants and purple cloth worn by the kings of Midyan and the chains around their camels' necks*. (Judges 8:19-26 CJB)

These are the three places "crescent" appears in Scripture, but it is never used in conjunction with the beginning of a month. Instead, we see the Midianites, the people who would eventually turn to a pure lunar calendar under Islam, were worshipping[16] the moon and sanctifying

---

15 More properly, YHWH will rule over you.
16 Moon watching for its own sake, exclusively and without other mechanisms, was demonstrably condemned by YHWH. The first city in Canaan that YHWH gave over to Joshua's hand was Jericho, it's name is derived from yareakh = moon. The people of the "Moon City" were totally destroyed down to its last bit of livestock and grain. The method of it destruction mimicked the absolute weekly Shabbat, marching around until the 7th day!

the crescent. It's also interesting to note that the historical origins of the Karaites, modern day moon watchers, is Iraq, which is of a moon-watching[17] Islamic culture. In reality, when "new" appears in conjunction with "moon", it is always compared to darkness. We saw this before in Isaiah 48, 65 and 66 references. Now let's see it in the NT too:

> Let no (one) therefore judge you about food and drink, or about the distinctions of festivals *and new moons and Shabbats which were shadows* of the things then future; but the body of Mashiyach.- Colossians 2:16 (AENT)

New moons and Shabbats are *literally* "shadows" because the month and the week end in darkness! Here it is again:

> …They who minister in the emblem and shadow of the things in heaven: as it was said to Moshe when he was about to build the tabernacle, See and make every thing according to the pattern which was showed you in the mount. Hebrews 8:5 (AENT)

It is also important to note that I've thoroughly cross-checked every time "new moon" *chodesh*, is used in Tanakh, with every Aramaic version of Tanakh known—including all the Targumim and the Peshitta complete version done in Babylon. Every single time the word that can sometimes mean "crescent" *sahar* was scrupulously avoided by the translators in favor of *yarakh* (generic moon or month) said to be "in renewal" or else dropped from the sentence altogether with synonyms meaning "renewal/first cycle". That cannot be a coincidence.

Sahar-crescent may be fine when describing the glory of a shining moon or a full moon, but never for describing the start of the month. Apparently, the Babylonian Jews then who were responsible for both the Peshitta Tanakh and the Talmud, along with authorizing the Onkelos and Jonathan ben Uzziel Targums for the Torah and the Prophets, knew exactly what they were doing. It is these same people who say that *kisa* in Psalm 81:3 cannot mean "full moon", and I for one believe them.

---

17 In recent years a small community of "Lunar Sabbatarians" has joined the moon watching ranks, please see Lunar Sabbath in the appendix.

Another Way to Look at the Evidence

Here is one final exploration of the evidence before concluding this section. Every potential calendar system must also show how the ancients kept it with their own tools and methods rather than have us moderns "hide" behind our computers, telescopes and satellites that the ancients did not have. I am therefore using a model that speaks to as much of the available evidence as possible, including that from calendrical systems I don't support. In other words, we need to understand where the right ideas started, as well as discuss how the application of those ideas may have gone off track.

That is why I view the barley as an *effect* of the year, rather than its cause, that was noted by the ancients before it became fully formed into its own calendar theory. The same holds true for sighting the crescent as "new" even though astronomically speaking it is not new. But I definitely see an advantage in having the people of Israel participate with their leaders to set the beginning of the new months. If certain individuals would say, "It was too cloudy for us, we didn't see the New Moon" they would still rest assured knowing that in previous months they were able to bring evidence forward and it was accepted, and for the months they didn't see it, other fellow countrymen did.

The reason I bring this up is for practical considerations stemming from one undeniable fact: *If ancient Israel argued about when the month began as often as we in "the Believing" community do today, there is no way the nation could function! Somehow, all lines of evidence had to be put together so that the nation as a whole could proceed with its business!*

Even at the time of writing this, the current year of 2010 provides an example of the kind of chaos that Israelites avoided when setting the new moons for their nation. On March 15th, the moon was astronomically new—that is in conjunction-darkness. However, the crescent was not sighted in various parts of the world until the 16th, and those in Israel had to wait until the 17th before they saw it. *As a result, some were saying Pesach was on the 29th, others the 30th, still others the 31st and even a few even went with April 1ˢᵗ. Imagine this kind of chaos happening every month or so in ancient Israel?* In terms of calendar setting, that's a train wreck! You throw off Pesach and you have also thrown off the entire Hebrew year!

Festivals of the Full Moon Includes Shavuot-Pentecost!

One of the issues that Philo helped clarify is that when he means to restrict a certain classification, he clearly says so. For example, Philo specifically says that Pesach and Sukkot are tied to their respective equinoxes, but in terms of Great Feasts or "festivals" as he terms them, he seems content with this general language:

> [169] For some of them are offered up every day, and some on the days of the new moon, and at the *festivals of the full moon; others on days of fasting; and others at three different occasions of festival.* (On the Special Laws, 1:169)

Now, in the Hebrew year, Pesach and Sukkot are clearly "festivals of the full moon". But notice also that Philo references "days of fasting" which would include Yom Kippur and also part of Purim? Further, if we put that phrasing aside what is left are two portions that clearly seem to relate to one another:

> *And others at the festivals of the full moon, at three different occasions of festival.*

"Three different occasions of festivals of the full moon" can only mean that all three Great Feasts are connected to the full moon. But if so, how does Shavuot fit into the mix given its odd start time? To answer that, we need to look at how both Josephus and Philo viewed the omer count and the timing of Shavuot in the first place:

> *When a week of weeks has passed over after this sacrifice, (which weeks contain forty-nine days,) on the fiftieth day, which is*

Pentecost, but is called by the Hebrews Asartha[18], which signifies Pentecost, they bring to God a loaf, made of wheat flour, of two tenth deals, with leaven; and for sacrifices they bring two lambs... (Antiquities 3:252)

Now when that feast, which was observed after seven weeks, and which the Jews called **Pentecost (i.e. the 50th day) was at hand, its name being taken from the number of the days [after the Passover]**, the people got together, but not on account of the accustomed divine worship, but of the indignation they had [at the present state of affairs]. (Wars of the Jews 2:42)

And also the day on which is offered the sheaf of corn, as an offering of gratitude for the fertility and productiveness of the plain, as exhibited in the fullness of the ears of corn. And the day of pentecost, which is numbered from this day by seven portions of seven days, in which it is the custom to offer up loaves, which are truly called the loaves of the first fruits, since, in fact, they are the first fruits of the productions and crops of eatable grain, which God has given to mankind, as the most tractable of all his creatures. (The Decalogue, 1:160)

The solemn assembly on the occasion of the festival of the sheaf having such great privileges, is the prelude to another festival of still greater importance; for from this day the fiftieth day is reckoned, making up the sacred number of seven sevens, with the addition of a unit as a seal to the whole; and this festival, being that of the first fruits of the corn, has derived its name of pentecost from the number of fifty, ('pentecostos'). And on it it is the custom to offer up two leavened loaves made of wheat, as a first fruit of the best kind of food made of corn; either because, before the fruit of the year is converted to the use of man, the first produce of the new crop, the first gathered corn that appears is offered as a first fruit, in order that by an insignificant emblem the people may display their grateful disposition; (The Special Laws, 2:176 PHE)

---

18 Asartha in Hebrew, like Pentecost in Greek, refers to fifty days.

For the fiftieth year, as the year of Pentecost or the Jubilee, is called remission in the giving forth of the law, as then all things are given their liberty, whether living or inanimate. And the mystery of the seventh year is one of quiet and profound peace to both body and soul. For the seventh is the recollection of all the good things which come of their own accord without industry or labor, which at the first creation of the world nature produced of herself; but the number forty-nine, consisting as it does of seven times seven, indicates no trifling blessings, but rather those which have virtue and wisdom, in such a degree as to contribute to invincible and mighty constancy. (On Creation, 3:39)

It seems rather straightforward which side of the omer count debates these men fall. Philo in particular also "kills two proverbial birds with one stone" by also affirming a 50 year Jubilee interval, which Josephus also endorses elsewhere.

For now though the most important fact is this: When the debate about how to count the omer comes up, the number one source that is cited for the Saduccean-Karaite point of view is the *Septuagint* translation of the relevant Torah passage. *In the ancient world, there were no better experts on the Septuagint as it originally was 2,000 years ago than Josephus and Philo, and both men have said here that they interpret the omer count from there as being precisely and exclusively 50 days! Both men have also said they start the omer count from the 16th of Abib:*

[162] There is also a festival on the day of the paschal feast, *which succeeds the first day*, and this is named the sheaf, from what takes place on it (The Special Laws, 2:162).

[250] *But on the second day of unleavened bread, which is the sixteenth day of the month, they first partake of the fruits of the earth, for before that day they do not touch them.* And while they suppose it proper to honour God, from whom they obtain this plentiful provision, in the first place, they offer the firstfruits of their barley, and that in the manner following: (Antiquities 3:250)

As a result, modern Karaite efforts to suggest a "real" LXX reading in favor of their view of the omer count fail the test of the experts who bore witness to the most ancient form of that translation which was known to exist! And for understanding the halachic view of both of these experts— whether one agrees with them or not—it is important to establish as I have that they are both on the same timetable.

That being said, there is only one way all this evidence can work together, and that is to say that Josephus, Philo, the Pharisees and the rest of first century Israel which would include Mashiyach Y'shua all sanctified the new moon over a two day period!

While Shavuot is a one day festival, it still counts as a Great Feast and sanctifies the week it appears in requiring special requirements that direct impact priestly service. In other words, all courses need to appear to help all of Israel do their sacrifices on that day and on the weekly Shabbat immediately following. As a result, it feels like an eight day period just as with Pesach and Sukkot and the Talmud seems to echo that sentiment for that whole week of the year:

> At three periods of the year money is drawn from the treasury (of the Shekalim); viz.: Half a month before Passover, **half a month before Pentecost**, and half a month before the Feast of Booths. The same dates are also the terms for the obligation of cattle-tithing, so says R. Aqiba. Ben Azai says: **"The dates for the latter terms are the twenty-ninth of Adar, the first of Sivan**, and the twenty-ninth of Abh." **R. Eliezer and R. Simeon both say: "The first of Nissan, the first of Sivan, and the twenty-ninth of Elul."** But why do they say the twenty-ninth of Elul why not the first of Tishri? Because that is a feast-day, and it is not allowed to tithe on a feast-day; therefore they ordained it for the preceding day, the twenty-ninth of Elul. (Rodkinson, Shekalim 3:1)

It is easy to see how the other dates match precisely with their Great Feasts. The last day of Adar (or first of Abib) would be exactly two weeks before Pesach and the last day of Elul would be two weeks and a day before Sukkot because, as the Talmud correctly says, you could not tithe on 1 Tishri as it is Yom Teruah.

But the "two weeks before Shavuot" is not literally two weeks. *It is the first of Sivan, only five days before that feast!* What's going on?

The answer is a bit startling. One of the innovations in the Rabbinic calendar was that the months were forever fixed to start at 30 and alternate to 29 and back to 30 days throughout the year. That means in any given Rabbinic year Abib must always be 30 days, Iyar 29, Sivan 30 and so on.

But when we look at Shavuot we see something very bizarre in the ancient sources: *While the ancient historians are unanimous that the 50-day omer count begins at 16 Abib, they nowhere mention that it must end only on 6 Sivan!* Part of the reason for 6 Sivan never showing up anciently as the "official" date for Shavuot may be found here:

> [3] The House of Shammai say: A peace-offering may be brought without laying the hands on them, but not burnt-offerings. But the House of Hillel say: Both peace-offerings and burnt-offerings may be brought, and also lay the hands on them. In the case of Pentecost, which falls upon the eve of a Sabbath, the House of Shammai say: The day for sacrificing is after the Sabbath. But the House of Hillel say: There is no day for sacrificing after the Sabbath. Both, however, admit that if it fall upon a Sabbath the day for sacrificing is the day after the Sabbath. And on that day (which is called the day of sacrificing) a high-priest is not to clothe himself in his costly garments, unless in case of a mourning or of a fast. The prohibition was in order not to confirm the words of those who say, Pentecost is after the Sabbath (only). (Rodkinson, Hagigah 2:3)

This small paragraph is describing a lot. It is refuting the Karaite position on Shavuot only happening on a Sunday as "the morrow after the Shabbat" directly. Instead, it is explaining that if the 50th day of the omer count hits Shabbat (Saturday) that part of the sacrifices that they would have done for the festival must be delayed to the following day, the first day of the week (Sunday). This is precisely what appears to have happened in the year 30 when Y'shua died! There is little doubt that Pesach in that year was a Wednesday and the first day of the Feast of Unleavened Bread a Thursday. That would mean the omer count had to have begun for them Thursday at sunset; for us the daylight period after, Friday, counting midnight to midnight.

Now, that means each subsequent Friday is another seven days, or a full week, in the omer count. To use Gregorian dates for convenience, that computes to Friday, April 5th, 30 CE. Then we count:

1) April 12th
2) April 19th
3) April 26th
4) May 3rd
5) May 10th
6) May 17th
7) May 24th

So then, the next day, May 25th, should be Shavuot right? But according to the book of Acts the sacrifices done on that day were "the first day of the week"—Sunday—meaning 7 Sivan a day later! The Shabbat intervened, delaying part of the Shavuot process from being completed, and this also explains other sources that talk of an occasional two-day Shavuot.

The other variant that would rule against a guaranteed 6 Sivan Shavuot as they counted in the first century is this:

> And this brings up yet another difficulty. The Jews calculated the month according to the phases of the moon, each month consisting of either twenty-nine or thirty days, and beginning with the appearance of the new moon. But this opened a fresh field of uncertainty. It is quite true that every one might observe for himself the appearance of a new moon. But this would again partly depend on the state of the weather. Besides, it left an authoritative declaration of the commencement of a month unsupplied. And yet not only was the first of every month to be observed as 'New Moon's Day,' but the feasts took place on the 10th, 15th, or other day of the month, which could not be accurately determined without a certain knowledge of its beginning. To supply this want the Sanhedrim sat

in the 'Hall of Polished Stones' to receive the testimony of credible witnesses that they had seen the new moon. To encourage as many as possible to come forward on so important a testimony, these witnesses were handsomely entertained at the public expense.

If the new moon had appeared at the commencement of the 30th day—which would correspond to our evening of the 29th, as the Jews reckoned the day from evening to evening—*the Sanhedrim declared the previous month to have been one of twenty-nine days, or 'imperfect.' Immediately thereon men were sent to a signal-station on the Mount of Olives, where beacon-fires were lit and torches waved, till a kindling flame on a hill in the distance indicated that the signal had been perceived*. Thus the tidings, that this was the new moon, would be carried from hill to hill, far beyond the boundaries of Palestine, to those of the dispersion, 'beyond the river.' Again, if credible witnesses had not appeared to testify to the appearance of the new moon on the evening of the 29th, the next evening, or that of the 30th, according to *our* reckoning, was taken as the commencement of the new month, in which case the previous month was declared to have been one of thirty days, or '*full.*' **It was ruled that a year should neither have less than four nor more than eight such full months of thirty days**. (Alfred Edersheim, *The Temple: Its Ministry and Services, Chapter 10.*)

So unlike the Rabbinic calendar which is one that has fixed the months and is meant to be used by Jews in exile, this system in the first century could have months vary in length so that what was a 30 day month in year 1 could be a 29 day month in year 2. This is also why we don't see 6 Sivan "fixed" to Shavuot before the establishment of the Rabbinic calendar!

In other words, by this system the first two months of the Hebrew year could also have consecutive 29 day or consecutive 30 day lengths, making 6 Sivan merely an average; the 50th day of Shavuot could then be as early as 5 Sivan and as late as 7 Sivan, depending on the timing of the lunar conjunction with the next sunset and subsequent sighting of the crescent moon!

Nevertheless, with 6 Sivan as the "average time" for Shavuot, the Temple authorities did reckon "2 weeks before Shavuot" as 1 Sivan, because by the 14-15th day the moon would be full! This is, albeit indirectly, also a festival of the full moon in the sense that by the time all the things associated with this holiday work out, that is with all the priests arriving the Friday before to assist or what may happen if it falls on a Shabbat, the process is guaranteed to be over and done with by the first appearance of the full moon!

Chapter 5

The Perfect
Fixed Hebrew Calendar

THEN THE GLORY OF YHWH DEPARTED FROM
THE THRESHOLD OF THE TEMPLE AND STOOD OVER
THE CHERUBIM. WHEN THE CHERUBIM DEPARTED,
THEY LIFTED THEIR WINGS AND ROSE UP FROM THE EARTH
IN MY SIGHT WITH THE WHEELS BESIDE THEM;
AND THEY STOOD STILL AT THE ENTRANCE OF THE
EAST GATE OF YHWH'S HOUSE, AND THE GLORY OF
THE ELOHIM OF ISRAEL HOVERED OVER THEM.
EZEKIEL 10:18-19-(MATARA)

Aries and the Vernal Equinox Are the Same Thing!

Today, we can track the equinoxes to the very second they occur. The ancients however couldn't see the equinoxes directly, which is fine because YHWH wanted it that way. But let's give technology and computer precision a rest and step back into the minds of priests and sages from 3,500 years ago.

YHWH has declared, as we have referenced often, that signs, seasons, days and years, in that order, is His ordering not man's. A sign is something that must be seen, which is why the constellations—*mazzaroth* in Job 38:31-34—are given the task of telling us that the equinoxes had happened, as opposed to happening right then and there.

With the Vernal Equinox, the return of Aries happens along with the setting of seven other stars, known in Hebrew as ***Kiymah*** (the Pleiades), and these are mentioned directly in Scripture too:

> He who made the Pleiades and Orion and changes deep darkness into morning, Who also darkens day *into* night, Who calls for the waters of the sea and pours them out on the surface of the earth? YHWH is His Name! Amos 5:8 (Matara)

> Who commands the sun not to shine, and sets a seal upon the stars? Who alone spreads out the heavens and treads down upon the waves of the sea? Who makes the Bear, Orion and the Pleiades, and the chambers of the south? Who does great things, that cannot be uncovered and extraordinary works without number?
> Job 9:7-10 (Matara)

Notice again this imagery of "darkening into morning" matches perfectly Adar being the month of darkening and giving way to the time of morning or ripening in the next month of Abib? *There is no such thing coincidence in Scripture!*

Similarly, the constellation of Libra and the Autumnal Equinox are also the same thing in the way the ancients tracked the seasons and determined when to plant and harvest their crops. How convenient then that Sukkot is scheduled to align with this time generally and in or "template year" of the Exodus in 1447 BCE which we will see momentarily, how convenient that the month Sukkot happens in and the very day of the sacred seventh moon of Yom Teruah is the precise time Libra, the autumnal equinox, just as Philo predicted!

Will the Real Zodiac Please Stand Up?

In both the ancient past and in today's New Age pop culture, the mythical counterfeit Zodiac draws people away from YHWH and into the worship of the created rather than the Creator. One of the titles of haSatan (the Adversary) is the Morning Star as opposed to the Star of Jacob who is Mashiyach Y'shua (Numbers 24:17, Revelation 22:16)!

The counterfeit Zodiac features things like rams, bulls and un-kosher shellfish (Cancer the crab), one of the subtle underlying messages therein is that kosher or un-kosher is irrelevant. Virgo is a pagan deity, one of the many deities invented within the sun worship pagan culture that denies that YHWH is One. Had Israel associated with pagan portrayals of the stars they would likely have been enticed into the pagan world, which is why the priests kept elements of the constellations private or hidden. Or, at the very least, they preferred Israel track the stars by looking up at constellations that corresponded to important dates in their own history.

The pagan or counterfeit Zodiac also runs out of time, as shown with the Mayan calendar running out of time in 2012. Each division of the sky—or house—is a 30 degree slice of a great Sky Circle. Hipparchus in 128 BCE proved conclusively that the equinoxes "precess"—or move away from our view—so that what the ancients saw 3000 years ago is not what we see today. Every century, the constellations move one degree from their previous place, so in about three millennia the fake Zodiac's signs are off by a month while the real ones are never even late, let alone off by a month or more!

This is also why modern astrology is a fraud, because it is based on constellations that appeared in the sky in the distant past not what appears in the skies at the time of our "birthdays" now.

Freeze Dried Dates Track the Year
(The Absolute-Kosher Zodiac)

> While the earth remains, seedtime and harvest and cold and heat, and summer and winter, and day and night shall not cease. (Genesis 8:22 NAU)

As we saw earlier, even if we were confined to Noah's Flood alone, it would still be possible for Israel to construct a perfectly working Zodiac year where they simply remember X constellation coincided with Y event.

However, in Moshe's day the calendar orientation changed, and so it is also fair to ask if a modified Kosher Zodiac was also commissioned to represent the new order. Just like Noah's version, the constellations would only be named for their seasons, and not false deities or un-kosher crabs, scorpions and so on.

This Absolute or "Kosher" Zodiac would also have the benefit of never going out of date, as it will always point to the first constellation of a season and "fix it" there regardless as to how it might have been called. This Absolute Zodiac would be so easy to use because the Israelites were remembering these dates anyway either because the constellations gave valuable information about the seasons, weather and agriculture or because an important event happened in a stellar month. It could be as simple as this:

> Constellation 1: Vernal Equinox (Barley/Pesach)
> Constellation 2: Summer Solstice (Figs)
> Constellation 3: Autumnal Equinox (Grapes/Feast of Ingathering)
> Constellation 4: Winter Solstice (Wait for spring)

From there, it would be natural for even casual observers to realize that the star patterns directly above them would change about every 30 days, and when that third "changing" was done, so was the season. So from here, we can get to all 12 constellations without a single pagan name thusly:

> Constellation 1: Vernal Equinox
> Constellation 2: 2nd spring month
> Constellation 3: 3rd spring month
> Constellation 4: Summer Solstice
> Constellation 5: 2nd summer month
> Constellation 6: 3rd summer month
> Constellation 7: Autumnal Equinox
> Constellation 8: 2nd autumn month
> Constellation 9: 3rd autumn month
> Constellation 10: Winter Solstice
> Constellation 11: 2nd winter month
> Constellation 12: 3rd winter month

As time goes on, certain historical and agricultural events then can get fixed to their signs:

Constellation 1: Vernal Equinox (Pesach)
Constellation 2: 2nd spring month (2nd Pesach)
Constellation 3: 3rd spring month (Shavuot)
Constellation 4: Summer Solstice
(Time of figs; Babylon breaks thru outer wall)
Constellation 5: 2nd summer month
(Aaron dies 1 Ab, Temples burned 9 Ab)
Constellation 6: 3rd summer month (Creation days 1-5)
Constellation 7: Autumnal Equinox
(Yom Teruah/Atonement/Sukkot)
Constellation 8: 2nd autumn month (Rainy season begins)
Constellation 9: 3rd autumn month
(Dedication and Re-dedication of Temples[1])
Constellation 10: Winter Solstice
Constellation 11: 2nd winter month
(Moshe Begins Last Discourse)
Constellation 12: 3rd winter month (Moshe's Dies)

As a result, the combination of historical events and agricultural necessity was powerful enough to give the Israelites all the "memory dates" needed to track the Kosher Zodiac of YHWH. All the Israelites had to do was look up and see the constellation associated with their event, and then track it for thousands of years as it came back on the exact same date of the solar calendar!

This is also why both Josephus and Philo continuously refer to the first constellation of spring as Aries, even though they knew that in their time—seventy years before Philo was born and nearly two centuries before Josephus compiled his writings—the spring constellation had shifted to Pisces. In their mind, what mattered was that something was always reliably in the sky to start spring and bring their times of memory into motion, to remember YHWH's covenant and what He did for Israel.

---

1 Haggai 2:10-18 has the Second Temple dedicated on the 24th of Kislev, and John 10:22 has Y'shua celebrate Hanukkah which was done on 25 Kislev, in accordance with the expulsion of the Syrian army under Judah Maccabee.

When you build a year in this manner, the full moon and new moon times will always synchronize to YHWH's timing for His ordained feasts. In fact, lets build that year right now!

The Hebrew Year According to the Kosher Zodiac

Okay, first thing to do is find the times of the equinoxes. We can easily do this for 2011 with the help of the web: http://www.imcce.fr/en/grandpublic/temps/saisons.php. Type in 2011 and hit "calculate" this is what comes up:

> Spring 20 March 2011 à 23h20m UT
> Summer 21 June 2011 à 17h16m UT
> Autumn 23 September 2011 à 9h4m UT
> Winter 22 December 2011 à 5h29m UT

You can also provide your local time zone if you choose, I am simplifying slightly for the sake of clarity of process.

But by ancient reckoning, remember they track the equinoxes by when their associated constellations appear, so that is our clock, at March 21st and September 22nd because we still have the day end at sunset.

In order to find the beginning of the Festivals though, we need to find the New Moon nearest the Vernal Equinox, which will also almost always be the first Full Moon on or after that equinox. Let's bring in NASA to do this, at http://eclipse.gsfc.nasa.gov/phase/phases2001.html which provides:

Apr 3 14:32 UT

That moon is sanctified over Israel 2 hours later, 16:32 or 4:32 PM. Because we are in our own times there are no errors to compensate for. *The next sunset after this time, wherever you live, is your time for Abib 1.* In my case, I live in the Eastern United States, so I need to look up that time zone at http://www.timeanddate.com/worldclock/. In my time zone

Abib 1 will begin at the sunset after April 3, 9:32 AM EST (Jerusalem is 7 hours ahead).

Your Abib 1 will begin the next sunset after you have also converted April 3, 4:32 PM into your time zone. Of course, should you do the mitzvah—good deed—of visiting Israel on the correct dates, you would then be able to observe them at the exact moment YHWH intended. That is why all pious Jews say, no matter how happy they are elsewhere, "This year we celebrate our Set-Apart time here, but next year we hope to do so in the Land of Israel."

Using these calculations then, sunset on April 3rd begins Abib 1 in Hebrew time. The first daylight period of my New Hebrew year would be April 4th.

From there: Pesach must happen on the first appearance of the full moon and 14 days later, or as NASA puts it: Apr 18 02:44 UT.

Fifty-two days from that point is Shavuot: June 6th (also 6 Sivan).

At this point we can track the rest of the year one of two ways. We can either go "new moon to new moon" and fix the first and last days of each month and fill them in later. Or, we can track the sacred occasions based on the full moons and count backwards or forwards to the next (or previous) equinox.

In other words, we know that Sukkot must happen around the time of the Autumnal Equinox but squarely on the 15th day of the seventh month that is also at the first appearance of the full moon. So NASA again will tell us when this is: Oct 12 02:06 AM UT (15th of Tishri)

If we count back 15 days, that means Tishri 1 is September 27th, when there should be a new moon, and so there is: Sep 27 11:09 AM UT (1st of Tishri, Yom Teruah)

Now if we want to skip to the end of the year, Purim will occur in late February of 2012 at the last full moon before the Vernal Equinox. So we count from the New Moon of September 27th knowing that is Tishri:

Oct 15 12:02 UT (Heshvan)
Nov 13 22:08 UT (Kislev—Happy Hanukkah 25 days later!)
Dec 13 08:42 (Tevet)
Jan 11 19:44 (Shevat in 2012)
Feb 10 07:20 (Adar)
Mar 11 19:51 (Abib)

So we need to schedule Purim by counting the 14th day of Adar as the first appearance of the full moon:

Feb 25 20:26 UT

Many thanks to NASA!

Notice this is 15 days from the astronomical new moon on February 10th. That's because the full moon happens on average 14.75 days from the time of the start of the lunar conjunction, so depending on what day that is, it will either be 14 or 15 days from there.

That is why our last day must end not just at the lunar conjunction but at the sunset from that day it occurred. So let's say the sun sets on February 10th around 5:20 PM, or exactly 8 hours later. Now February 11th will be the first daylight period of Adar and guess what? By that count, February 25th will be 14th day of Adar and the first appearance of the full moon!

Once a person practices this a few times, it becomes relatively easy to do. And the great thing is, everything we are doing the ancient also did, official records confirm this!

By the fourth century this simple system, tied to fixed phenomena that anyone could utilize, had been obscured by later traditions and half-remembered legends. The rabbis of that time picked a fixed 19 year lunar cycle that for the most part did the same thing, because it didn't appear to directly contradict their traditions. Put simply, if the vast majority of Jewry couldn't agree, there would be no calendar for the exiled nation of Israel! Apparently, they did the best they could with what they could remember and what was available to them.

The calendar system described in this section isn't contingent upon varying lengths of months. The months simply change the sunset after conjunction day and are never less than 29 or more than 30 days long, which makes sense given an average 29.53 solar day period from new moon to new moon.

Chapter 6

The Priestly Calendar

A RIVER OF FIRE WAS FLOWING
AND COMING OUT FROM BEFORE HIM;
THOUSANDS UPON THOUSANDS WERE ATTENDING (שמש)
HIM, AND MYRIADS UPON MYRIADS WERE STANDING
BEFORE HIM; THE COURT SAT,
AND THE BOOKS WERE OPENED.
DANIEL 7:10 (NAS)

Origins and Purpose from the Exodus

One of the most challenging elements when researching this material is in understanding how different calendars were synchronized to different events. As we saw with Pre-Metonic and Prophetic calendars, they were oriented from the creation of Adam. But the Priestly system, like the Moedic before it, was oriented from the time of the Exodus.

Taken collectively, these four calendars showcase the full redemptive promises of YHWH. First He tells us to be fruitful and multiply and fill the earth and then, in His timing, He institutes His feasts and proclaims a new system to keep them on time. However, this calendar is "priestly" in a very rarified and surprising way: It has nothing to do with when the priests may have actually served! Instead, it is a matrix that is derived from priestly patterns as expressed in Biblical mathematics.

I have recovered the entire matrix for every single week since the Exodus to long after the Second Temple was destroyed in CE 70.

We can describe this pattern with 100% mathematical and scientific accuracy, but I leave it to you the reader, your good judgment, and understanding to determine the spiritual ramifications of what this pattern means.

Most of the contents of this book could not have been possible without applying Biblical mathematics. For example, a literal interpretation of 1 Kings 6:1 helped uncover the year of the Exodus. Then, it was up to the best calendar and astronomical software to recover the actual day of the Exodus which revealed patterns of sevens that hit across the board, exclusively on that day.

From there, researching Scripture, Josephus and Philo showed the YHWH-based Zodiac system, or Wheel of Stars. The priests tracked the Zodiac in their garments and in every way possible. They froze the Exodus night sky in eternal memory that was lovingly cherished and passed on until the Second Temple was destroyed. From there, it survived as fragmentary and sometimes confusing legends, that only now, with this math revealed, make complete sense. I truly believe what I am about to share with you now has not been fully understood since the 9th of Ab, 70 CE, or perhaps a few decades later. This is by far the greatest Scripture pattern I have ever witnessed.

Let's see how it works.

A Small Clue

The first tiny piece of evidence that led me to the bigger picture came more than 15 years ago when I noticed a curious word in Scripture:

> For, because of the Mashiyach's work, he came near to death and little regarded his life that he might fulfill what you lacked in the *ministration* (שמש) to me. Colossians 2:30 (AENT)

> But of the Son He said, You have loved righteousness and hated iniquity; therefore Elohim, your Elohim, has anointed you with the oil of rejoicing more than your associates. And again, *You have from the beginning laid the foundations of the earth and the*

heavens are the work of your hands: they will pass away, but you endure; and they all, like a robe, wax old; and like a cloak, you will fold them up. They will be changed; but you will be as you are, and your years will not be finished. And to which of the Messengers did He ever say: Sit you at My right hand until I will place your enemies a footstool under your feet? Are they not all spirits of *ministration* who are sent to *minister* (שׁמשׁ) on account of them that are to inherit life? Hebrews 1:8-14 (AENT)

Now look at this:

9992 שׁמשׁ

שׁמשׁ: **pael**: impf. pl. sf. יְשַׁמְּשׁוּנֵּהּ: **serve** Dn 7₁₀. † (pg 423)

9993 שֶׁמַשׁ

*שֶׁמַשׁ or *שֶׁמֶשׁ: Heb. שֶׁמֶשׁ: det. שִׁמְשָׁא: **sun** Dn 6₁₅. † (pg 423) – Holladay's Hebrew and Aramaic Lexicon of the OT

The clue concerned the word *shemesh* or "sun" which is directly related to priestly service via the exact same root, and manifesting in Aramaic as *shamash* which means: "to be in service, ministry". The one place it appears in Tanakh is in the Aramaic part of Daniel:

A river of fire was flowing and coming out from before Him; Thousands upon thousands were **attending** (שׁמשׁ) Him, And myriads upon myriads were standing before Him; The court sat, And the books were opened. (Daniel 7:10 NAS)

In fact, the Aramaic speaking Church of the East has always called her deacons with the title of *shamasha*! When multiple meanings of a word/root are used in this manner it becomes a *remez* or hint. Somehow the ministry of the priests and the sun were related, and the only logical thought on the subject was that somehow the priests or their ministry patterns were meant to represent the sun. As I delved into the Tanakh a little deeper, I found precise confirmation of this idea:

[16] "And the responsibility of Eleazar the son of Aaron the priest is the oil for the light and the fragrant incense and the continual grain offering and the anointing oil--the responsibility of all the tabernacle and of all that is in it, with the sanctuary and its furnishings." (Numbers 4:16 NAS)

Here's the first key in the code: When were the sons of Aaron supposed to light the lamp for the Tabernacle and later the Temple? When were they supposed to physically show the representation on earth of YHWH's living presence through this ritual?

[2] "Command the sons of Israel that they bring to you clear oil from beaten olives for the light, to make a lamp burn continually. [3] "Outside the veil of testimony in the tent of meeting, Aaron shall keep it in order *from evening to morning*… (Leviticus 24:2-3 NAS)

One thing that sometimes puzzles scholars and lay people alike is this: We know the day begins at sunset, but in several key places the time marker of evening, or *ereb* is used. This word means, as we have seen several times already, the mixing of shadow and light after the sun is directly overhead (Jeremiah 6:4). As the shadows of afternoon (after the sun is overhead lengthen), it is tied to the last three astronomical hours of daylight, or roughly 3 PM. An astronomical hour is simply one-twelfth of the total time of the day, from sunrise to sunset. This is how the ancients understood hours and why Y'shua said, "*Are there not twelve hours of daylight?*" (John 11:9).

Pesach, for example, is timed to begin at *ereb* on the 14th, after which the lamb is slaughtered in between the evenings, or between sunset and darkness:

הָעַרְבַּיִם בֵּין *between the two evenings*, i.e. prob. between sunset and dark (v. Thes [various views fully given]; otherwise Di:Ex 12:6; on form as poss. only expanded pl. v. Ges:§ 88 c), † Ex 12:6, 16:12, 29:39, 29:41, 30:8, Lv 23:5, Nu 9:3, 9:5, 9:11, 28:4, 28:8 †. **c.** other phrases are: צַלְלֵי 'ע Je 6:4 (dist. fr. צָהֳרָיִם and לָיְלָה v:5), (הָ)עֶ(רֶב) מִנְחָה † 2 K 16:15, Ezr 9:4, 9:5, Psalm 141:2, Dn 9:21 †; זְאֵבֵי 'ע v. 1. זְאֵב; for all combin. with בֹּקֶר

morning, v. **׳ב 1 d, e. 2.** (late poet.) = *night,* עֶרֶב Jb 7:4; cf. בְּנֶשֶׁף בְּעֶרֶב
יֹום Pr 7:9 (‖וַאֲפֵלָה בָּאִישֹׁון לַיְלָהן) –Brown Drivers Briggs

So why would this word *ereb* be used by YHWH to mean late afternoon
and other times mean sunset? Furthermore, why are the most sacred days
scheduled to start at sunset but, Pesach and Yom Kippur are scheduled
just before the sun goes down?

The answer, as we have seen before, is that both Pesach and Yom Kippur-
Sukkot are tied to the times of their equinoxes in their Set-Apart months.
The double meaning of *ereb* is meant as a clue for us today. It is meant to
show that YHWH has commanded the *shemesh* (sun) to give power over
to the *shamash* (priests) as it is setting. The sons of Aaron then begin
the process of taking the sun's light and mimicking it on earth, as if to
say, that during the daytime the *shemesh* declares His glory but at night
the *shamash* does. Let's look again at the "sense" of Daniel 7:10. In
Scripture the heavenly court is often compared to the stars, and here we
see the myriads of the heavenly host bowing down, standing in service
to YHWH, the Ancient of Days, just as the priests on earth were meant
to do.

The Code of 24

The division of the priests into 24 courses is no fluke. It is patently obvious
that the only repeatable marker of time, based on 24, are the hours in the
day. ***Such an arrangement may in fact have been well known also the
writers of the Talmud:***

> Therefore did the elder prophets institute twenty-four watches
> (divisions): each watch always had a section of standing men,
> composed of priests, Levites, and Israelites, stationed at Jerusalem.
> When the turn of each watch came around to go up (from their
> cities to the Temple), the priests and Levites went up to Jerusalem,
> and the Israelites who belonged to that watch assembled in (the
> synagogues of) their cities to read the history of the creation (i.e.,
> the first chapter of Genesis). (Rodkinson, Babylonian Talmud,
> Taanit 4:1)

With those thoughts in mind, what I am going to show you is how that first division Jehoiarib, whose name means "YHWH pleads", can be thought of as an hour hand on the Constellation Clock. In due time, Jehoiarib will hand over his responsibility to the previous course and in so doing mimic the relationship between the earth and her constellations.

While the ancients would not have reckoned an "hour" as being 60 minutes as we do today. They would have observed the length of the daylight period (sunrise to sunset) and divided it by 12.

The Code of Aries

[248] *In the month of Xanthikos, which is by us called Nisan, and is the beginning of our year, on the fourteenth day of the lunar month, when the sun is in Aries,* (for in this month it was that we were delivered from bondage under the Egyptians,) the law ordained that we should every year slay that sacrifice which I before told you we slew when we came out of Egypt, and which was called the Passover; and so we do celebrate this passover in companies, leaving nothing of what we sacrifice till the day following. (Antiquities 3:248)

There is only one possible day that is both on the 14th of the lunar month of Abib and in the time of Aries: March 22nd, 1447 BCE. This is the day of the Vernal Equinox, adjusted for the Hebrew day beginning at sunset. Therefore, it is the following daylight period that is referenced. Only with this language, with a stellar coordinate also synched to the lunar cycle, could we recover the date with 100% certainty. What really matters is how it bears eternal witness to us in ways that go well beyond the accuracy of any calendar now known.

The sign of Aries is the sign of the YHWH-based Zodiac which has not been perverted by pagan practice. That is why the priests, and only the priests, were charged with keeping the full process hidden from the rest of Israel! Now, "for such a time as this", as Daniel foretold, "knowledge will increase, seal up the book for the time of the end". Only now could the pattern be revealed and only now could science and technology confirm it.

Remembering the Constellation Clock

Twelve is the perfect number, of which the circle of the zodiac in the heaven is a witness, studded, as it is with such numbers of brilliant constellations. The periodical revolution of the sun is another witness, for he accomplishes his circle in twelve months, and men also reckon the hours of the day and of the night as equal in number to the months of the year. (Philo, On Flight and Finding 1:184)

As we saw earlier, the intervals of time and the constellations come into season add up to the perfect representation of the tropical year. In fact, this was the most accurate measure of the year that the ancients could see and touch and even today with the precision of our modern computers and space telescopes, it is very difficult for us to get a more accurate measurement of the year! From the perspective of the ancients who had to rely on visual data to fix their solar year, the YHWH-based Zodiac was the only game in town.Let's look at the months on our Constellation Calendar:

Aries: March 21-April 20
Taurus: April 21-May 20
Gemini: May 21-June 20
Cancer: June 21-July 20
Leo: July 21-August 20
Virgo: August 21-September 20
Libra: September 21-October 20
Scorpio: October 21-November 20
Sagittarius: November 21-December 20
Capricorn: December 21-January 20
Aquarius: January 21-February 20
Pisces: February 21-March 20

While YHWH clearly commanded the moon to keep track of sacred occasions, He has also made it abundantly clear from Job 38:31-34 that we shouldn't forget about the *constellations* (*mazzaroth*) that herald the seasons. In fact the numbers YHWH provides, tell us how to draw the real Zodiac for His intended purposes and timings. I use modern Zodiac titles only for reference purposes, most certainly ***never*** to "divine" any aspects of future events, or remove YHWH from our central focus. Prophetic revelation rests solely with YHWH Himself.

Winding the Constellation Clock

In order to get YHWH's Great Timepiece to start ticking and witnessing for His glory, we need to assemble the pieces in the order He has given them. The Aramaic understanding of Job 38:31-34 correctly identifies the first of these pieces: Aldebaran and Antares. These two stars form a line from one part of the visible universe to the other in the night sky. When we connect these two dots, we have something called "the ecliptic", or the circuit that the sun takes throughout the year:

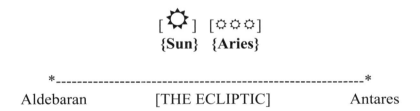

This simple depiction is what the ancients would have seen and experienced: The sun returning to its zero point every Vernal Equinox. Astronomical bodies are never at a precise "zero point" per se, but we are talking about how ancient priests would have viewed this phenomenon from the earth. In matters of sacred understanding and practical survival the constellations would tell them when to plant and harvest. If they were wrong, planting and harvesting times wouldn't correlate with YHWH's calendar!

The next piece of the winding mechanism is to put the Shabbat Week count outside of the processes of the sun and the moon, because YHWH counted the Creation Week before the sun and the moon were created. This also hints at the idea that the other stars/constellations were made on day 1 marking His "Real Time"! Our sun and moon made on day 4 enshrine the time for sacred observance on earth. Both clocks must align perfectly to showcase YHWH's ultimate glory.

Therefore, the week is understood in the context of its relationship to the constellation of Aries. The week or Shabbat count must point to the first Friday sunset to Saturday sunset period of the constellation of Aries. From that Friday-Saturday daylight period, the 24 "hours" of the day where represented by the priests mimicking the solar cycle in a perfect circuit and cycle of return.

Two separate celestial systems began in 1447 BCE. The first, is the start of the lunar month tracking sacred time (Abib 1), as fixed by YHWH without any sighting of celestial phenomena or barley to confirm it. The second, is the start of the "constellation year" as Philo says, at the beginning of the vernal equinox two weeks later. In order to correlate the two properly and for all time, the Shabbat day count for the week also had to be synchronized. This is why Abib 1 and 15 are on the seventh day. The sevens, as we witnessed before, bring a coordinating series of "perfections" to finish out the old calendar and inaugurate the new.

In other words, we can use the first priestly course, YHWH pleads, to tell time from YHWH's perspective. Henceforth we will assume a continuous and eternal and self-balancing system of 24 courses/hours repeating across the full spectrum of time from 1446 BCE (the year the actual priests began serving one year after the Exodus) to the destruction of the Second Temple in 70 CE. Let's wind the Clock now and see where it leads us.

Finding the Two Beginnings

One of the biggest challenges in this research has been to understand that this is a self correcting "Constellation Clock" with two beginnings. What I mean by this system, this may be just the first of many potential patterns in the matrix. The priests began the year after the Exodus, but the day 1/ year 1 was the year before. What that means is that this recurring pattern places 1446 BCE start in the middle of a longer cycle.

In order to show this undeniable pattern clearly, we need to take ourselves back to 1469 BCE, and put our theoretical course 1 precisely at Friday, March 21st. This is Cycle 1, from 1469 to 1446 BCE. The same exact date will pop up again 23 years later, Friday, March 21st, 1446 BCE, as shown below Cycle 2 begins here:

Cycle 2

	12/29	12/30	12/31	1/1	1/2	1/3	1/4	14
1446-1445	12/29	12/30	12/31	1/1	1/2	1/3	1/4	14
	1/5	1/6	1/7	1/8	1/9	1/10	1/11	15
	1/12	1/13	1/14	1/15	1/16	1/17	1/18	16
	1/19	1/20	1/21	1/22	1/23	1/24	1/25	17
	1/26	1/27	1/28	1/29	1/30	1/31	2/1	18
	2/2	2/3	2/4	2/5	2/6	2/7	2/8	19
	2/9	2/10	2/11	2/12	2/13	2/14	2/15	20
	2/16	2/17	2/18	2/19	2/20	2/21	2/22	21
	2/23	2/24	2/25	2/26	2/27	2/28	3/1	22
	3/2	3/3	3/4	3/5	3/6	3/7	3/8	23
	3/9	3/10	3/11	3/12	3/13	3/14	3/15	24
	3/16	3/17	3/18	3/19	3/20	*3/21*	3/22	*1*

The First Constellation Cycle

We have seen how the courses of the priests coincided with path of the sun, and there is no better time of the year to express this than the time of the Vernal Equinox and the return of the constellation of Aries from the ancient perspective, and which is now Pisces in our own day.

With 24 courses of priests then, these "hours" are expressed as years. In the 24th year, at the end of the 23rd, is the key cycle on which this clock runs. The best part is that it is totally constructed from Biblical mathematics. This creates what we might describe as a "Priestly Astrolabe".

So let's wind forward another 23 years and see what is there:

Cycle 3

1423-1422

12/28	12/29	12/30	12/31	1/1	1/2	1/3	**14**
1/4	1/5	1/6	1/7	1/8	1/9	1/10	**15**
1/11	1/12	1/13	1/14	1/15	1/16	1/17	**16**
1/18	1/19	1/20	1/21	1/22	1/23	1/24	**17**
1/25	1/26	1/27	1/28	1/29	1/30	1/31	**18**
2/1	2/2	2/3	2/4	2/5	2/6	2/7	**19**
2/8	2/9	2/10	2/11	2/12	2/13	2/14	**20**
2/15	2/16	2/17	2/18	2/19	2/20	2/21	**21**
2/22	2/23	2/24	2/25	2/26	2/27	2/28	**22**
3/1	3/2	3/3	3/4	3/5	3/6	3/7	**23**
3/8	3/9	3/10	3/11	3/12	3/13	3/14	**24**
3/15	3/16	3/17	3/18	3/19	**3/20**	3/21	**1**

In this case, the Friday day, which is when the courses change, is now pointing to 3/20.

Now let's move on to the next 23 year cycle:

Cycle 4

1400-1399

12/28	12/29	12/30	12/31	1/1	1/2	1/3	14
1/4	1/5	1/6	1/7	1/8	1/9	1/10	15
1/11	1/12	1/13	1/14	1/15	1/16	1/17	16
1/18	1/19	1/20	1/21	1/22	1/23	1/24	17
1/25	1/26	1/27	1/28	1/29	1/30	1/31	18
2/1	2/2	2/3	2/4	2/5	2/6	2/7	19
2/8	2/9	2/10	2/11	2/12	2/13	2/14	20
2/15	2/16	2/17	2/18	2/19	2/20	2/21	21
2/22	2/23	2/24	2/25	2/26	2/27	2/28	22
3/1	3/2	3/3	3/4	3/5	3/6	3/7	23
3/8	3/9	3/10	3/11	3/12	3/13	3/14	24
3/15	3/16	3/17	3/18	3/19	**3/20**	3/21	**1**

Again the Friday date for course 1 is 3/20. For what follows, let's do a survey of all the charts for this "small" cycle before we continue.
Let's wind through, 23 years at a time:

Cycle 5

1377-1376

12/28	12/29	12/30	12/31	1/1	1/2	1/3	14
1/4	1/5	1/6	1/7	1/8	1/9	1/10	15
1/11	1/12	1/13	1/14	1/15	1/16	1/17	16
1/18	1/19	1/20	1/21	1/22	1/23	1/24	17
1/25	1/26	1/27	1/28	1/29	1/30	1/31	18
2/1	2/2	2/3	2/4	2/5	2/6	2/7	19
2/8	2/9	2/10	2/11	2/12	2/13	2/14	20
2/15	2/16	2/17	2/18	2/19	2/20	2/21	21
2/22	2/23	2/24	2/25	2/26	2/27	2/28	22
2/29	3/1	3/2	3/3	3/4	3/5	3/6	23
3/7	3/8	3/9	3/10	3/11	3/12	3/13	24
3/14	3/15	3/16	3/17	3/18	*3/19*	3/20	*1*

Cycle 6

1354-1353

12/27	12/28	12/29	12/30	12/31	1/1	1/2	14
1/3	1/4	1/5	1/6	1/7	1/8	1/9	15
1/10	1/11	1/12	1/13	1/14	1/15	1/16	16
1/17	1/18	1/19	1/20	1/21	1/22	1/23	17
1/24	1/25	1/26	1/27	1/28	1/29	1/30	18
1/31	2/1	2/2	2/3	2/4	2/5	2/6	19
2/7	2/8	2/9	2/10	2/11	2/12	2/13	20
2/14	2/15	2/16	2/17	2/18	2/19	2/20	21
2/21	2/22	2/23	2/24	2/25	2/26	2/27	22
2/28	3/1	3/2	3/3	3/4	3/5	3/6	23
3/7	3/8	3/9	3/10	3/11	3/12	3/13	24
3/14	3/15	3/16	3/17	3/18	*3/19*	3/20	*1*

Cycle 7

1331-1330

12/26	12/27	12/28	12/29	12/30	12/31	1/1	14
1/2	1/3	1/4	1/5	1/6	1/7	1/8	15
1/9	1/10	1/11	1/12	1/13	1/14	1/15	16
1/16	1/17	1/18	1/19	1/20	1/21	1/22	17
1/23	1/24	1/25	1/26	1/27	1/28	1/29	18
1/30	1/31	2/1	2/2	2/3	2/4	2/5	19
2/6	2/7	2/8	2/9	2/10	2/11	2/12	20
2/13	2/14	2/15	2/16	2/17	2/18	2/19	21
2/20	2/21	2/22	2/23	2/24	2/25	2/26	22
2/27	2/28	3/1	3/2	3/3	3/4	3/5	23
3/6	3/7	3/8	3/9	3/10	3/11	3/12	24
3/13	3/14	3/15	3/16	3/17	*3/18*	3/19	*1*

Cycle 8

1308-1307

1/1	1/2	1/3	1/4	1/5	1/6	1/7	15
1/8	1/9	1/10	1/11	1/12	1/13	1/14	16
1/15	1/16	1/17	1/18	1/19	1/20	1/21	17
1/22	1/23	1/24	1/25	1/26	1/27	1/28	18
1/29	1/30	1/31	2/1	2/2	2/3	2/4	19
2/5	2/6	2/7	2/8	2/9	2/10	2/11	20
2/12	2/13	2/14	2/15	2/16	2/17	2/18	21
2/19	2/20	2/21	2/22	2/23	2/24	2/25	22
2/26	2/27	2/28	3/1	3/2	3/3	3/4	23
3/5	3/6	3/7	3/8	3/9	3/10	3/11	24
3/12	3/13	3/14	3/15	3/16	**3/17**	3/18	*1*

Cycle 9

1285-1284

12/26	12/27	12/28	12/29	12/30	12/31	1/1	14
1/2	1/3	1/4	1/5	1/6	1/7	1/8	15
1/9	1/10	1/11	1/12	1/13	1/14	1/15	16
1/16	1/17	1/18	1/19	1/20	1/21	1/22	17
1/23	1/24	1/25	1/26	1/27	1/28	1/29	18
1/30	1/31	2/1	2/2	2/3	2/4	2/5	19
2/6	2/7	2/8	2/9	2/10	2/11	2/12	20
2/13	2/14	2/15	2/16	2/17	2/18	2/19	21
2/20	2/21	2/22	2/23	2/24	2/25	2/26	22
2/27	2/28	2/29	3/1	3/2	3/3	3/4	23
3/5	3/6	3/7	3/8	3/9	3/10	3/11	24
3/12	3/13	3/14	3/15	3/16	*3/17*	3/18	*1*

Cycle 10

1262-1261

1/1	1/2	1/3	1/4	1/5	1/6	1/7	15
1/8	1/9	1/10	1/11	1/12	1/13	1/14	16
1/15	1/16	1/17	1/18	1/19	1/20	1/21	17
1/22	1/23	1/24	1/25	1/26	1/27	1/28	18
1/29	1/30	1/31	2/1	2/2	2/3	2/4	19
2/5	2/6	2/7	2/8	2/9	2/10	2/11	20
2/12	2/13	2/14	2/15	2/16	2/17	2/18	21
2/19	2/20	2/21	2/22	2/23	2/24	2/25	22
2/26	2/27	2/28	3/1	3/2	3/3	3/4	23
3/5	3/6	3/7	3/8	3/9	3/10	3/11	24
3/12	3/13	3/14	3/15	3/16	*3/17*	3/18	*1*

Cycle 11

1239-1238

12/31	1/1	1/2	1/3	1/4	1/5	1/6	15
1/7	1/8	1/9	1/10	1/11	1/12	1/13	16
1/14	1/15	1/16	1/17	1/18	1/19	1/20	17
1/21	1/22	1/23	1/24	1/25	1/26	1/27	18
1/28	1/29	1/30	1/31	2/1	2/2	2/3	19
2/4	2/5	2/6	2/7	2/8	2/9	2/10	20
2/11	2/12	2/13	2/14	2/15	2/16	2/17	21
2/18	2/19	2/20	2/21	2/22	2/23	2/24	22
2/25	2/26	2/27	2/28	3/1	3/2	3/3	23
3/4	3/5	3/6	3/7	3/8	3/9	3/10	24
3/11	3/12	3/13	3/14	3/15	*3/16*	3/17	*1*

Cycle 12

1216-1215

12/30	12/31	1/1	1/2	1/3	1/4	1/5	15
1/6	1/7	1/8	1/9	1/10	1/11	1/12	16
1/13	1/14	1/15	1/16	1/17	1/18	1/19	17
1/20	1/21	1/22	1/23	1/24	1/25	1/26	18
1/27	1/28	1/29	1/30	1/31	2/1	2/2	19
2/3	2/4	2/5	2/6	2/7	2/8	2/9	20
2/10	2/11	2/12	2/13	2/14	2/15	2/16	21
2/17	2/18	2/19	2/20	2/21	2/22	2/23	22
2/24	2/25	2/26	2/27	2/28	3/1	3/2	23
3/3	3/4	3/5	3/6	3/7	3/8	3/9	24
3/10	3/11	3/12	3/13	3/14	*3/15*	3/16	*1*

But now look what happens:

Cycle 13?

1193-1192

12/30	12/31	1/1	1/2	1/3	1/4	1/5	15
1/6	1/7	1/8	1/9	1/10	1/11	1/12	16
1/13	1/14	1/15	1/16	1/17	1/18	1/19	17
1/20	1/21	1/22	1/23	1/24	1/25	1/26	18
1/27	1/28	1/29	1/30	1/31	2/1	2/2	19
2/3	2/4	2/5	2/6	2/7	2/8	2/9	20
2/10	2/11	2/12	2/13	2/14	2/15	2/16	21
2/17	2/18	2/19	2/20	2/21	2/22	2/23	22
2/24	2/25	2/26	2/27	2/28	2/29	3/1	23
3/2	3/3	3/4	3/5	3/6	3/7	3/8	24
3/9	3/10	3/11	3/12	3/13	*3/14*	3/15	*1*

Did the sequence just go out of order? Hardly! Instead, it's much more precise and beautiful than one might see at first glance.

Course 1, after being on duty for 276 years (23 x 12), is passing on his responsibilities for the week to Course 2:

3/16	3/17	3/18	3/19	3/20	*3/21*	3/22	**2**

It is easy to see this extends into the following week, and that Friday has once more cycled back to March 21! This is therefore, the new Cycle 1.

Now let's see what happens next:

-1170-Cycle 2

3/16	3/17	3/18	3/19	3/20	*3/21*	3/22	2

-1147-Cycle 3

3/15	3/16	3/17	3/18	3/19	*3/20*	3/21	2

-1124-Cycle 4

3/14	3/15	3/16	3/17	3/18	*3/19*	3/20	2

-1101-Cycle 5

3/14	3/15	3/16	3/17	3/18	*3/19*	3/20	2

-1078-Cycle 6

3/14	3/15	3/16	3/17	3/18	*3/19*	3/20	2

-1055-Cycle 7

3/13	3/14	3/15	3/16	3/17	*3/18*	3/19	2

-1032-Cycle 8

3/12	3/13	3/14	3/15	3/16	*3/17*	3/18	2

-1009-Cycle 9

3/11	3/12	3/13	3/14	3/15	*3/16*	3/17	2

-986-Cycle 10[1]

3/12	3/13	3/14	3/15	3/16	*3/17*	3/18	2

-963-Cycle 11

3/11	3/12	3/13	3/14	3/15	*3/16*	3/17	2

-940-Cycle 12

3/10	3/11	3/12	3/13	3/14	*3/15*	3/16	2

So is course 2 retired after its 276 year "service week"?

-917-Cycle 1 (for course 3)

3/9	3/10	3/11	3/12	3/13	*3/14*	3/15	2
3/16	3/17	3/18	3/19	3/20	*3/21*	3/22	3

Magnificent! It keeps going exactly this way, returning to Friday 3/21, the historical solar day that the real priests began their service. Every macro cyle of courses will then have the exact same 276 years to "serve" YHWH.

One might ask might how is this a "Constellation Clock"? Isn't this data more likely to present something totally different, like a Solar-Priest clock?

---

1 It is interesting that the Friday dates toggled from 3/17 to 3/16 and back to 3/17, however this is due to our Gregorian calendar and various leap year rules it employs. The cycle is eternal in the way it recycles back to 3/21 on a Friday, and that is the overall point; Shabbat illustrates a balance in the timing when the priests come on duty Friday afternoon.

As noted earlier the priesthood is represented by the sun in its journey, collectively speaking. Individually, however, each course has another role of representing the constellations. Like the heavenly bodies, each course takes its turn rising and falling from service. In other words, this is the real **Wheel of Stars**!

You can examine the full data set for yourself at www.wheelofstars.com.

Here are two more cycles in shortened form:

1) -917 course 3@3/21	1) -641 course 4@3/21
2) -894 course 3@3/22	2) -618 course 4@3/21
3) -871 course 3@3/21	3) -595 course 4@3/21
4) -848 course 3@3/20	4) -572 course 4@3/20
5) -825 course 3@3/19	5) -549 course 4@3/19
6) -802 course 3@3/19	6) -526 course 4@3/19
7) -779 course 3@3/18	7) -503 course 4@3/18
8) -756 course 3@3/17	8) -480 course 4@3/18
9) -733 course 3@3/16	9) -457 course 4@3/17
10) -710 course 3@3/16	10) -434 course 4@3/17
11) -687 course 3@3/16	11) -411 course 4@3/16
12) -664 course 3@3/15	12) -388 course 4@3/15

And so it goes…

The Double Mechanism: How Forwards is also Backwards

While my research on the Constellation Clock is in some ways just beginning, it would be amazing to discover anything with more poetic grace and beauty than this "Double Mechanism". Here YHWH's signature design is perfectly exemplified. If a man were to build a pocket-watch he would either have one gear tick back and forth or two separate gears alternating back and forth. YHWH engineered one gear to tock back and forth simultaneously.

After 276 years, course 2 now points to Friday 3/21. What happened to course 1? It now points to the week before: Friday 3/14. The same 23 year cycles that apply for course 2 in its current position also apply to course 1 on its new day of Friday 3/14.

What that means is that while it takes 276 years for course 2 to advance to the next week, it takes four times as long for the previous course to recess 1 month backwards. When that happens, course 1 will then be pointing to the previous constellation of Pisces while course 5 will be on duty for Friday, 3/21.

Here a 276 year cycle is simultaneously expressed backwards and forwards as an 1,104 year cycle. The Constellation Clock mirrors the earth's own precession away from the constellations! Forward motion relates to Mashiyach's return and backwards motion relates to the Earth's actual journey through space! Obviously, only YHWH as Master Architect could do this and make forwards and backwards the exact same movement at the exact same moment in time.

Wheel of Stars: The Coin?

About a decade ago I came across an interesting debate about the Star of Bethlehem. It was one of the first things I researched extensively on the Internet. A man named Michael Molnar had found a curious coin that had been struck in Israel more than 2000 years ago. There's a picture of it on the back cover of this book. You may visit his website at http://www.eclipse.net/~molnar, he presents a few ideas I may not share, but I most certainly give him credit for finding this and seeking to make sense of it.

My exception with Mr. Molnar boils down to this: Rabbinic documentation is a more ancient source and unanimous that the Zodiac sign which represented Israel and Syria has always been Pisces. This is why the rabbinic writer Abarbanel spends so much effort writing about a conjunction of Jupiter and Saturn in Pisces. Famed astronomer Johannes Kepler found those writings and was astonished to witness this same alignment in 1603.

Molnar insists this *one* coin indicates that the real sign of the Jews is Aries. It seemed as he had ignored the testimony of Josephus who wrote about the Exodus happening in Abib and while Aries was in the sky. This coin, minted during Roman occupation and persecution, was a veiled threat to Roman authority. Hebrews might once again be freed under the sign of Aries, perhaps during the Passover season. A certain procurator named Pontius Pilate seemed particularly nervous about this. Later, Molnar found a similar coin and wrote about it on his website:

> Bronze coin of Quadratus issued in AD 55-56 ***showing Aries with a star & crescent that symbolized majesty or sovereignty*** - Molnar Collection - RPC 4287

My question is: Majesty or sovereignty of whom? I believe the answer must be YHWH Himself! Israel would then be depicted as waiting to be delivered from Roman persecution, as they were from the Egyptians under the leadership of Moshe, once again, under the sign of Aries.

But as with all such suggestions and assertions, time will tell what the ultimate truth of that matter may be.

Chapter 7

Reading the Beginning from the End

HE HAS MADE ALL BEAUTIFUL AND BECOMING
TO ITS TIME; ALSO, HE HAS GIVEN MANKIND
AN AWARENESS OF ETERNITY; BUT
IN SUCH A WAY THAT THEY WILL
NOT FULLY FATHOM, FROM
BEGINNING TO END,
THE WORKS THAT ELOHIM DOES.
ECCLESIASTES 3:11 (MATARA)

Creation and Pre-Creation Scriptural Calendars

As we draw near the end, in more ways than one, it's fair to inquire about other cycles of time. What about, "before the beginning", the time before Adam?

Isaiah tells us plainly, that YHWH's thoughts are not our thoughts and His ways are higher than our ways. In other words, YHWH placed a limit on what we are allowed to understand: pre-Adam. The Creation calendar that YHWH used was "practical" only for Him. The calendar (including the weekly Shabbat, Feast days, etc) helps us recognize our need to be transformed into the "image of Elohim". The sciences are pointing to what YHWH has revealed in Scripture from Ancient of Days, through Irriducible Complexity, Intelligent Design, Dark Energy, or awesome patterns of mathematics within the Wheel of Stars all of "conspiracy" proportion.

Certainly, there is speculation that 24-hour days did not count prior to the sun and moon being created on day 4. YHWH's "Creation calendar" is His 6 days of symmetrical creative periods. But, since a day to Him is as a thousand years to us, I would rather stay with what is revealed in Scripture, but on this subject Scripture is silent.

I suggest we focus on and fully understand what we do know, rather than speculate on what YHWH may choose to reveal later. We know that His Week was meant as the template for our own week. We know that He has kept time on time for us, without losing a day. We know that all His commandments for His covenant are held within His creation. We can see this in Hebrew with the words *breet* (covenant) and *bereshit* (in the beginning). In addition, both Hebrew and Aramaic indicate that there is *light* / ⲓⲟⲭ (aur / or) in *Torah* / ⲭⲇⲩⲓⲟⲭ Everything that has happened since the beginning has been set in YHWH's timing according to His Word as shown in Scripture.

As for Pre-Creation, we have even less information. To me it is clear that YHWH meant Creation to be the start of time itself and that anything before that must, by definition, be for YHWH alone.

There was a story about St. Augustine (354-430 CE) the philosopher. A scoffer asked him what YHWH was doing before He made the world and Augustine is said to have answered, "He was busy creating hell for people who ask questions like that!" Such an answer might provide more insight into Augustine than YHWH, but in another place Augustine said: "there was no time and no space before the beginning".

That doesn't mean there isn't any further information on this topic. We can logically infer and answer Augustine's heckler at the same time thusly: When YHWH wasn't creating, He was thinking about creating. That is apparent in Genesis 1 where YHWH spoke and it happened, that He would "think" of it before "speaking it" into being.

The other aspect comes from a mystical assessment of something Solomon said. When he finished the Temple he looked up to YHWH and asked, *"But will Elohim really dwell on earth? The heavens— the highest heavens—cannot contain You, let alone the house that I have built!"*[1] In Hebrew, the word *shmayim* (heavens) can also mean

---

1 1 Kings 8:27.

"universe" as opposed to just "sky" or "outer space". So if the heavens, the limits of the physical universe, cannot contain YHWH, it stands to reason there must be another "place" that has "the rest of Him". That place is likely referred to by Y'shua when he said that *no one has seen the Father except the Son who came down from heaven*. Scripture tells us it is the *Word* that became the Son who came down from heaven! If so, that place would not have a physical dimension. It would be the "highest heaven," or to borrow from the Zohar, *"the dwelling of He Who Has No Boundary"* (Ein Sof). This may also explain why Y'shua would never tell us directly what His Father's Kingdom actually was. Instead he would say what it was not, what it was like, that it was inside us or at hand. To provide understanding, he "translated" his experience as the Word made flesh, as a pre-incarnate Spirit being, to provide a reference point for us. Since YHWH is everywhere, so must His Kingdom be, and yet, His *house has many rooms*, therefore, each one of us might have a unique perspective that is just as valid and accurate as any other.

In the end, Y'shua is our only witness to this Pre-Creation time because He was there as the *Thought* and then the *Word*. Only He came down from highest heaven and only He could open His mouth in parables and talk of secrets from the founding of the universe. For those reasons, I suggest that when we observe the Torah as Y'shua did we will become his brothers and sisters and mothers as he said, that we may enter that house with *many rooms* and see these wonders for ourselves one day.

Eight Days a Week?

As we have progressed through this vast topic, I have attempted to show how significant and recurring numbers are reflected in YHWH's timing. We have seen how units 7, 40, 50 and 100 are all multiplied out and used as balancing mechanisms for the four calendars.

There is one recurring number I have not dealt with until now: The number 8.

This number is important because it happens to be the length of the Great

Feasts of Pesach and Sukkot instituted by YHWH under Moshe and also for Hanukkah, which Y'shua himself kept in John 10. In the cases of Pesach and Sukkot, the 8th day is a special annual Shabbat regardless of the day of the week. The question is: Why?

I believe the answer has to do with a pattern in the first two chapters of Genesis. We see just now how "creation" is in "covenant" and how "Let there be light" can be also thought of as "Let there be Torah". These themes have always been a part of the Hebrew Bible, and certain ancient traditions expressed in the Targums and mystical literature. The most significant of these themes being that Zion is the real origin of the creation of Adam and that he was placed in Eden later, or that the Temple itself is the completion/perfection of YHWH's creative process.

What I noticed in Genesis was that there were two ways to track creation:

- Six day creative intervals ending with humanity's creation, followed by the seventh day on which YHWH rests, OR...
- Six day creative intervals ending with humanity's first creation, followed by the Shabbat of YHWH's rest, followed by Adam and Eve in Eden...on day 8.

Over the years, I would ask this question: Why does it look like 6-7 days in the traditional view, but 8 days if you follow the text literally? I never gave my opinion. I was simply asking the question to see where others stood. Since first observing this, I strove to resolve the "contradiction".

Let me provide an answer to that query now. Yes, there is only one creation of man. Yes, that time is best understood as a detailed account in Genesis 1 and re-capped in Genesis 2.

At the same time, other ancient sages understood that, from YHWH's viewpoint, both could be true depending on what method is used. That is why the great sage Onkelos translated the Hebrew of Genesis into a very literal Aramaic style that eventually became the Targum authorized by the rabbis for the Torah. He used the plural phrase *be-kadmin* rather than *bereshit* (in the beginning). As it turns out, *be-kadmin* literally means "***in*** *the beginnings*, Elohim created the heavens and the earth"! I view that as a "prophetic remez" or hint about a deeper mystery.

The mystery is simply that, while in one sense, all calendars go back to the beginning, they also begin anew with a different cycle caused by the beginning. From there, I have only one more observation. There are 8 calendars:

1) Pre-Creation
2) Creation Week
3) Prophetic
4) Solar Pre-Metonic
5) Equinox Pre-Metonic [Moedic]
6) Priestly
7) Babylonian Metonic
8) Rabbinic Metonic

In the case of the last two, I have added the innovations of the astronomer Meton who found that 19 year lunar cycle that was later adapted by Rabbinic Judaism. So in essence, YHWH already knew a total of 8 calendars and that 8 ways of counting the days would be relevant to the elect and the Hebrew people. Those 8 ways of counting the days are then symbolized in the 8 day Feasts that YHWH gave to Israel in her long history[2]. The fact is that three of these 8 day feasts adds up to the sum 24, the number of priestly divisions. Taking into account the last 8 day feast: Hanukkah (the Festival of Lights), we see direct evidence that this was the time Y'shua (the Light of the World) was conceived!

From thence He would "dwell" or, to use a Hebrew expression, "tabernacle" among us around the time of Sukkot, the Feast of Tabernacles. Then He would die at Pesach as the Passover Lamb and have his resurrection thematically linked by the apostles as the First-Fruit of the resurrection on the Day of Firstfruits (Bikkurim). After these things, YHWH would send His Ruach haKodesh (a title for Him[3] a.k.a. "The Holy Spirit") to

2 That is to say, the feasts of Pesach, Sukkot and Hanukkah are each 8 days. Shavuot is only for the 50th day, but the Talmud says certain sacrifices for that day can be deferred to the following day if it falls on Shabbat.
3 See Psalm 51:1-11 and Isaiah 63:1-11 for full context.

come to the apostles at Shavuot (Feast of Weeks/Pentecost), and bring the world to its current stage in the redemptive saga that the Father has set.

Now, only one cycle remains in terms of the Great Feasts (Sukkot), the same time as his first appearance. Additionally, only one cycle remains that speaks of Y'shua's return (the Jubilee); thus bringing all calendars together in one single, magnificent clarifying message:

> *"I am YHWH. I will not give My glory to another or My praise to idols. Walk with me and be perfect, and follow My Son as the embodiment of My True Torah and My true High Priest. Then wait, for when the Land is supposed to have its captives set free and revert to its original owner, so too will I send back My Son to again claim what is Mine for my glory and your salvation!"*

What Did the Israelites Know and When Did They Know It?

One issue that I've always wondered about is this: why did information from the Book of Signs (if it was, in fact, a book) get forgotten in the first place?

This is one of those issues where we only have hints to work with so we must take bits of Scripture and piece them together.

We know from direct reference that the Israelites did not keep the Land Shabbats on time after the Assyrians took the Northern Kingdom into captivity in 722 BCE. Whether they ignored the 7 year Land cycle or the whole Jubilee coming at the wrong time or not at all"cycle" is not immediately clear. That they did not observe the 7 year cycle is unquestionable since YHWH took those Sabbaths back that they were supposed to give to the Land:

> [34] Then the land will enjoy its sabbath years all the time that it lies desolate and you are in the country of your enemies; then the land will rest and enjoy its sabbaths. [35] All the time that it lies desolate,

the land will have the rest it did not have during the sabbaths you lived in it. (Leviticus 26:34-35 NIV)

The best answer for Judah's apostasy was that 90% of the nation had been taken into captivity. Because their entry into Canaan originally was in great numbers, and because the Jubilee was not required of them until they lived in the Land, some leaders might have reasoned that the lack of Israelites also meant that the Jubilee was no longer necessary. They were, literally, dead wrong.

Apparently, there was a deliberate refusal to follow that instruction; a kind of stubborn and pernicious apathy as opposed to passive ignorance. The closest Scriptural proof we get on this matter may be these famous words from the prophet Hosea:

> [6] My people are destroyed for lack of knowledge; because you have rejected knowledge, I will also reject you, that you will be no priest to Me; seeing you have forgotten the law of your Elohim, I also will forget your children."(Hosea 4:6 JPS 1917)[4]

What is most interesting is that Hosea was preaching to the corrupt kings of the Northern Kingdom just before the Assyrian invasion. Nevertheless, Hosea would never have transferred the priestly duties away from Levi and the kingdom of Judah, and he rebukes both Judah and Israel equally:

> [10] The princes of Judah are like them that remove the landmark; I will pour out My wrath upon them like water. [11] Oppressed is Ephraim, crushed in his right; because he willingly walked after filth. [12] Therefore am I unto Ephraim as a moth, and to the house of Judah as rottenness. (Hosea 5:10-12 JPS 1917)

Going back to the first verse, it seems by about 722 BCE, the priests had actively rejected the knowledge of YHWH. It may simply have been that there were not enough of them who were exclusively loyal to the jealous El who would brook no sharing of power. Certainly, the worst of

---

4 This is used for convenience, with sacred names restored and archaic English verbs replaced with you/your, etc. This translation is public domain.

Judah's kings at this time, Hezekiah's son Manasseh, didn't help matters by trying to introduce pagan feast days into their Yahwistic faith.

The most likely scenario is this: the priests knew exactly when the Exodus was and exactly when to fulfill their duties. As seasons came and went, it would have been easy for them to notice the flow of the courses in this manner.

But their Jubilee pattern may have been based on a faulty assumption. Instead of always counting 50 year intervals from the right entry date into Canaan, the priests in this period succumbed to religious relativism and pagan syncretism. This was not only true when 90% of their nation was gone; it was also the case centuries earlier:

> [18] And there was no passover like to that kept in Israel from the days of Samuel the prophet; neither did any of the kings of Israel keep such a Passover as Josiah kept, and the priests, and the Levites, and all Judah and Israel that were present, and the inhabitants of Jerusalem. [19] In the eighteenth year of the reign of Josiah was this Passover kept. (2 Chronicles 35:18-19 JPS 1917)

Having no Passover would, likely, mean a lapse in priestly duties as well, but when they were ready, the Book of Signs would be waiting:

> *And establish yourselves in the order of your clans and according to your divisions as prescribed in the writing of King David of Israel and in the document of his son Solomon, and attend in the Set-Apart place, by clan divisions, on your brotherhood and the lay people and according to the clan divisions of the Levites. Having made yourselves set-apart, slaughter the Pesach sacrifice and prepare it for your brothers (in service), according to the word of Elohim given by Moshe.* 2 Chronicles 35:4-6 (Matara)

Here is the main point after showing all these pieces: Leviticus 26:34-35 says that the land enjoys the Shabbats for all the time it is abandoned. This means that during the time since Solomon set up the Temple, YHWH expected the Land Sabbaths to be kept. Now, after years of research, we arrive at a sobering and very surprising conclusion:

The Land Shabbat/Jubilee was never kept in the First Temple period at all!

Note: Solomon began to build the Temple in 967 BCE, finished it 7 years later or 960 BCE (1 Kings 6:38) and it was destroyed in 586 BCE. From here, a little simple math will finish the story:

$$960 - 586 = 374 \text{ years}$$

Or, we can count the time from when the building began since the priests were already there, and get 383 years (from 967 BCE).

Remember that the total period of apostasy, i.e. not keeping Land Shabbat-Jubilee, was much longer than either figure:

$$70 \times 7 = 490 \text{ years}$$
$$586 + 490 = \mathbf{1076 \text{ BCE}}$$

Let's remember that; *"not since the days of Samuel the prophet had such a Passover been kept"*. Is it any wonder then that such longstanding (or at best inconsistent) practice would create confusion as to when to do this occasion in the Second Temple period, if they were doing it at all? Bottom line: we must go all the way back to the Judges to find when the Land Shabbats were kept properly.

1 Samuel 7:13-14 tells us that YHWH's hand was against the Philistines "all the days of Samuel", and that if Israel kept the Torah, that YHWH would extend rest to Israel from her enemies. That offer was made throughout the First Temple period but seemed to be ignored, starting with David, even though, in other respects, he was a man after YHWH's heart.

But did you also notice that 70 years of Land Shabbats resulted in 490 years, the exact same interval between Daniel's prophecy and the coming of Y'shua? Again, there are no coincidences in Scripture!

490 years is given from before David's time to completely keep YHWH's Jubilee. When they refused to obey, the Temple was destroyed. The

Land then takes its Shabbats back for 70 years. Once the word is issued to rebuild all of Jerusalem, guess what happens? Another 490 years is prophesied for Israel to finish all transgression and anoint the most holy! Put simply, the more we dig the more we find. [5]

Then, in the fullness of time, YHWH sent: "(He who) is to us as an anchor that retains our soul so that it stays fixed; and it enters into that within the veil where Y'shua has previously entered for us and has become a priest forever, after the likeness of Melchisedec," Hebrews 6:19-20 (AENT).

Since we who are in the faith know that Y'shua is that High Priest, perhaps we should also see the one final place where He proclaims the true Jubilee:

> "The Spirit of Master YHWH is upon me and because of this, He has anointed me to declare hope to the poor. ***And He has sent me to heal the brokenhearted and to preach release to the captives and sight to the blind. And to free those who are oppressed (by the power of) forgiveness, and to preach the acceptable year of Master YHWH***. And he rolled up the scroll and gave it to the minister and went and sat down. And all of those in the assembly, their eyes were fixed on him. And he began to say to them that, ***"This Scripture in your ears is fulfilled today."*** Luke 4:18-22 (AENT)

From the time He said those words, there would be only one more Absolute Yovel (Jubilee) before the end of the Second Temple, CE 45. The judgment of YHWH never coincided with any Jubilee directly; rather, the warning would go out in advance that at some time in the near future the desolations had been decreed.

---

5 We should bear in mind that larger cycles have sway over smaller ones. The Babylonian Captivity happened because the Israelites did not give the land proper rest once every seven years. As a result, their return to the Land in 515 BCE was synched to when the Land Shabbat period had ended, not to when the cycle reset back to course 1. Nevertheless, the courses mentioned in Ezra 6:18 were restored "in their orders for the service of Elohim in Jerusalem, as it is written in the book of Moshe", which means they still could count back to the Exodus and determine which course was supposed to be on duty that first Pesach back from Babylon.

Tracking the Book of Signs

After that Adam started reading Nisis [the Book of Signs] before his sons. And when Enoch heard it, he prayed unto God and he was sixty five years old. And Enoch walked with God. And he (Enoch) rebuilt the altar of his fore-father Adam. And he begat Metushelah and Metushelah Lamech and Lamech Noah in (the month of) Nisan. *And on the fourth day of his birth was seen a sign in the middle of the heavens and all the inhabitants of the world were frightened and they came to Adam. And Adam arose in the height of his wisdom and he foretold the Flood, and he also proclaimed the statement that so long as Enoch was alive it would not happen*.- Samaritan Asatir, or Secret Book of Moses, p. 202.[6]

I will let Scripture speak for itself in terms of this special priestly material which is mentioned, but not always spelled out in the official record. First, from Moshe to David:

This was their appointed order of service when they entered the Temple of YHWH, *according to the regulations prescribed for them by their ancestor Aaron, as YHWH, the Elohim of Israel, had commanded him*. 1 Chronicles 24:19 (Matara)

Next, from David to Josiah:

Josiah kept the Pesach for YHWH in Jerusalem; the Pesach sacrifice was slaughtered on fourteenth day of the first month. *He re-established the Cohanim (priests) in their shifts and encouraged them into the service of the House of YHWH. He said to the Levites who were Set Apart unto YHWH*, who taught all Israel: "Put the Set Apart Ark in the House that Solomon the son of David, king of Israel, built. You will no longer carry it on your shoulders so now tend to the service of YHWH your Elohim and His people, Israel. *And establish yourselves in the order of your clans and according to you divisions as prescribed in the*

---

6 Published by the Royal Asiatic Society of London and translated by Moses Gaster, PhD (1927).

writing of King David of Israel and in the document of his son Solomon, and attend in the Set-Apart place, by clan divisions, on your brotherhood and the lay people and according to the clan divisions of the Levites. Having made yourselves set-apart, slaughter the Pesach sacrifice and prepare it for your brothers (in service), according to the word of Elohim given by Moshe. 2 Chronicles 35:1-6 (Matara)

After this, from Josiah to Ezra:

And the sons of Israel, the Cohanim (priests), the Levites and the rest of the exiles, celebrated the dedication of this house of Elohim with joy. They offered for the dedication of this temple of Elohim 100 bulls, 200 rams, 400 lambs, and as a sin offering for all Israel 12 male goats, corresponding to the number of the tribes of Israel. *Then they appointed the priests to their divisions and the Levites in their orders for the service of Elohim[7] in Jerusalem, as it is written in the book of Moshe.* Ezra 6:16-18 (Matara)

Where in the Torah does it say 24 courses? It doesn't. But according to Tanakh, that was the original instruction also from Moshe and Aaron. Now we have tracked the Book of Signs by direct reference from 1447 to 515 BCE or 932 years; and that's just from Tanakh!

The question is, what happens after Ezra? This is where the trail seems to go cold. After this time, certain mistakes seem to creep into the official record. The Talmud not only refers to this directly, but makes a few of those mistakes itself.

Taking the latter statement to task first, we saw how ancient Israel neglected or guessed wrong collectively on the timing of the Land Shabbats and/or Jubilee cycles in the First Temple period. In that case, it simply may have been that the information was missing or that the nation had mixed too thoroughly with the paganism around her and stopped keeping feasts like Pesach altogether. This happened from Moshe to David's time and again from David to Josiah's time. The Talmud also

---

7 Actually *Elah*, singular form. The more familiar plural "Elohim" is used for convenience.

ascribes the destruction of the Second Temple to 432 BCE even though modern scholarship has proven that this was patently impossible and ultimately accepted 586 BCE as the proper year.

After the Captivity in Babylon, it was clear that the book itself was still extant. Some time afterwards, bad practices began creeping in alongside Festival keeping. Ironically, one of these practises may have been sighting the crescent moon as the sole beginning point of the month! I say this because, YHWH commanded us not to worship the sun or the moon but began His Set-times in darkness. Yet crescentists insist that, even if crescent sighting in the First Temple period is not directly stated, they are "absolutely sure" it happened in the Second Temple period. If that is true, then the Pharisees and Y'shua must have also used the sighted crescent to determine the start of the month.

There's one big problem with that scenario: History says no! What is clear is that there were controversies between Pharisees and Sadducees as to how to keep the calendar. Josephus tells us that in the previous century, before the Common Era, these two sects were in a power struggle. Historians suggest that Herod the Great played the two groups off against each other to his political advantage.

During that long process of acrimony and competition, extremists on both sides made assessing the historical truth rather difficult. One such extremist, a thousand later, Saadia Gaon, took such a hard line (that calculations were being done from Moshe's time forward), that he was sharply rebuked by his own colleagues, including Maimonides! What is also clear is that just prior to the first Century, a clear and convincing winner in the contest had emerged, and it was the Pharisees:

> [288] However, this prosperous state of affairs moved the Jews to envy Hyrcanus; but they that were the worst disposed to him were the Pharisees, {b} who were one of the sects of the Jews, as we have informed you already. *These have so great a power over the multitude, that when they say anything against the king, or against the high priest, they are presently believed.* (Antiquities 13:288)

What I would now explain is this, that the Pharisees have delivered to the people a great many observances by succession from their fathers, *which are not written in the laws of Moses; and for that reason it is that the Sadducees reject them*, and say that we are to esteem those observances to be obligatory *which are in the written word, but are not to observe what are derived from the tradition of our forefathers.* [298] *And concerning these things it is that great disputes and differences have arisen among them*, while the Sadducees are able to persuade none but the rich, and have not the populace favorable to them, *but the Pharisees have the multitude on their side*. (Antiquities 13:297-298)

So while Herod the Great murdered those of both camps, the Pharisees had control of the nation as far as sacred occasions and practices were concerned. There were surely disputes, but at the end of the day, the Pharisees had won the theological battle.

The high priests, however, were of the Sadducees. It was their job to make atonement for the nation. Crescentists speculate that both Pharisees and Sadducees would go off together on crescent sightings, at least for a while. I do not believe this to be true, but I offer it for discussion purposes. If that were the case, Talmudic tradition tells us that something very bizarre had been happening:

> According to the Talmud, during the First Temple period of about 410 years, there were only 18 High Priests. During the Second Temple period of 420 years, there were more than 300 High Priests! We know (from Talmud, Yoma 9a) that Yochanan was High Priest for 80 years, Shimon was High Priest for 40 years, and Yishmael ben Pabi was High Priest for 10 years. That means in the remaining 290 years there were at least 300 priests -- one every year or so. What accounts for that?

> The Talmud tells us that the Holy of Holies was forbidden ground, except for Yom Kippur. On that *one* day only, the High Priests entered to perform special rites before God. But if he himself was

not spiritually pure and unable to focus, he would not be able to stand the intense encounter with God and would die on the spot. (Rabbi Ken Spiro, History Crash Course #25: The Second Temple, from Aish.com)

And here are the Talmudic references:

The Second Temple stood for 420 years[8], *ve-shimshu bo yoter mi-shelosh meot Kohanim*, and more than 300 served as High Priest over that period. Take out forty years in which Shimon the Tzaddik was the High Priest and deduct another 80 years in which Yochanan the Kohen Gadol served, and ten more years that Elazar b. Charson served." **That leaves 300 priests over 290 years.** "*Kol echad ve-echad lo hotzi shenato*, none of them lived out their year in office.

Rabba bar bar Hana in the name of R. Johanan said: It is written [in Proverbs x. 27]: "The fear of the Lord increases man's days, but the years of the wicked will be shortened." "The fear of the Lord increases the days"; that refers to the first Temple, during whose existence of four hundred and ten years there were only eighteen high-priests. "The years of the wicked will be shortened," refers to the second Temple, which existed four hundred and twenty years, and more than three hundred high-priests succeeded each other during that period. Subtract the forty years during which Simeon the Righteous ministered, eighty years of Johanan the high-priest's ministry, and ten years of Ishmael b. Favi--according to others, eleven years of R. Eleazer b. Harsum--and compute, *you will see that not even one high-priest completed his year*. -Yoma 9a

This idea is consistent throughout Tanakh. If the Israelites approached Mount Sinai at the wrong time they would die. If the sons of Aaron offer fire in the wrong manner or at the wrong time, they would also die, and if the high priest comes into the Holy of Holies at any time other than Yom Kippur, guess what? He dies too!

In Talmud, the number of years for the Second Temple standing is off by

---

8 Actually this figure is off by 150 years as the Talmud wrongly identifies 432 BCE rather than 586 BCE as is proven in history.

more than a century and a half, but the rest of the story is accepted as fact because it is "tradition". The real date for the rebuilding of the Temple was about 515 BCE, and then it was destroyed by Rome in 70 CE, so it is standing now roughly 584 years.

Nevertheless, for about 300 years, the high priests kept dying. Clearly, the priesthood had lapsed into pagan traditions and possibly, kept missing the correct Day of Atonement. If that were the case, could it have been that they had adopted the crescent moon calendar that was based on paganism?

If the Talmud is open and honest about the problem, it also tells us the solution.

In the famous book Magid Harakia, to cite just one of many possible examples, the tradition tells us that the rabbis of this period had carefully guarded the real secret of calculating the beginning of the month, and that the crescent was simply a kind of public relations exercise. Admittedly, we may never fully know how or why certain aspects of the Book of Signs were not followed or how they related to other parts of "oral law" that ultimately got preserved centuries later.

What is definitely well-known and beyond dispute is what happened with Hillel the Elder. This Hillel is not to be confused with the fourth century rabbi of the same name who inaugurated the current Rabbinic calendar in 359 CE. But Hillel the Elder, as the chief Pharisee, was in charge of this secret information of how to intercalculate the month so that the crescent would appear shortly thereafter, providing the sky was clear and allowed for the confirmation. It is interesting that the Babylonian Talmud (Tractate Sanhedrin 11a) calls Hillel the Elder, the successor to Ezra, the last person to have access to the Book of Signs!

> ***Our Rabbis taught: Since the death of the last prophets, Haggai, Zechariah and Malachi, the Holy Spirit [of prophetic inspiration] departed from Israel***; yet they were still able to avail themselves of the Bath-kol. Once when the Rabbis were met in the upper chamber of Gurya's house at Jericho, a Bath-kol was heard from Heaven, saying: ***'There is one amongst you who is worthy that***

the Shechinah should rest on him as it did on Moses, but his generation does not merit it.' The Sages present set their eyes on Hillel the Elder. And when he died, they lamented and said: 'Alas, the pious man, the humble man, the disciple of Ezra [is no more].'
Rodkinson, Babylonian Talmud, Sanhedrin 11a

It is also noteworthy that the loss of knowledge after the death of Malachi roughly coincides with the 300 years of apostasy when the high priests began dying on Yom Kippur!

In 10 BCE, Hillel the Elder prevailed in restoring calculation as the primary means for determining the month, so that, by Y'shua's day, they were celebrating the feasts on the correct day! That may also be why Y'shua said:

> *The scribes and the Pharisees sit on the seat of Moshe.*
> Matthew 23:2 (AENT)

That means, they were the inheritors of the tradition of Moshe and Aaron and the Book of Signs was still extant at that time. The Mishnah records the two-day uncertainty of the New Moon, which is best explained as a result of these two elements: 1) the new month beginning at sunset after the conjunction and 2) the confirmation of this by the first visible crescent. Whatever the case at that time, only 40 years remained until the destruction of the Temple. Except for some periods of apostasy, *we have tracked the "Book of Signs" for a whopping 1,516 years!*

Naturally, nothing lasts forever, and disaster struck. In the year 70 CE Jerusalem was destroyed by the Romans just as Y'shua predicted. It was a disaster from which Israel has not yet recovered. And yet, a tiny remnant of her ancestral faith stayed under Roman permission, as Yochanan ben Zakkai persuaded the General Titus to set up a learning academy in the Galilee after predicting he would become emperor.

Only sixty years later, rebellion was again in the air. The charismatic leader, Shimon Bar Kosiva, was re-named "Bar Kochba" (son of the star) by Rabbi Akiba. In 132 CE he proclaimed freedom from Rome and minted coins saying: "Year One of the New Israel". But by 135 CE Rome came down on him with a vengeance. The devastation to Israel was even worse than when the Temple was destroyed. Lamentations Rabba, a rabbinic account of the time, says that in one town alone, hundreds of schools with 300 Torah students each were put to the sword. The Jews were in turmoil, and those that didn't become slaves to Rome escaped to Babylon.

At this point, many Babylonian influences pervade the early efforts to codify oral traditions into what would later be called: The Talmud. For example: they began to read the Torah and Prophets through in one year rather than all 3 parts of the Tanakh over three years as had been done in Israel. This voluntary "Babylonian captivity" resulted in them keeping time the same way the Babylonians did, with the 19 year Metonic cycle that became the basis of the Rabbinic calendar.

In the intervening centuries, many more Jews came back to Israel. By 359 CE, the overwhelming practice was to adapt the Babylonian calendar. Sadly, the Sanhedrin ordained this inaccurate calendar and approved its universal usage. This inherently flawed calendar construct continues to be used even in our day.

In a very curious development, the Sanhedrin that had existed from Moshe's time, that Y'shua knew as well, dissolved shortly after the Hillel Calendar was adapted in 359 CE. The last few years have witnessed the re-emergence of the Sanhedrin in Israel. With a new Sanhedrin the question becomes: What do they do with the Hillel 2 calendar, the calendar used by Israel in exile, now that many more Jews are back in the Land?

Some are suggesting that the answer is to junk the Hillel calendar and begin sighting the first visible crescent.

I would imagine there would be plenty of skepticism about such discussions being undertaken. The more salient question would be: why re-establish a Sanhedrin for the first time in 1600 years if not for the re-establishment of Israel as a religious state for the Jewish people? That's what one of the roles of the Sanhedrin was in the first place: To proclaim the sacred season for the Hebrew people from Jerusalem!

For those who are acquainted with these matters the question is: "If they are considering sighting the moon again, wouldn't that demand they do it by the crescent?" My answer: Yes…and no!

When we consult the official records of the Talmud, what we find that there is no authoritative and unifying opinion about where to proclaim the beginning of the month precisely during a two-day period. That is why, in many cases, the Rabbinic calendar delays certain Feast days by two days or, in other cases, grants toleration to those who choose to celebrate a feast on one of two days. *Would they need to be so "tolerant" if their records had a final answer?*

The Sanhedrin may choose to go with the crescent alone, or maybe find, as I did, that the role of the crescent is simply to confirm that the month had begun a short time beforehand. One thing is certain: The true meaning of the crescent could easily disappear from history, while the memory of sighting it from days gone by would remain intact. Time will tell what the Sanhedrin will do, but whatever it is, it will be another chapter in the 6,000 year calendar saga, and debates about this topic are not likely to disappear any time soon.

The Woman in Revelation 12

The first century of our Common Era was a critical one in terms of Biblical calendar history. With Hillel the Elder's calendar being accepted in the land from 10 BCE until the destruction of the Second Temple, the significance of historical sources agreeing on what that calendar contained can hardly be overstated. Even more important than testimony from credible eye-witnesses like Josephus and Philo, who were descended from Hebrew priests, was the fact that our Master Y'shua Mashiyach never disagreed with the Pharisees' timing of Shabbat or other special occasions (Matthew 15; 23:1).

One burning question still remains: Since the early Jewish followers of Y'shua came out of first century Judaism, is there any evidence that their knowledge of the Hillel the Elder calendar might have included the secret calculations of that time? To begin to answer this question, let's look at this interesting line from the book of Acts:

> "And the Word of Elohim spread and increased the number of disciples in Urishlim greatly, and many people of the Yehudeans were obedient to the faith." Acts 6:7 (AENT)

Those members who came from the religious upper classes, mostly Pharisees and some priests, would not likely have joined a Jewish movement that kept Torah holidays on a different schedule from what they knew and agreed to. Priests who became followers of Y'shua, assuming they knew the secret calculations, would have carried them into their Nazarene observance of Torah.

There is another elite scholar and calendar expert that we must hear from:

> "You have heard then, regarding my previous conduct in (traditional) Judaism, especially about how I followed the congregation of Elohim and greatly devastated it. And how greatly advanced I was in (Orthodox) Judaism, superior to most of my countrymen who were also my kin. And, in particular, how zealous I was with respect to the teaching of my fathers." Galatians 1:13-14 (AENT)

There is little doubt that Rav Shaul (Apostle Paul) was extremely well connected to the same elite religious hierarchy. Historians have even suggested that he was being groomed to be the next Chief Rabbi of Israel before becoming Nazarene. Acts 22 tells us that Apostle Paul learned Torah from the grandson of Hillel the Elder himself! In addition, when he was persecuting the early believers, Rav Shaul did so with the full authority and support of the Sanhedrin who, in turn, presided over these same calendar calculations. As a result of all this, one would be hard pressed to demonstrate how this knowledge could not have passed to the Nazarene followers of Y'shua in the first century. However, the ultimate test of this idea is this: Does the knowledge of the secret calendar show up in their actual writings? Yes, I believe it does, hiding in plain sight in the most controversial book of them all:

> "And a great wonder was seen in heaven; a woman clothed with the sun, and the moon under her feet, and on her head a crown of twelve stars. And, being with child, she cried and labored, and had the pangs of giving imminent birth. And there appeared another wonder in heaven; and behold, a great fiery dragon which had seven heads and ten horns, and upon his head seven diadems. And his tail drew along the third part of the stars of heaven, and cast them on the earth. And the dragon was standing before the woman, who was about to bring forth so that, when she should bring forth, he might devour her child. And she brought forth a male child who was to rule all nations with a rod of iron. And her child was caught up to Elohim and to His throne. And the woman fled into the wilderness where she had a place which was prepared for her by Elohim; so that they might nourish her there a thousand and two hundred and sixty days." Revelation 12:1-6 (AENT)

This language is evocative of Daniel in particular, where the evil forces try to change the times and occasions of the Torah and those faithful to Torah are persecuted for following the ancient path. More fundamentally however, we have distinct ties to the Tanakh, the ancient Israelites, and the stars:

> "I see him, but not now. I behold him, but not close by. A star shall come forth from Ya'akov. A scepter shall rise up from Israel and shall crush the forehead of Moab and tear down all the sons of chaos (Sheth). Numbers 24:17 (Matara)

> "And he dreamed another dream, and told it to his brothers, and said, Behold, I have dreamed another dream: and, behold, the sun and the moon and eleven stars made obeisance to me. And he told it to his father, and to his brothers; and his father rebuked him, and said to him, What is this dream that you have dreamed? Shall I and your mother and your brothers indeed come to bow down ourselves

to you to the earth? And his brothers envied him; but his father kept the saying in mind." Genesis 37:9-11 (Matara)

So we see here by direct scriptural reference that Ya'akov has his own star enshrined in the heavens. More than that, Joseph's dream about stars bowing down to him was understood to relate to the twelve tribes. These same twelve stars are above the woman's head in Revelation 12! Therefore, if we take that last image literally, we have the moon at her feet, the sun above her feet that she is clothed in and the twelve stars above everything because they are in charge! The Nazarenes too had this secret knowledge about the Zodiac setting the year, and this is confirmed by our other historical sources:

> 6 And it may be well at all times to begin our instruction with the first instances. Now the first dreams are those which Joseph beheld, receiving two visions from the two parts of the world, heaven and earth. From the earth the dream about the harvest; and that is as follows, "I thought that we were all binding sheaves in the middle of the field; and my sheaf stood up." [Genesis xxxvii. 7.] 7 And the other relates to the circle of the zodiac, and is, "They worshipped me as the sun and the moon and the eleven stars." And the interpretation of the former one, which was delivered with great violence of reproof, is as follows, "Shall you be a king and reign over us? or shall you be a lord and lord it over us?" The interpretation of the second is again full of just indignation, "Shall I, and thy mother, and thy brethren come and fall down upon the ground and worship thee?" (Philo, On Dreams 2:6-7)

> 15 Now Jacob was pleased with the dream; for, considering the prediction in his mind, and shrewdly and wisely guessing at its meaning, he rejoiced at the great things thereby signified, because it declared the future happiness of his son; and that, by the blessing of God, the time would come when he should be honored, and thought worthy of worship by his parents and brethren, 16 as guessing that the moon and sun were like his mother and father; the former, as she that gave increase and nourishment to all things, and the latter, he that gave form and other powers to them; and that

the stars were like his brethren, since they were eleven in number, as were the stars that receive their power from the sun and moon. (Josephus, Antiquities 2:15-16)

186 And for the twelve stones, whether we understand by them the months, or whether we understand the like number of the signs of that circle which the Greeks call the Zodiac, we shall not be mistaken in their meaning. And for the mitre, which was of a blue color, it seems to me to mean heaven;

187 for how otherwise could the name of God be inscribed upon it? That it was also illustrated with a crown, and that of gold also, is because of that splendor with which God is pleased. Let this explanation {d} suffice at present, since the course of my narration will often, and on many occasions, afford me the opportunity of enlarging upon the virtue of our legislator. (Josephus, Antiquities 3:186-187)

Once again we see this secret information winding its way through all sacred history and hiding in plain sight for those who might one day have the discernment to see it!

What's it all for?

I once heard a rabbi say, "The question is not whether these things happened in the Bible exactly as you think. Rather, the question is, what difference do those events make in your life?" I think he was quite correct. Not that Moshe, the Exodus and countless other dramas were not real or important, but what we do as believers, Jewish, Christian, and Netzari alike, **because** of those events is most important. After all, we are told that without our belief in the resurrection of Y'shua, our preaching is worthless and the stake may be emptied of its power in our lives. Therefore, in order to have the Word truly mean something, it must change us for the better and reform our lives unto YHWH. Otherwise it's a dead letter.

My best answer to this question is that the calendars described herein are no substitute for Scripture study or for living a righteous life. They are meant, like the Scripture itself, to showcase the eternal nature of YHWH and the eternal benefit of His Son, Y'shua the Mashiyach, through whom we receive the waters of life eternal.

I would never suggest that anyone forgo the Rabbinic or even secular calendars and retreat to a cave or mountaintop to keep appointed times, though that might be an interesting plan. In fact, except for Lunar Shabbat and employing barley alone to set the year[9], I encourage open, fair and balanced discussion on how all these systems came to be. I now offer my own perspective on that process in this next and last section.

In the final analysis, I endeavor to show that Bible math works, and it works perfectly when we simply go step by step with simple reverence for YHWH's instructions. Therefore, if anyone has discovered another system that takes all these factors into account, as is done here, and which also accomplishes everything as effortlessly as this system does, I would be delighted to learn of it and review it.

As someone who studies the ancient world, I am aware of history's pitfalls when it comes to bad assumptions. Ptolemy, the famous Greek astronomer who wrote the *Almagest*, had developed a system for tracking the planets that worked absolutely perfectly, but was wrong in its core assumption of the Earth being the center of the solar system. When Copernicus came along two millennia later with the right data, his equations balanced much more easily, but in terms of the end result, both men were accurate in their details. Then, in the stream of time came Galileo and Newton to add more data; until all of them would have their ideas turned upside down by Albert Einstein, who said that Elohim did not play dice with the Universe. Even in Relativity, it seems there is at least one absolute truth.

I'm not certain if what I did here is more like Ptolemy or Einstein's work or neither, but I do know the math works. If the worst case scenario is that I have had Ptolemy's success only to be later overthrown, I will be content with that. In every generation the source of all knowledge

---

9 But very open to discussing how all schools of thought on Biblical timekeeping, including Lunar Sabbath and the veneration of the barley, came about as the result of ancient interpretive disputes.

exclusively resides with YHWH. Therefore I ultimately stand for a call to study His Word, even if your reason for doing so would be to try and prove me wrong.

A Call for Perspective and Unity

For the last stop on this journey, I want to, first and foremost, thank you the reader for your patience and fortitude in sticking with this challenging material. I pray that I have, at least, given you a few things to think about, even if, in the end, we agree to disagree.

I wrote at the outset that this work is never truly finished. That is a truer statement now than when I wrote it earlier in this book. We all stand on the shoulders of giants and sages and rabbis. I could not do this work without their efforts and just as importantly, there will be others who will take up this subject after we are gone, for such must be the case until Mashiyach returns, unless of course he does come sooner than later.

It is also true that we must know where we have come from to know where we are going. After researching all the available information on history, linguistics, mathematics and astronomy as seen through the prism of the early 21st century, I have developed a model of how the current schools of calendar thought came to be, but, more importantly, to garner respect for the calendar we have today and the one we will have in the Seventh Millennium.

YHWH wants us to keep track of the seasons. We can see clearly in Scripture how food production is tied to Biblical Feasts, and that He also wants us to have reliable harvests that ensure our survival. But even beyond that, the Feast days point to cycles of life, even within our own spirits, that point to our own spiritual development and understanding of our purpose on this planet. As empires rose and fell and the dark shadows of catastrophe engulfed ancient Israel, it is easy to see what would be remembered and what would be forgotten and what would only have a partial and confused memory remaining. Perhaps, it's not so much that people chose wrong things as that they didn't protect the right things, and didn't have access to the information or context to fully know how to do right.

Let's contrast the barley references in relation to the Exodus. Even though barley is nowhere referenced as setting the year, the assumption is made that it does by Karaites and others because green ears are mentioned at the time of the actual event. My response is: of course green ears are mentioned, it was springtime, the time of year when things ripen. It is no surprise that spring occurs in a month called "Abib" anymore than it should surprise anyone that the previous month, Adar, references the darkness of late winter.

Therefore, it's both natural and expected that the ripening barley would be a sign that some would want to look for. When we investigate in greater detail, we realize that YHWH had set the year anyway by using the sun, moon and stars for Moedim (Set Times) according to Genesis 1:14, thousands of years before barley is added in Scripture.

Similarly, the Lunar Sabbath[10] idea was born in very modern times by enthusiastic New Moon seers who postulated: If we can do it for the month, why not the week days in that month? Once again, Scripture must be taken into account, YHWH counted the first week without the sun and moon present until day 4.

Additionally, the displacement of the nation of Israel on two occasions, the incursion of paganism and rival shrines and priesthoods even in the Monarchic period makes it easy to see how much confusion came about.

During the Second Temple period, matters got even worse. Something as tumultuous as the Maccabean Revolt would drive home the need to guarantee that the priests could restore services to their original cycles. And finally, my hope is that we may see Mashiyach return and the Temple rebuilt, speedily and in our days, so that all will have opportunity to serve YHWH—even as was done from the time of Moshe.

---

10 Please see Lunar Sabbath in the appendix.

The Final Surprise

This publication would not have come about had I not discovered the "Master Pattern" from my own personal quest for answers about the calendar, that could be validated. This is not my "theory" per se. It is simply the sum total of what I discovered about the Wheel with an explanation of how it works. I thought that I had said all that needed to be said.

Nevertheless, only hours after I was "finished", a final surprise found its way to me. It showed me a Message behind the Constellation Clock; a Message that I believe has been waiting to be delivered for a very long time; a time such as this. I think this Message is the whole point of the Wheel in the first place and while *I don't necessarily feel that I am so worthy to deliver it, I do know that such is the requirement for finding the Wheel. I also believe that most will agree that such an interpretation is only possible by and for those who have faith in the Perfection of the unadulterated Original Hebrew and Aramaic based Faith.*

We have seen throughout all this that the heavens do literally declare the glory of YHWH; but it is also clear that Scripture does the same thing with mathematics derived from those same heavens. This is why one of the greatest mystics of all time, Sir Isaac Newton, was also one of the greatest scientists who ever lived. Secret papers were discovered in his old desk at Cambridge in the 1930's that calculated Mashiyach's return in this century. To him, Scripture, science, physics and faith were all one, and so they are to me.

In any case, that isn't the Message—the math is:

23 years x 12 = **276 years**
for a total course's service.

276 x 24 = **6,624 years**
(1 for each course's service time in the heavens)

Do you see anything remarkable about 6,624 years?

It's quite okay if you don't, at first, I didn't either. Until we add *one* more course cycle to it:

6,624 + 276 = 6,900

Which brings us back to:

> "Daniel, I have now come to give you insight and understanding. As soon as you began to pray, an answer was given, which I have come to tell you, for you are highly esteemed. Therefore, consider the message and understand the vision: Seventy 'sevens' are decreed for your people and your holy city to finish transgression, to put an end to sin, to atone for wickedness, to bring in everlasting righteousness, to seal up vision and prophecy and to anoint the most holy. Know and understand this: *From the issuing of the decree to restore and rebuild Jerusalem until the Anointed One, the ruler, comes, there will be seven 'sevens,' and sixty-two 'sevens.' It will be rebuilt with streets and a trench, but in times of trouble. After the sixty-two 'sevens,' the Anointed One will be cut off and will have nothing. The people of the ruler who will come will destroy the city and the sanctuary.* The end will come like a flood: War will continue until the end, and desolations have been decreed. He will confirm a covenant with many for one 'seven.' In the middle of the 'seven' he will put an end to sacrifice and offering. And on a wing of the temple he will set up an abomination that causes desolation[11], until the end that is decreed is poured out on him." (Daniel 9:22-27-NIV)

It is 69 weeks in the cycle of Y'shua's first coming and, as we saw with the Prophetic calendar earlier, Y'shua's return is tied to an event happening soon after the completion of the 69th remaining cycle, that of the Jubilee. In this case, it is really 69 cycles of 100 years each rather

---

11 As mentioned in Andrew Gabriel Roth's *Ruach Qadim*, this prophecy was fulfilled when the Romans put their pagan ensigns on the burnt remnants of the destroyed Temple, as was recorded by Josephus. This also explains the shadow and type of Anti-Mashiyach that is referred to by Rav Shaul in his letters.

than 6,900 years with 100 years to go before 7,000 because the 100 year generational cycle holds a special place in the Wheel of Stars!

Let's analyze what the Message is for us today. Through His infallible and perfect mathematical precision, YHWH has brought all of us to the end of 69 century cycles. We now await the imminent commencement of the 70th century cycle. What's missing between that last little cycle and Mashiyach's return is the 25th course to bring us the rest of the way. This being the case, who is the 25th priest?

It's not Y'shua, because the Constellation Clock points to a time after His return, at which point, the heavens may be shaken and the rules of time could be suspended.

I believe a portion of YHWH's Message from His Word, from Tanakh and NT, is left for the Wheel to prove, through math and astronomy, what philosophers, rabbis and theologians have been unable to. His mathematics, I believe, absolutely prove His existence by the utter perfection of the numbers that are correlated by the Wheel of Stars.

Surely, *"I am that I am, I will be who I will be"*, could not be the sum total of this Message, could it? That's what Torah is for and Moshe's message, though well known, may have only scratched the surface.

Perhaps, Rav Shaul (Apostle Paul) was closer to the truth than even he may have realized when he said that faith is the belief in the unseen and the knowledge of that which is incomplete. YHWH, through His Wheel, has said, "I have brought all you this far. I have called you out and shown you right from wrong. I have given you the ways of life and goodness and even sent My Son to die for your sake. All this I have done, but the one thing I will not do, is force you to believe in Me."

Therefore, my dear reader, it's apparent that:

You are the 25th priest

YHWH stands and waits for <u>you</u> at the end of time.

You are the one who is chosen and called to take the remaining steps that are set before you, into light, peace, love towards yourself, your family, your neighbors, and your planet, and, most importantly, into the love of YHWH your Elohim. The reason the Wheel then seems "incomplete" is because you have the free will to decide whether to bridge the gap now or walk away and say, "I need more proof."

With what you have read in this book, is it not obvious that YHWH is the Master Architect of Creation?

So it was written. So it shall be done.

Epilogue on the Road to 2012

I remember well a decade or so ago, the last time "apocalyptic fervor" hit the world with the approach of the year 2000. I was, happily I think, insulated from all this pandemonium for a variety of reasons.

For one thing, I knew that the year 2000 was an artificial date. Knowing the true time of Mashiyach's birth as 5 BCE, I fully expected that his return 2000 years later would have manifested itself in 1995 or 1996. So much for "date setting".

In the 1990's I had spent more than a year learning computer programming, COBOL in particular, so when rumors began to spread that September 9, 1999 was "a universal COBOL shut off code for all computers (99999), I knew that was total bunk, as did many friends that I had studied with.

Nevertheless, others thought they would be "cute" by saying, "Andrew, hey no year 0, it could be 2001!" And once again I said, "Hey guys. Not yet." Now that the talk is all about the fascination with December 21, 2012, and since it will inevitably be linked with this work, let's set a few things straight right here.

The Mayans were incredible astronomers, probably the best the ancient world ever produced. Their work was a boon to the Wheel of Stars in the sense that they proved just how much ancient man could accurately predict celestial events without telescopes or computers. The next time someone suggests to you that simple nomadic farmers in ancient Israel couldn't track the equinoxes and other heavenly cycles, ask them if they think the same was true of ancient farmers in Mexico, Central and South America.

The fact is, the Mayans accurately predicted a major and incredibly rare astronomical event; the ultimate sky sign, in a way. On December 21, 2012 our sun will rise in alignment with the Dark Rift at the center of our galaxy.

Somehow, the image of the sun being swallowed up terrified them, as much as we would be terrified if that super-massive black hole at the center of our galaxy suddenly switched on. Fear not! Our sun is in no danger, and even Hollywood didn't try to suggest otherwise when they made their recent movie on the phenomenon. If it's too incredible for even a Hollywood director to imagine and profit from, I doubt that anyone need worry about it either.

Let's look at what the Mayans didn't know. They didn't know that they were in no real danger on that day. They weren't even able to predict their own destruction at their own hands, although historians aren't sure what really happened.

I do admire the Mayan data; I just don't share their "theology" about a flying snake returning to teach me about the universe. Nevertheless, religious issues aside, I am certain they felt the same awe and deep respect for YHWH's heavenly bodies as I do and I'm sure they would approve of my looking at celestial alignments as a possible roadmap to the future.

In other words, they also saw the Wheel of Stars and discerned the deep patterns and messages from it. All of us humans understand the impulse to look up and see how those "lights" affect us on earth. As long as we don't turn the created things into gods, I have no problem with trying to see YHWH's glory in whatever way is possible. Ultimately, it is the **unseen**, rather than the seen, that moves us the most.

As we progress through what most believe will be an extremely difficult and painful 21st century, I understand the longing to explain the unexplainable which is at the root of all such studies whether I agree with the messenger or not. We wait as a species for a "New Age" but it is the really the return of the Old one. It is at this "crossroad" where we are given the chance to "choose wisely" and bow before the throne of the One Master of the Universe.

I believe the Enemy, HaSatan, wants to coerce the world into picking a contrary belief system or condoning indifference, relativism or even contempt for the beauty and Perfection of Creation.

On the "bright" side, truth and love, is also present. YHWH wants us to know that however dark our lives get, His sun, moon and stars will shine their light for us into those deep recesses. Thus we will know He is there and in control, no matter what! The human race will become non-existent as we know it, according to the best science and Holy Scripture. But, whatever course we individually take, and personal choices we make, we know that it is through His will and love for us that each of us are given free choice to choose Him or not.

With the heavenly orbs as His witnesses, we can all say with one voice:

YHWH is the same yesterday,
today and forever!

Appendixes

Aramaic Basics and History

Y'shua (Jesus) and all the Apostles spoke Hebrew and Aramaic and also wrote in their native language. Although the West has developed many religious ideals according to Greek primacy, Greek was the *vehicular* not the *vernacular* language of Israel. Additionally, the West has put much emphasis on the teachings of the Greek based "post-Apostolic" founders of the Church, but the fact is, until recently, precious few have accessed the original Aramaic and Hebrew teachings; the very Words of Y'shua and his Apostles.

How is the Aramaic English New Testament different?

Most New Testaments come from Greek translations that were originally translated from Hebrew and Aramaic texts. However, the Aramaic English New Testament (AENT) by Andrew Gabriel Roth comes directly from Aramaic. The meaning of an entire verse can easily be altered by the most minor translational error, for example; the Greek "Kurios" is often rendered as "Lord", however there is both "LORD" (the Father) and "Lord" (the Son), which the translator must choose. However the Father (YHWH) and Son are clearly distinguished in Aramaic, there is no confusion about the speaker or Who is being addressed.

Mashiyach (Messiah) was and is revealed in ancient Hebrew and Aramaic terms that are nonexistent in Greek, therefore, Greek translators were forced to coin Greek terms or try to make existing ones fit, regrettably, in many cases original meaning was lost. Aramaic has direct Hebrew cognates that flow between the Hebrew Tanakh (Old Testament) and the New Testament that provide much more precise understanding. Within the AENT, these rare and important Aramaic terms are explained in detailed footnotes and appendices for the reader.

In many cases, the Aramaic English New Testament harmonizes verses that otherwise seem contradictory in other Bibles. There are numerous examples in the New Testament that reveal a Greek cultural and religious bias that eventually became "the Gospel". The AENT however, employed a diverse group of scholars and Bible students from Christian and Jewish backgrounds who scrutinized the AENT, the objective being to keep this translation as devoid as possible of any theological bias.

Where does the Aramaic come from?

The Aramaic text is derived from the most ancient Aramaic sources within the family of Eastern Peshitta texts (including the Khabouris Codex), the most ancient readings are restored in the Aramaic and then translated into English. There are copious amounts of footnotes within the AENT that explain differences within the Aramaic family of texts. The AENT strives for consistency and accuracy and therefore uses bracketed words to enhance English sentence structure. The reader is provided with a "literal-as-possible" translation without losing the English flow.

A few examples of Aramaic Renewed Covenant Primacy

There are literally hundreds of places that show evidence of mistranslation from Aramaic originals into the Greek "families" of manuscripts. These inconsistent readings in Greek are often used by Jewish counter-missionaries to prevent Jews from accepting Y'shua as Mashiyach and Savior. In many places the Greek text shows itself unreliable when attempting to carry over ideas from the Tanakh (Old Testament) into the New. As a former counter-missionary, I know where the proverbial bodies are buried.

In my former life as a counter-missionry, one of my favorite "attack points" was with Matthew 26:6-7 which says: a LEPER (present tense) had dinner parties two miles from Jerusalem where Jews freely attended. A servant girl came by the "leper party" and presented Y'shua with an expensive alabaster jar of perfume, all of which is impossible under Torah law in Israel (Leviticus 13:45-46)!

Neither Christian friends nor Greek manuscripts could provide an answer for such an implausible contradiction. Some suggested, rather weakly, that the "leper" had been healed by Y'shua and he was celebrating his healing with a dinner. However, no one who had been cured of leprosy would be called a leper or allow himself to continue being called a leper. Rather, under both Torah and Jewish tradition, he would have been pronounced clean by the priests otherwise he wouldn't have be able to rejoin the community nor do any work in Israel!

As it turned out, the answer came with two words in Aramaic, spelled the same way, but pronounced differently. One of these words meant "leper" and the other "jar maker". Clearly, "jar maker" makes more sense, not just legally and historically, but because the Gospels have Y'shua receive a jar while he was there!

Other odd readings came about in John's Gospel where Aramaic grammar appears mangled in the Greek. For example, Aramaic has no "the" as opposed to "a/an", the Greek rendering got confused to read "a prophet doesn't come from Galilee". The Tanakh names half a dozen prophets from the Galilee. Instead, the Aramaic reads, "THE Prophet (the one Moses predicted in Deuteronomy 18) WILL NOT come out of Galilee." The context was this: The Pharisees assumed Y'shua was born in Galilee because he came from there. They were expecting THE PROPHET, i.e. the Messiah, would come out of Bethlehem, which of course Y'shua did, but they didn't understand that.

In another place in John, the Greek doesn't understand that one Aramaic word can mean both "slave without monetary compensation" and "servant working off a debt" and so the Greek has the Pharisees say something totally idiotic: "We were never SLAVES", denying the Exodus itself! Instead Y'shua, in Aramaic, was saying that they were in debt because he who is in sin is a "slave" to sin.

For each example here, I could provide hundreds of others. While many would not even see this as a problem, the totality of evidence for Aramaic primacy, as shown in the AENT, will prove overwhelming to anyone who is honestly researching the issue on a critical level.

Lunar Sabbath

All forms of Judaism and the vast majority of Christians understand that the counting of days for the weekly Shabbat began before the sun and moon existed and over 3,000 years of history confirms this. However, in modern times a very small minority of individuals (whose mother tongue is English) have begun postulating that the weekly Sabbath should be ruled by the cycles of the moon, rather than according to it's own sovereign weekly cycle since Creation. One of the follies of such a theory is that lunar based weeks often produce more than seven days between Sabbaths!

History of the Lunar Sabbath

The Judeo-Christian Lunar Sabbatarian movement began within the last two decades when Believers (Christians) began celebrating a rest day on the head (Rosh) of the month (Chodesh); at the time of the new moon. As we've discussed in this publication, YHWH clearly changed the Biblical New Year from the fall to the spring, as stated in Exodus 12:2:

הַחֹדֶשׁ הַזֶּה לָכֶם רֹאשׁ חֳדָשִׁים רִאשׁוֹן הוּא לָכֶם לְחָדְשֵׁי הַשָּׁנָה

"This month shall be to you the רֹאשׁ חֳדָשִׁים (rosh chodeshim-beginning of months): it shall be the first month of the year to you."

However, YHWH never commanded rest days on Rosh Chodeshim (New Moons) as He does for the weekly or annual Shabbat rest days. Only on the Feast of Trumpets (Yom Teruah a.k.a. Rosh HaShana) the first day of the seventh month, does YHWH command a cessation from work as on the seven annual Shabbats of the Moedim (Appointed Times) and weekly Shabbat.

The Lunar Sabbatarian movement was born through a misunderstanding of Bible verses that speak of New Moons and Sabbaths, like Isaiah 66:23:

"...from one new moon to another, and from one Shabbat to another, all flesh will come to worship before Me, says YHWH."

YHWH commanded that we base the timing of annual festivals: Passover, Feast of Unleavened Bread, FirstFruits, Pentecost, Feast of Trumpets, Day of Atonement and Feast of Tabernacles, on the cycles of the sun, moon and stars. However, Lunar Sabbatarians have customs much like those of Wiccans, Pagans, Muslims and Karaites who elevate the importance of new moon sightings over and above the other two witnesses of the sun and stars.

In modern and ancient times those within Orthodox Judaism and the Messianic Jewish movement recognize and celebrate Rosh Chodeshim (new moons) by counting and numbering each month, saying a short prayer and being together with family and friends for a meal. The emphasis is not upon celebrating the occurrence of new moons, but rather the role that new moons play in calculating Feast Days. As we will see, there are times when manual labor is allowed on the New Moon day that is not permitted on the weekly Shabbat. The Scriptural record indicates that that day of the New Moon has an in-between status, higher than a normal day, yet lower than a Shabbat or Great Feast.

The issue has been exacerbated as there are neither Hebrew nor Aramaic scholars who support this folly or any history of this theory ever being discussed. It is much like breaking down the data for the Saturday Shabbat vs. Sunday conspiracy which takes a significant education in history to appreciate how it evolved. Much of this foundational material has been addressed in a *Path to Life* essay on my website www.aramaicnttruth. org, in the section "The 18 Most Misunderstood New Testament Terms." This addresses the Sabbath so let's begin there, with its relationship to the Christian world view, and then work our way to the absolute truth versus the lunar reckoning of the sacred week.

1) "Shabbat" means "seven":

One of the foremost misconceptions about Shabbat is the idea that any day of the week could serve as a "Shabbat" if we seek "God" with all our hearts. Therefore, Christians say, since we pray on Sunday, this is all we need to do to please YHWH. Scripture says the very opposite:

On the seventh (*shebayee*—שְׁבִיעִי) day Elohim completed the work
that He had been doing, and He ceased on the seventh (*shebayee--*
שְׁבִיעִי) day and declared it Set-Apart, because on it Elohim ceased
from all the work of creation He had done. Genesis 2:2-3 (Matara)

We see clearly that "Shabbat" is derived from שְׁבִיעִי or "seven", and
the "seventh day" simply becomes a title. Literally, we could say that
Shabbat means to "seventh" yourself. Therefore, there are no substitutes,
for those who want to be obedient to the Word of YHWH, neither should
we accept any.

2) Shabbat means a day of rest.

So we come to the perfect transition for the next fact, Shabbat as a day of
rest defined in Scripture.

Observe the Shabbat day to keep it Set-Apart, as YHWH your
Elohim has commanded you. Six ***days will you labor and do all
your work but the seventh*** (*shebayee--* שְׁבִיעִי) ***is a Shabbat*** (שַׁבָּת) of
YHWH your Elohim. You will not expand your domain[1] through
profit-making work—not you nor your daughter nor your male or
female slaves, nor your ox nor your donkey or even any of your
cattle or the stranger residing with you, so that your male and
female slaves may rest just as you will.
Deuteronomy 5:12-14 (Matara)

There is a wordplay between "Shabbat" and "seventh". More to the
point, Scripture also tells us that certain occasions also are "Sabbaths",
regardless of the day of the week on which they fall. The reason for this
injunction: You are not supposed to work on those special appointed days
either!

These are the appointed times of YHWH, the Set-Apart occasions,
which you will celebrate at their appointed times. In the first month,
on the fourteenth day of the month, at twilight, there shall be a
Pesach offering to YHWH, and on the fifteenth day of that month

---

1 Again, as we saw in Exodus, the word for "work" is actually "kingdom / domain" (מְלָאכָה).

YHWH's Feast of Unleavened Bread. You will eat unleavened bread for seven days. On the first day you will celebrate a Set-Apart occasion; you will not work at your occupations. Seven days you will make offerings by fire to YHWH. *The seventh day shall be a sacred occasion; you shall not work at your occupations.* Leviticus 23:4-8 (Matara)

On that same day (Shavuot, Pentecost) you will hold a celebration; it will be a Set-Apart occasion for you; *you shall not work at your occupations*. This is a Torah-instruction for all time in your cities and towns throughout the ages. Leviticus 23:21 (Matara)

YHWH spoke to Moshe saying, "Speak to the Israelite people and say: In the seventh month, on the first day of the month, you will observe a total rest, a Set-Apart occasion commemorated with loud (*shofar*) blasts. You will not work at your occupations; and you will bring an offering by fire to YHWH. YHWH spoke to Moshe saying, *"Mark, the tenth day of this seventh month is the Day of Atonement. It shall be a sacred occasion for you; you will deny yourselves and you will bring an offering by fire to YHWH; you will do no work for that entire day.* For it is a Day of Atonement, on which expiation is made on your behalf before YHWH your Elohim. Leviticus 23:24-29 (Matara)

So far, we have seen that days of rest, in addition to Shabbat are required as a matter of Torah. However we will see that this day of *rest*, even if it falls on another day of the week, is still called Shabbat. Let us continue with the rest of this passage:

Indeed, any person who does not practice self-denial throughout that day will be cut off from his people, and whoever does any work throughout that day, I will cause that person to perish from the midst of his people. *Do no work whatever; it is a Torah-instruction for all time, throughout the ages in all your settlements. It shall be a Sabbath (שׁבת) of complete rest for you, and you will practice self denial*; on the ninth day of the month at evening, from evening to evening, you shall observe this your Shabbat (שׁבת)!
Leviticus 23:30-32 (Matara)

Finally, and if the English text is not strong enough here, the Hebrew actually doubles the emphasis with a wordplay on the same root! And so what comes out to our ears as "Sabbath of complete rest" actually reads in Hebrew as *Shabbat shabbaton* (שבת שבבתון). Obviously there is something more going on here with this phrase.

3) There is more than one kind of Shabbat.

What we see here is that there are two types of days of rest, both called Shabbat. The first, obviously, is the weekly variety that comes every seventh day. The second is equally important, as special days of worship should never be desecrated from by us having to do any kind of regular work.

4) The Mechanics of the Heresy:

So what then is a Lunar Sabbath? Simply put, it is the belief that a weekly Sabbath can only occur on certain days of the Hebrew month. The lunar portion of the Hebrew calendar is keyed, for example, to begin at the cycle of the New Moon. In the Jewish world this is called Rosh Chodesh, or "head of the month", and even in English this linkage exists as "month" comes from "moon".

So, to make each Hebrew month begin with a New Moon, each unit has to be either 29 or 30 days long. Since the lunar year is only 354 days, it is necessary to synchronize the months to the solar cycle to keep the Spring and Fall Festivals occurring at their intended times. While the Rabbinic versus Karaite calendar issues are addressed elsewhere in this book, the current Jewish calendar, following ancient Middle Eastern customs from places like Babylon, uses intercalculary months as a direct interpretation of Genesis 1:14, which says:

> And Elohim said, "Let there be lights in the expanse of the sky to separate the day from the night, and let them serve as signs to mark *seasons and days and years...*"

As the passage continues, these two lights are revealed to be the sun and the moon. We will dig deeper into another aspect of this very shortly. *For now, the key point here is that both the sun and the moon are used to mark the seasons,* days and, most critically, the years! This means that we must somehow reconcile between the lunar and solar systems or this key commandment is not complete. We can certainly debate as to how to do this, but the fact that we *have to do it* cannot be denied. At the end of the *yom* (day) the biblical year has the lunar yielding to the solar. How that happened in Biblical times has been a mystery until now.

Unfortunately, *Lunar Sabbath proponents ignore the fact that both the sun and the moon mark time together*, pointing instead to places in the Psalms where the moon is called a faithful witness and so on. *But again, it's just a witness, not a judge*! These same advocates go even further, claiming that a "Sabbath" can only happen on the 8th, 15th, 22nd or 29th of the month. If a "Sabbath" occurs at a certain juncture, these folks claim it is possible to have eight or even nine days pass between the "weekly" occasions, which is lunacy! (Or "lunarcy", if you prefer.)

There are verses in Scripture which indicate that some Shabbats fell on one of those dates, but if that is their strongest argument, then the opposite must also be true. If Scripture shows absolute proof of a biblical Shabbat that doesn't occur on one of these days, then that invalidates the whole Lunar Sabbath theory. The fact is, there are several clear Scriptural examples that invalidate Lunar weekly Shabbats, which we will get to shortly.

For now, let me make this observation. The significance of Genesis 1:14-19 is twofold: First, it tells us clearly that both the sun and the moon mark time in general terms. Job 38:31-34 tells us clearly that YHWH has set the rules of the heavens above the earth and Revelation tells us of the lady who has the sun in her crown and the moon at her feet, showing that the sun rules over the moon. This idea is also supported in Ecclesiastes where judgment is "under the sun", not the moon. In Hebrew, judgment and power are expressed in the same word.

The second key point in Genesis 1:14-19 has to do with what is missing. The text says that the sun and the moon mark signs, seasons, days and

years; in that order. Where is the week listed? It is nowhere! Why? We
will see…

5) "Six Days Shall You Work"

As mentioned earlier, the Lunar Sabbath system often produces more than
seven days in a "week". However, this idea is contradicted by Scripture:

> "Guard and keep the Shabbat, because it is Set-Apart to you.
> Anyone who pollutes it must be put to death. Whoever does any
> work on that day must be cut off from the midst of his people. For
> in six days work may be done, but the seventh day is a Shabbat
> of rest, Set-Apart unto YHWH. Whoever does any work on the
> Shabbat day must be put to death. The Israelites are to guard and
> observe the Shabbat, celebrating it for the generations to come as a
> lasting covenant. *It will be a sign between Me and the Israelites
> for ever, for in six days YHWH made the heavens and the earth
> and on the seventh day He stopped working and rested*." When
> YHWH finished speaking to Moshe on Mount Sinai, He gave him
> two tablets of the Testimony, the tablets of stone that were written
> by the finger of Elohim. Exodus 31:14-18 (Matara)
>
> *There are six days when you may work, but the seventh day is a
> Shabbat of rest*, a day of Set-Apart assembly. You are not to do any
> work; wherever you live. Leviticus 23:3 (Matara)

We see Torah clearly stating that there are always 6 days of work to one
day of rest, mirroring the creative and resting periods of YHWH Himself.

6) Genesis 1:14-19 says the sun and the moon do NOT mark the week!

*Returning once again to Genesis 1:14, both the sun and the moon
are supposed to mark "seasons, days and years"--but the week isn't
mentioned for either of them!* The day is marked by the rising and
setting of both the sun and the moon. The "seasons" are marked by the
month, beginning with the new moon, because it is from the New Moon
that we also reckon the days of the festivals, such as Passover on 14

Nisan, which must be a full moon. The "years" are actually marked by the sun however, but that is a topic for later. Sufficed to say, the lunar year ends up bowing down to the solar year, having the sun bring it into synchronization for the start of the year.

So where is the week in all this? The answer is that the week is an **absolute cycle**, meaning it parallels the six days of creation and the one day that YHWH rested. It is, literally, above the lunar calculation; an absolute rendering from the beginning of time until now that has not lost a single day.

If we consider this deeply, it makes more sense, in that no month or year ends with the exact number of weeks completed. There is always a remainder.

Here's what I mean: The year 2012 ends on a Monday and 2013 begins on a Tuesday. When the year recycles, we do NOT begin counting towards Shabbat from day zero. We resume counting from Monday (the second day of the week) until Friday night. That is what YHWH did and this is what He commanded us to do.

We must also bear in mind that YHWH did not count from when the sun and moon were created but when He began creation itself. The sun and the moon are not made until day four, it is the third day from the sun and moon's creation that YHWH honored as Shabbat! The Lunar Shabbat theorists would then have their next Shabbat falling on the 11th day since creation, if Shabbat began when the moon was "first visible". Furthermore, this cessation of work on the seventh/Shabbat day is the reason YHWH told us also to rest every seventh day, so, obviously, we must count the way YHWH did, independently from the sun and the moon and from an absolute count commencing on Creation Day 1.

Again, Exodus 31 says:

> "Guard and keep the Shabbat, because it is Set-Apart to you. Anyone who pollutes it must be put to death. Whoever does any work on that day must be cut off from the midst of his people. For

in six days work may be done, but the seventh day is a Shabbat of rest, Set-Apart unto YHWH. Whoever does any work on the Shabbat day must be put to death. The Israelites are to guard and observe the Shabbat, celebrating it for the generations to come as a lasting covenant. *It will be a sign between Me and the Israelites for ever, for in six days YHWH made the heavens and the earth and on the seventh day He stopped working and rested.*"

7) Tanakh disproves the Lunar Sabbath

Going from the main Lunar Sabbath argument, it certainly does seem like plenty of Shabbats are recorded on the 8th, 15th, 22nd and 29th days of the month. But, we must bear in mind that we are dealing with a few dozen recorded instances over a very long period, so extrapolating those few times in an area like biblical chronology is very simplistic at best and it leads to error.

The Lunar Sabbath system is a flawed theory because there are multiple witnesses from Scripture that completely overturn it from each part of the Bible. Let's begin in Exodus:

> The whole Israelite community set out from Elim and came to the Desert of Sin which is between Elim and Sinai, *on the fifteenth day of the second month after they had come out of Egypt.* In the desert the entire community grumbled against Moshe and Aaron. Exodus 16:1-2 (Matara)

Clearly, on this 15th day of the second month (now called Iyar) it wasn't a Shabbat. The Israelite community was certainly not instructed by YHWH to break camp and travel on a Shabbat! However, according to my calculations the 15th of Abib, the day of the Exodus in 1447 BCE, is both a weekly Shabbat and the first day of Unleavened Bread. So, wouldn't the Israelites be breaking Shabbat by leaving Egypt on that day? Not at all, more than four centuries of continuous bondage ended on a glorious Shabbat, and surely that was the overriding and important message YHWH wished to convey to them and for all of us today! All souls who observe Shabbat today understand this vitally important spiritual and practical principle. However, once freed from Egypt, it would not be a casual matter to pack up and travel on Shabbat, unless of course it was a matter of life and death. Now let's look at another fact:

> Then YHWH said to Moshe: "I will rain down bread from the heavens for you. The people are to go out each and gather just enough for that day. In this way I will test them to see whether they will follow My instructions. *On the sixth day they are to prepare what they bring in and that is to twice the amount as they gather on the other days of the week.*" Exodus 12:45 (Matara)

A double portion of manna arrived on the *sixth day* to make up for no portion arriving on the seventh day, Shabbat. There is never an indication of a period of time being longer than six days between Shabbats. But remember, the question is, was there ever a time when we could reconstruct the calendar and prove that Shabbat happened on non-Lunar Sabbbath days? Let's take a look:

> *On the evening of the fourteenth day of the month*, while camped at Gilgal on the plains of Jericho, the Israelites celebrated *the Passover. The day after the Passover, that very day, they ate some of the produce of the land: unleavened bread and roasted grain. The manna stopped the day after they ate this food* from the land; there was no longer any manna for the Israelites, but that year they ate of the produce of Canaan. (Joshua 5:10-12 NIV)

Let's break this clear chronology down:

1) Passover—evening (end of) of the 14th of Nisan.
2) The day after Passover, or first day of Feast of Unleavened Bread—15th of Nisan.
3) The day after that, the 16th, the manna stops.

Now, when was the *only* day the manna stopped? Again, we are told:

> *On the sixth day*, they gathered twice as much--two homers for each person--and the leaders of the community came and reported

this to Moshe. He said to them, "This is what YHWH commanded: *'Tomorrow is to be a day of rest, a Set-Apart Shabbat unto YHWH…".* *Eat it today,"* Moshe said, *"because today is a Shabbat unto YHWH. You will not find any of it on the ground today.* Exodus 16:22-23, 25 (Matara)

The only day the manna did not fall was after the double portion on the sixth day.

But, we just saw in Joshua 5:10-12 that the manna stopped on the 16th day of the month. That means the 16th was a Shabbat, and clearly not the 8th, 15th, 22nd or 29th day of the month!

If Shabbat always fell on the 8th, 15th, 22nd or 29th, then YHWH gave the prophet Ezekiel one very nasty and un-restful Shabbat!

In the twelfth year, on the fifteenth of the month, the word of YHWH came to me saying, *"Son of man, lament bitterly for the hordes of Egypt* and bring it down, her and the daughters of the powerful nations, to the nether world, with those who go down to the pit; 'Whom do you surpass in beauty? Go down and make your bed with the uncircumcised.'…"*Though I instilled a terror of him in the land of the living, yet he will be made to lie down among the uncircumcised along with those slain by the sword, even Pharaoh and all his hordes*," declares YHWH Elohim. Ezekiel 32:17-19, 32 (Matara)

Read the rest of this chapter and then imagine after all that torment YHWH saying, "And by the way Ezekiel; Shabbat Shalom!" For those who are not familiar with Shabbat observance it must be pointed out that Shabbat is a time of intimate prayer, singing, reading Scripture, eating good biblically kosher food, intimate fellowship with family and friends, and, of course, *rest*. To get up and go down to those who don't observe Shabbat is an unthinkable thing! Here's another example from Tanakh:

On the first day of the first month the work of making the House Set-Apart was started, *and on the eighth day they came to the covered way of YHWH. In eight days they made YHWH's House Set-Apart and on the sixteenth day of the first month the work was completed.* 2 Chronicles 29:17 (Matara)

This verse also proves the foolishness of the Lunar Sabbath theory. Work began on the first day of the first month, which is a day that some modern Lunar Sabbatarians hold as their Sabbath! Also notice this, these pious and righteous men were traveling on the 8th day of the month, there is *no way* it was a Shabbat. Absolutely unthinkable!

Lunar Sabbath is clearly a fallacy which doesn't hold up to any serious scrutiny from the Scriptures. Let's investigate some New Testament verses as well.

8) Y'shua himself disproves Lunar Sabbath!

The vast majority of Biblical scholars agree that Y'shua was a native Aramaic speaker who also spoke Hebrew in synagogue and, possibly, knew enough Greek to get by in business. Regardless of the levels of Greek fluency among first century Jews, Torah scrolls have always been written in Hebrew. There is a vast difference between secular fluency and sacred choice for language.

Josephus describes how his countrymen did not encourage Greek learning (Antiquities 20.9.11) and that sentiment was echoed 200 years later in the Talmud with; "Better to feed your son swine flesh than have him learn Greek wisdom." In this same time period, rabbis instituted a fast day to mourn the time of the Septuagint's creation. There is plenty more documentation that could be offered, but I summarize for the sake of brevity.

A massive 75% of the Gospels contain *oral teachings* of Y'shua that most scholars agree had to be delivered in Aramaic. The Aramaic words that survive even in the Greek New Testament translations prove this. Talitha qumi (Mark 5:41) is Aramaic and not Hebrew, the same can be said of other words like Epatha, Corban, and so on. There are much more detailed lists available, along with grammatical peculiarities in the

Gospels that only make sense in Aramaic.

For now, the point is this: Y'shua himself disproved the Lunar Sabbath, and this is easily demonstrated from his own native dialect of Aramaic. In John 7:21, Y'shua says, "I did one miracle and you are all astonished." The word for "do/perform" in Greek is *poeio*, and it is in the Active Participial form. The Aramaic equivalent is also in the Active Participial form. On the Aramaic side, which is admittedly much more rigid than the Greek, but the Greek doesn't contradict it, Active Participial means "an event in the immediate past that unfolds into the present." That is my definition, but any good Syriac Grammar lexicon, like *Thackston's*, will bear this out. You can also find out more at www.peshitta.org.

What that means is this: The miracle, by direct mention, happened on Shabbat, and that particular Shabbat is on the fourth or fifth day of Tabernacles, or the19th of Tishri. A Shabbat on the 19-20th day of the month disproves the Lunar Sabbath, which (depending on which Lunar person you ask) must happen on the 1st, 8th, 15th, 22nd and 29th days. This one instance, from Y'shua's own mouth, puts the Lunar Sabbath theory in peril. It would be prudent to take the words of Y'shua over those of man!

More proof of this is found here:

A Critical Note on the Aramaic Indefinite Plural of the Verb, James G. Williams *Journal of Biblical Literature*, Vol. 83, No. 2 (Jun., 1964), pp. 180-182 (article consists of 3 pages), Published by: The Society of Biblical Literature Stable www.jstor.org/stable/3264529

Please note that every Aramaic instance of Active Participial they give from the Aramaic portions of Tanakh fits this description of an event in the immediate past unfolding into the present: Daniel 2:18, 30; 4:22, 28, conf. in 30; 5:29; 6:17; 7:13; Ezra 6:1.

Edward Lipinski in his work, **Semitic Languages: Outline of**

Comparative Grammar, p. 433 says:

> "To express present, the present tense in (Biblical) Hebrew used the active participial in the normative clause, e.g., "the ark, Israel and Judah are abiding in booths (2 Sam 11:11)."

This means that they had just started abiding in booths (past) with the start of Sukkot and were still in booths, the two parts are in the same event (again Sukkot). The same is true in Y'shua's Aramaic.

See how this relates within the same cycle at http://net.bible.org/passage. php?passage=Ecc%201:5-11. The note properly points out:

> The Hebrew text has a perfect verbal form, ***but it should probably be emended to the participial form***, which occurs in the last line of the verse. Note as well the use of participles in vv. 4-7 to describe what typically takes place in the natural world. The participle זוֹרֵחַ (*zoreakh*, "to rise") emphasizes ***continual, durative, uninterrupted action (present universal use of participle): the sun is continually rising (and continually setting)*** day after day.

In this case, the cycle in question is the Shabbat since the start of Tabernacles, therefore, "performed" takes place in that confined circumstance and not prior to the start of that feast! ***Thus, there can be no doubt, either to the Hebrew speakers present or Aramaic speakers like Y'shua, that the Shabbat is rooted in the time stated: the fourth day of the Feast, 19 Tishri.***

9) One thousand nine hundred (1,900) year old Christian traditions that changed the Seventh Day Shabbat to Sunday prove the Lunar System was not the original.

This point would best require a review of several appendix articles in the Aramaic English New Testament, on how Constantine legislated Sunday, for his Christian worshippers, from the Seventh Day Shabbat to Sunday, the venerable day of the Sun. If Constantine changed it to Sunday, that means it wasn't Sunday originally, not even in apostolic times.

Roman records indicate that there were thousands of people put to the sword or excommunicated from the Church because their Seventh Day Shabbat conflicted with the Pagan *Sun Day* choice. Persecutions and/or pogroms continued long after Constantine's time and many Easterners fled to the Persian Empire as a result. For more on this see Dr. Asahel Grant's book "The Nestorians or Lost Tribes", which you can obtain freely at www.books.google.com.

For now, the point is: If there were Christians who opposed Constantine when he changed the day of worship from Shabbat to Sunday in 321 CE as the record says, where are the records of Jews who protested changing the Lunar Sabbath to the Seventh Day of the Week? There are no such historical records, there are no sects of Judaism that ever followed such practices, there are no Askhenaz, Sephardi, Yemenite, Romaniotes, Moroccan groups who did so.

The Talmud, which records arguments on every possible point of Tanakh, is silent on this issue, as is the archaeological record. Furthermore, if Christianity is right, where are their arguments on this matter, i.e. that the Jews themselves don't even agree on when Shabbat is, so why bother us? Wouldn't they have used that argument if it was available to them?

The fact is, there is no way that the Lunar Sabbath issue wouldn't have been debated among the Jews. Had there been any issues with the current Seventh day Shabbat, *plenty* of argumentation and discussion would have followed, as it did in the case of the Eastern Christian church fighting Constantine. Instead, there is not even a whisper in either the Talmud or the wider historical-archaeological record of such a controversy.

First Day or 29th Day Lunacy

Within the Lunar Sabbatarian flock, some hold to the first day of the month as a Sabbath, others to the last day or 29th. However, there is plenty of clear evidence in Scripture where work was being done on the first day of the month, which invalidates it as a potential lunar based Sabbath. Here are a few examples:

> "On the first day of the first month you shall set up the tabernacle of the tent of meeting. "You shall place the ark of the testimony there, and you shall screen the ark with the veil. "You shall bring in the table and arrange what belongs on it; and you shall bring in the lampstand and mount its lamps. "Moreover, you shall set the gold altar of incense before the ark of the testimony, and set up the veil for the doorway to the tabernacle. "You shall set the altar of burnt offering in front of the doorway of the tabernacle of the tent of meeting." (Exodus 40:2-6 NAU)

Sounds like a lot of hard work doesn't it? There's a lot more labor intensive tasks happening throughout the rest of Exodus 40 as even a very cursory glance will easily reveal, for example:

> Now in the first month of the second year, on the first day of the month, the tabernacle was erected. Moses erected the tabernacle and laid its sockets, and set up its boards, and inserted its bars and erected its pillars. He spread the tent over the tabernacle and put the covering of the tent on top of it. (Exodus 40:17-19 NAU)

My favorite is this one, because it is so unusual:

> And Ezra the priest selected men who were heads of fathers' households for each of their father's households, all of them by name. So they convened on the first day of the tenth month to investigate the matter. (Ezra 10:16 NAU)

Why did these men convene on the first day of the tenth month? It wasn't for prayer, check it out:

> They finished investigating all the men who had married foreign wives by the first day of the first month. Among the sons of the priests who had married foreign wives were found of the sons of Jeshua the son of Jozadak, and his brothers: Maaseiah, Eliezer,

Jarib and Gedaliah. They pledged to put away their wives, and being guilty, they offered a ram of the flock for their offense. (Ezra 10:17-19 NAU)

So according to the Lunar Sabbatarian first day theory, the heads of the people violated two first day Shabbats to investigate which men would have to leave their wives and children. So how's that for some Shabbat Shalom?

Conclusions for this Topic

In closing, we will briefly restate the main points. However, it is also important for the reader to understand that there is a Biblical celebration called Rosh Chodesh (New Month)

The Shabbat has always been the seventh day of the week and is the only day of the week with a proper name. From ancient Hebrew culture until today, week days are named according to their sequential relationship with Shabbat:

Yom Rishon = "first day" (Sunday)
Yom Sheni = "second day" (Monday)
Yom Sh'lishi = third day (Tuesday)
Yom Revi'i = fourth day (Wednesday)
Yom Chamishi = fifth day (Thursday)
Yom Shishi = "sixth day" (Friday)
Shabbat

YHWH blessed the Shabbat and ordered us to observe it as He did, counting from Day 1 (Yom Rishon) of creation to Shabbat. Since the sun and the moon were made on day four (Yom Revi'i), they cannot be used to track the week. Genesis 1:14-19 excludes mentioning the "week" for this reason. Even when keep the months and years change, we keep counting to the next Shabbat, proving that Shabbat is outside of the year tracked by the sun and the moon.

There is no question that many Shabbats mentioned in Scripture happen on the 1st, 8th, 15th, 22nd and 29th days of the month. That means it only takes one Shabbat to happen on another day to disprove this theory, which Joshua 5:10-12 and John 7:21 clearly do. There are also Scriptures which indicate that work was being done on the 1st of the month which also disproves the Lunar Sabbath theory. Finally, there is no mention in any historical record, Jewish or Christian, of the Seventh day Shabbat being changed from a Lunar reckoning and creating arguments among the "original" adherents. On the other hand, we have plenty of evidence that when the Gentile Church thought they could change Shabbat to *Sun Day* many protested. Therefore, there is no way that a Lunar Sabbath could have been anciently supported and then abandoned without a whisper of controversy.

Mazzaroth

YHWH Names the Stars

He counts the number of the stars;
He gives names to all of them.
(Psalm 147:4 NAU)

Lift up your eyes on high and see Who has created these *stars*,
The One who leads forth their host by number,
He calls them all by name;
Because of the greatness of His might
and the strength of *His* power,
Not one of them is missing.
(Isaiah 40:26 NAU)

Stars require their individual names to be uniquely distinguished like everything else. One would expect that He Who created the stars would have the right to name and explain them, but, this is where much confusion about the stars entered. What was originally referred to as "Mazzaroth" (Hebrew for Wheel of Stars) became know as the "Zodiac". Pagan cultures equated the stars, sun and moon as dieties, rather than try to learn about Who created them and why.

Paganism has done an effective job of keeping the Judeo-Christian community away from the hidden messages within the stars. For many, learning about the Mazzaroth is a slippery slope, these same folks also tend to indict the Jews for becoming steeped in paganism, Jews like Philo who writes:

> For whatever is best among the objects of the external senses, the things by means of which the seasons of the year and the revolutions of time are brought to perfection in their appointed order, partake of the number seven. I mean that there are seven planets; that the stars of the Bear are seven, that the Pleiades are seven, and the revolutions of the moon when increasing and waning, and the orderly well-regulated circuits of the other bodies, the beauty of which exceeds all description. (Philo, The Special Laws 2:57)

Certainly there were Jews who imbibed in paganism, but history and archaeology also tells the story of those who didn't. When pagan cultures syncretized polytheistic worship and overlaid it on YHWH's original nomenclature and revelation, original knowledge of the sun, moon, and stars as YHWH intended was also retained. One of the reasons why ancient synagogues in the Middle East used the signs of the zodiac was because the modernist pagan brushstrokes of their day could not entirely displace the design and architecture of YHWH`s Hand.

Planets and the Days of the Week

> [The menorah] terminated in seven heads, in one row, all standing parallel to one another; and these branches carried seven lamps, *one by one, in imitation of the number of the planets*. These lamps looked to the east and to the south, the lampstand being placed obliquely. (Josephus, Antiquities 3:146)

> The candlestick was placed on the southern side of the tabernacle, since by it the maker intimates, in a figurative manner, the motions of the stars which give light; for the sun, and the moon, and the rest of the stars, being all at a great distance from the northern

parts of the universe, make all their revolutions in the south. And from this candlestick there proceeded six branches, three on each side, projecting from the candlestick in the center, so as altogether to complete the number of seven; *and in all the seven there were seven candles and seven lights, being symbols of those seven stars which are called planets by those men who are versed in natural philosophy*; for the sun, like the candlestick, being placed in the middle of the other six, in the fourth rank, gives light to the three planets which are above him, and to those of equal number which are below him, adapting to circumstances the musical and truly divine instrument. (Philo, On Moses 2:102-103)

Rather than name the days of the week after false deities, Hebrew has simply numbered the days. However, the ancient Hebrews also recognized that the sun, moon and the five visible planets (Mercury, Mars, Venus, Jupiter and Saturn) were each associated with a day of the week. The fact that modern astronomers have found several other planets in our solar system, in no way, diminishes the fact that YHWH designed seven visible moving bodies to match the days of the week.

The oldest known work on the subject, "The Chapters of Rabbi Eliezar", is more than 2,000 years old. It is one of the few surviving vestiges of the secret knowledge that the Sanhedrin kept to mark the time. This work would continue to be edited and updated well into the Middle Ages much like the Kabbalah and Zohar. The work even presumes to tell us which planet rules a given hour on a given day!

In English, a number of these associations with planets (as opposed to gods) remain, such as Saturn (Saturday), Sunday (the sun), Monday (the moon) and so on.

The full list is on the following page:

Common Name	Hebrew Name	Hebrew Meaning	Assigned Day[2]
Sun	Shemesh	Sun	Sunday
Moon	Lebanaw[3]	Moon	Monday
Mars	Maadim	Red	Tuesday
Mercury	Kokab Chama	Sun star (star nearest sun)	Wednesday
Jupiter	Zedek	Righteous[4]	Thursday
Venus[5]	Kokab Nogah	Bright star[6]	Friday
Saturn	Shabbatai[7]	Sabbath planet	Saturday

---

2 The Spanish and Latin languages preserve all of these associations: Dies solis (Sunday/Sun), Lunes (Monday/Moon), Martes (Tuesday/Mars), Miercoles (Wednesday/Mercury), Jueves (Thursday/Jupiter), Viernes (Friday/Venus), Sabado (Saturday/Saturn). In the case of the Latin name for "Sunday", modern Spanish calls it "Domingo".

3 This word, as seen elsewhere, actually references a full moon rather than a generic one.

4 Interestingly, pagan sources, owing to Jupiter being the largest of the planets, call it the King. This may be alluding to the idea of the righteous king, or Melchizedek.

5 Note that in the pagan version, this day is named after the Norse "god of thunder" or "Thor's day", as opposed to the planets that YHWH created for His own glory.

6 As "morning star" or *helel*, may be referred to in Isaiah 14:12.

7 Also known as "chiun" in Amos 5:26.

Other Astronomical Names in Scripture

Common Name	Hebrew Name	Hebrew Meaning	Scripture
Pleiades	Kimah כִּימָה	Seven Sisters (Star Cluster)	Amos 5:8; Job 38:31
Orion	Kesil כְּסִיל	Named after the ninth Hebrew month (?[8])	Isaiah 13:10; Amos 5:8; Job 9:9; 38:31
Aldebaran to Antares[9] "Great Bear" in Hebrew[10]	Ayish[11] עָיִשׁ	In Aramaic, "path of Aldebaran' refers to the ecliptic or line across the sky that includes Antares at the other end	Job 38:31-33
Wheel of Stars	Mazzaroth[12] מַזָּרוֹת	The full zodiac, all 36 constellations	Job 38:32
Milky Way Galaxy	Nehar d'Nur נְהַר דִּינוּר	Fire Stream	Daniel 7:10

The chart on the following two pages indicates how stars were matched with months and correlated with Scriptural concepts and events:

---

8 Perhaps related to Kislev, the timing of the laying of the foundation stone (Haggai 2) as well as its dedication after the Maccabean Revolt that led to Hanukkah.

9 Aramaic Job 9:9 and 38:31. Please see Holy Bible From the Ancient Eastern Text by George Lamsa.

10 Other authorities, "Arcturus".

11 Some authorities suggest it could also refer to at least part of Leo.

12 Also *ohel*, literally comparing the heavens to a tent or pavilion and *raqia*, an "expanse", describing the universe in Psalm 19:1-6.

Zodiac Name & Month	Hebrew Name	Hebrew Spelling	Hebrew Meaning	Scripture Reference	Comments
Aries-Abib	Taleh	טָלֶה	Lamb	Isaiah 65:25	Used metaphorically for paradise on earth and as sacrifice for Passover. Please note this is a young male lamb, as opposed to a full grown ram.
Taurus-Iyar	Shor	שׁוּר	Bull or Ox	1 Kings 18:1-46	In the famous contest between Elijah and the prophets of Baal, both sides sacrifice an ox to see whose El is real. Elijah also calls heavenly and earthly witnesses against Baal by building an altar of 12 stones for the tribes. Josephus and Philo contend, for the months/constellations as well (v. 31-33).
Gemini-Sivan	Tawma (Aramaic form)	תָאמָא	Twins	Exodus 20	Though not used directly, a synonym for "copy" is tied to this month since it is when the Ten Commandments were first given.
Cancer-Tammuz	Sarton	סַרְטָן	Cancer (both the crab and the disease)	Ezekiel 8:14	The one place this month appears as the name of a god, it is associated with "cancer"!
Leo-Ab	Ari	אֲרִי	Lion	Revelation 5:6	Before Mashiyach comes back in the fall, he will be the Lion of Judah, worthy to open the seals in heaven!
Virgo-Elul	Betula	בתוּלָה	Virgin	Genesis 1	The creation week for the "virgin" heavens and earth was in the last days of Elul. Man is created, according to tradition, on 1 Tishri.

Zodiac Name & Month	Hebrew Name	Hebrew Spelling	Hebrew Meaning	Scripture Reference	Comments
Libra-Tishri	Mozyanim	מֹאזְנַיִם	Scales (for weight)	Genesis 1	There is perfect balance in creation, and also at this time, autumnal equinox marking the beginning.
Scorpio-Heshvan	ʻAkraba	עַקְרָב	Scorpion	Deuteronomy 8:15 Ezekiel 2:6	Used as a trial YHWH helped Israel overcome and as a metaphor for enemies.
Sagittarius-Kislev	Kashet	קָשֶׁת	Archer	Genesis 21:20	Though associated in a positive sense, with Benjamin and Hanukkah, the first occurrence is with respect to Ishmael.
Capricorn-Tevet	Gedi	גְּדִי	Goat	Genesis 38	A young male goat is part of the sinful pact between Judah and Tamar. Yet Tamar, by Judah's own account, turns out to be more righteous than he.
Aquarius-Tevet	Dela	דְלָה	Water Drawer	Exodus 2:1-19	Moshe is heavily associated with this month. If he is precisely 120 years old before he dies, he would have been born then. Moshe's name was based on being drawn out of water and in 2:16-19 he helps draw water for Jethro's 7 daughters.
Pisces-Adar	Daga	דְּגָה	Fish	Jonah 1:17-2:10	Jonah is swallowed by a great fish (dark time). Out of the depths of Sheol he called unto YHWH and was released. The pattern of his confinement is the template for the Son of Man's time in the heart of the earth (Matthew 12:38-40). The month of Adar is named for the darkness of late winter.

Sefer Yetzirah Correlates the 12 Tribes with Signs

The sign of Nisan is Tleh/Aries/Ram corresponding to Judah and the faculty of Speech. This is the month in which the Jews overcame the Egyptian deity of the ram. Judah means "thanks", related to speech and on Passover in this month, the Pascal lamb was offered and we recite the haggada.

Iyar is Shor/Taurus/Bull corresponding to Issachar (Torah scholars) and the faculty of Thought. In this month, we must be as strong and stubborn as a bull in preparation to receive the Torah.

Sivan is Teumim/Gemini/Twins corresponding to Zevulun (Torah supporters) and the faculty of Motion. This is the month of Shavuot when we received the double Tablets and should strengthen our efforts to support Torah.

Tamuz is Sartan/Cancer/Crab corresponding to Reuven (means "see") and the faculty of Sight. Just as the crab hides, we should refrain from the distractions of this summer month and direct our sights toward spiritual pursuits.

Av is Ari/Leo/Lion corresponding to Shimon (means "hear") and the faculty of Hearing. In this month, the lion-like nations of Babylon and Rome destroyed the Temple and we must learn the lesson and return to G-d.

Elul is Betula/Virgo/Virgin corresponding to Gad and the faculty of Action. This is the month of repenting, to purify our thoughts and deeds in preparation for Rosh Hashana.

Tishrei is Moznaim/Libra/Scales corresponding to Ephraim (fruitful) and the faculty of Coition. In this month is Rosh Hashana, on which we are judged, and hope to merit a productive new year.

Cheshvan is Akrav/Scorpio/Scorpion corresponding to Menashe and the faculty of Smell. This month lacks a holiday and may be spiritually cold as venom, yet one must work hard to change the letters of Menashe to "neshama" (spirituality).

Kislev is Kashet/Sagittarius/Archer corresponding to Benjamin (warriors) and the faculty of Sleep. Here, we must direct and propel the inspiration from Chanuka through the rest of the winter to overcome spiritual slumber.

Tevet is Gedi/Capricorn/Kid corresponding to Dan (judge) and the faculty of Anger. The siege against Jerusalem began in this month as a result of baseless hatred among Jews. Here, we must be as steadfast as a goat to refrain from judging unfavorably which leads to anger and destruction.

Shevat is Dli/Aquarius/Water Drawer corresponding to Asher (wealth) and the faculty of Taste. By this month, most of the rain in Israel has fallen and we celebrate Tu b'Shevat by eating bountiful fruits.

Adar is Dagim/Pisces/Fish corresponding to Naftali and the faculty of Laughter. Just as fish are covered by the sea, in this month we observe Purim which celebrates the hidden miracles of G-d which bring salvation and joy to the Jewish people.

Name of YHWH

There are many reasons why the original followers of Y'shua (Jesus) never subscribed to the rabbinical ban on vocalizing and publishing the Name of YHWH. The very nature of Y'shua as Mashiyach is revealed in His name; through the Name of YHWH Y'shua's followers know that it is the Ruach haKodesh who gave him his authority, which was not of his human soul. The Spirit of Mashiyach is the Spirit of YHWH, and these are One.

Y'shua was clearly not vested with all the powers of his Father because Mashiyach is the Arm of YHWH revealed. This means that he serves his Father in everything to do with time and space, whereas his Father is outside of time and space. Y'shua clearly states that there are things that his Father has not revealed to him regarding the End of Days, but there are also many places where Mashiyach shows himself to be a reflection of the Father.

The "Arm of YHWH" provides a picture of Mashiyach being joined to YHWH as the instrument of YHWH to do His bidding. The "Word of YHWH" is a title that was given to Mashiyach, and the Netzarim restored the Name of YHWH accordingly.

The Spirit of Mashiyach is of YHWH and Mashiyach came in the authority of his Father. The titles "Word of YHWH" and "YHWH Tsidkenu" can only apply to Mashiyach; there is no man or messenger (angel) who could bear the Name of YHWH in this manner.

> "You shall not take the name of YHWH your Elohim in vain; for YHWH will not hold him guiltless that takes His Name in vain" Sh'mot/Ex. 20:7 (Matara).

This Commandment protects the Name of YHWH against being changed or distorted, or brought to nothing. Netzarim respect this Commandment by not substituting Hebrew or Greek titles in place of the Name of YHWH. As Andrew Gabriel Roth has clearly demonstrated in several publications, the title MarYAH definitively connects the usage of the Name of YHWH from the Tanakh and throughout the Ketuvim (writings) Netzarim.

Master YHWH was and is the designation that YHWH's Set Apart people have been instructed to refer to Him by. The Name of YHWH carries very specific Messianic insights when revealed with titles such as Raah (shepherd), Yireh (provider), M'kaddesh (sanctifier), Rapha (healer), Nissi (banner) and Tsidkenu (righteousness) which are all revealed to mankind through the Word of YHWH, who is known as Mashiyach. Therefore, contrary to religious opinions the Name of YHWH is Set Apart and to be proclaimed, published and lauded among the nations as the Name of the One True Elohim.

> "And these four creatures had, each of them, six wings around it: and within they were full of eyes: and they have no cessation, day or night, from saying: Kadosh, Kadosh, Kadosh, the Master YHWH, Elohim, the Omnipotent, who was, and is, and is to come" Revelation 4:8 (AENT).

Mainstream rabbinical Judaism decided that because of the sanctity of the Name and the fierce punishment required for abuse and blasphemy of the Name, that they would ban the pronunciation and say "Adonai" instead of the Name of YHWH. "Adonai" was then translated into the Greek "Kurios" which was then translated into the English "LORD." Some have been led to believe that YHWH instructed Jews to stop using His Name, but neither Scripture nor history bear this out. In fact, YHWH removed His Name from those who "profaned" His Name "among the heathen."

"And I scattered them among the heathen, and they were dispersed through the countries: according to their way and according to their doings I judged them. And when they entered unto the heathen, whither they went, they profaned My Holy Name, when they said to them, These are the people of YHWH, and are gone forth out of His land. But I had pity for My Holy Name, which the house of Israel had profaned among the heathen, whither they went. Therefore say unto the house of Israel, Thus says YHWH Elohim; I do not this for your sakes, O house of Israel, but for Mine Holy Name's sake, which you have profaned among the heathen, wherever you went. And I will sanctify My Great Name, which was profaned among the heathen, which you have profaned in the midst of them; and the heathen shall know that I am YHWH, says YHWH Elohim, when I shall be sanctified in you before their eyes. For I will take you from among the heathen, and gather you out of all countries, and will bring you into your own land" Ezekiel 36:19-24 (Matara)

The Most High YHWH has a Name that is Set Apart from all other names and He promises that the heathen shall know the Truth of His Name according to His Set Apart Righteous Authority and Will, regardless of what religions have to say about it:

"So will I make My Holy Name known in the midst of My people Israel; and I will not let them pollute My Holy Name any more: and the heathen shall know that I am YHWH, the Holy One in Israel" Ezekiel 39:7 (Matara).

> "O YHWH, my strength, and my fortress, and my refuge in the day of affliction, the Gentiles shall come unto thee from the ends of the earth, and shall say, Surely our fathers have inherited lies, vanity, and things wherein there is no profit. Shall a man make gods unto himself, and they are no gods? Therefore, behold, I will this once cause them to know, I will cause them to know My Hand and My Might; and they shall know that My Name is YHWH"
> Jeremiah 16:19-21 (Matara).

Furthermore, Y'shua the Mashiyach did not subscribe to the ban; rather, he proclaimed the Name of YHWH. However, when the teachings of Y'shua were put into the Greek language the theologians of the day readily adopted Greek terms that had previously been used to refer to Greek deities and which were also in line with conventions of the Pharisees within the Greek language.

> "I have heard what the prophets said, that prophesy lies in My Name, saying, I have dreamed, I have dreamed. How long shall this be in the heart of the prophets that prophesy lies? yea, they are prophets of the deceit of their own heart; Which think to cause My people to forget My name by their dreams which they tell every man to his neighbor, as their fathers have forgotten My Name for Baal" Jeremiah 23:25-27 (Matara).

This prophecy is literally fulfilled by a majority of Judeo and Christian religions. The equivalent word for Baal is "Lord," which is traditionally used to replace the Name of YHWH. Baal is used to reference many deities; Christians call upon the "Lord Gawd." There is a place name in Scripture called "Baal Gawd":

> "Even from the mount Halak, that goes up to Seir, even unto Baalgad in the valley of Lebanon under mount Hermon..."
> Joshua 11:17 (Matara)

Gad (pronounced "gawd" as in the English "god") means troop or fortune which is consistent with many Christians' belief that their God provides "good luck" and many carry "lucky" images of Mary, Jesus, angels, crucifixes, etc.

"Therefore hear the word of YHWH, all Judah that dwell in the land of Egypt; Behold, I have sworn by My Great Name, says YHWH, that My Name shall no more be named in the mouth of any man of Judah in all the land of Egypt, saying, Adonai YHWH Chai. Behold, I will watch over them for evil, and not for good: and all the men of Judah that are in the land of Egypt shall be consumed by the sword and by the famine, until there be an end of them. Yet a small number that escape the sword shall return out of the land of Egypt into the land of Judah, and all the remnant of Judah, that are gone into the land of Egypt to sojourn there, shall know whose words shall stand, Mine, or theirs. And this shall be a sign unto you, says YHWH, that I will punish you in this place, that you may know that My Words shall surely stand against you for evil" Jeremiah 44:26-29 (Matara).

It is a religious normative practice today to reference the name of "the LORD" to endorse all manner of false theology and lifestyle, which is also why YHWH removed His original Set Apart Name from the religious status quo in former times.

"But they rebelled against Me, and would not hearken unto Me: they did not every man cast away the abominations of their eyes, neither did they forsake the idols of Egypt: then I said, I will pour out My fury upon them, to accomplish My anger against them in the midst of the land of Egypt. But I wrought for My Name's sake, that it should not be polluted before the heathen, among whom they were, in whose sight I made Myself known unto them, in bringing them forth out of the land of Egypt" Ezekiel 20:8-9 (Matara).

Although there are clear prophetic directives that YHWH removed His Name because of rebellion He also promises to reveal His Great Name in the acharit hayamim (latter days). When Mashiyach Y'shua entered Jerusalem in the final days of his life, the people declared:

"Blessed be he that comes in the name of YHWH: we have blessed you out of the house of YHWH" Psalm 118:26 (Matara).

The Name of YHWH was openly declared by those who recognized Y'shua as YHWH's Mashiyach. This infuriated the Pharisaic elite because their authority had been brought to nothing. In Matthew 23:39 Y'shua states, "I say to you that you will not see me from now on until you say, 'Blessed is he who comes in the name of Master YHWH' indicating that a faithful remnant will return to the Ancient Paths within the Renewed Covenant and be awaiting Y'shua's return as Mashiyach ben David.

"But in the last days it shall come to pass, that the mountain of the house of YHWH shall be established in the top of the mountains, and it shall be exalted above the hills; and people shall flow unto it. And many nations shall come, and say, Come, and let us go up to the mountain of YHWH, and to the house of the El of Jacob; and He will teach us of his ways, and we will walk in His paths: for the Torah shall go forth of Zion, and the word of YHWH from Jerusalem. And He shall judge among many people, and rebuke strong nations afar off; and they shall beat their swords into plowshares, and their spears into pruning hooks: nation shall not lift up a sword against nation, neither shall they learn war any more. But they shall sit every man under his vine and under his fig tree; and none shall make them afraid: for the Mouth of YHWH of Hosts has spoken it. For all people will walk every one in the name of his god, and we will walk in the name of YHWH our Elohim for ever and ever" Micah 4:1-5 (Matara).

"I will also stretch out Mine Hand upon Judah, and upon all the inhabitants of Jerusalem; and I will cut off the remnant of Baal from this place, and the name of the Chemarims with the priests" Zephaniah 1:4 (Matara).

"Then they that feared YHWH spoke often one to another: and YHWH hearkened, and heard it, and a book of remembrance was written before Him for them that feared YHWH, and that thought upon His Name" Malachi 3:16 (Matara).

So, when people ask why I have "restored" the Name of YHWH in my writings, the answer is because it never left primary source materials in the first place! In particular, the Aramaic New Testament clearly distinguishes between the Father YHWH (LORD) and Master Y'shua (Lord) so this distinction is carried over into the English. There are much higher levels of clarity within the office of Mashiyach within the original language that is not available in the Greek or any other versions.

Pharisaic Calendar

The Pharisees (פרושים P'rushim "the set apart ones") were a political and social movement as well as the most popular religious Jewish sect during the times of Y'shua. As a well known follower of Y'shua, Apostle Paul considered himself to be a "Pharisee of Pharisees", even at the end of his life. While being critical of their religious traditions, Y'shua also upheld many of the social values and ideas they represented. Pharisees represented the interests of the working class, whereas their main rivals the Sadducees (צדוקים Tzedukim "the righteous ones") represented the elite and priestly classes.

As a large and popular sect (in the same sense that Roman Catholicism is today) the Pharisees had plenty of antagonists from all other Judeo-Christian religious sects. After the destruction of the Second Temple in 70 CE Pharisaic beliefs became the basis for what is today referred to as Orthodox Judaism. We should bear in mind that even as we see diverse religious expressions within Judaism today, that ancient Judaism also had its own diversity.

Pharisaic control of the calendar

Our best evidence from the first century by far, is the historian Josephus, who writes the following on the extent of Pharisaic power:

> This Simon was of the city of Jerusalem, and of a very noble family, of the sect of the Pharisees, which are supposed to excel others in the accurate knowledge of the laws of their country. (Life, 1:191)

But then as to the two other orders at first mentioned, the Pharisees are those who are esteemed most skilful in the exact explanation of their laws, and introduce the first sect. These ascribe all to fate [or providence], and to God, 163 and yet allow, that to act what is right, or the contrary, is principally in the power of men, although fate does co-operate in every action. (The Jewish War, 2:162-163)

On account of which doctrines, [the Pharisees] are able greatly to persuade the body of the people; and whatever they do about divine worship, prayers, and sacrifices, they perform them according to their direction; insomuch that the cities give great attestations to them on account of their entire virtuous conduct, both in the actions of their lives and their discourses also. (Antiquities 18:12-15)

However, this prosperous state of affairs moved the Jews to envy Hyrcanus; but they that were the worst disposed to him were the Pharisees, {b} who were one of the sects of the Jews, as we have informed you already. These have so great a power over the multitude, that when they say anything against the king, or against the high priest, they are presently believed. (Antiquities,13:288)

What I would now explain is this, that the Pharisees have delivered to the people a great many observances by succession from their fathers, which are not written in the laws of Moses; and for that reason it is that the Sadducees reject them, and say that we are to esteem those observances to be obligatory which are in the written word, but are not to observe what are derived from the tradition of our forefathers. And concerning these things it is that great disputes and differences have arisen among them, while the Sadducees are able to persuade none but the rich, and have not the populace favorable to them, but the Pharisees have the multitude on their side. (Antiquities, 13:297-298)

So she made Hyrcanus high priest, because he was the older, but much more because he cared not to meddle with politics, and permitted the Pharisees to do everything; to whom also she ordered the multitude to be obedient. She also restored again those practices which the Pharisees had introduced, according to the traditions of their forefathers, and which her father-in-law, Hyrcanus, had abrogated. (Antiquities, 13:408)

[Queen Alexandra] was a sagacious woman in the management of great affairs, and intent always upon gathering soldiers together; so that she increased the army the one half, and procured a great body of foreign troops, till her own nation became not only very powerful at home, but terrible also to foreign potentates, while she governed other people, and the Pharisees governed her.
(The Jewish War, 1:112)

Calendar Observations from Mainstream Jewish Sources

The Jewish calendar was put in its present form over 1600 years ago. Until 359 CE the Sanhedrin functioned in Jerusalem as the supreme judicial body in Jewish life. It was the Sanhedrin, through a special calendar council called Sod Ha-Ibur (literally "secret of calendar intercalation"), that decided when a leap year would occur and whether the month Hesvan and Kislev should have 29 or 30 days.

The process of intercalating (adding to the calendar extra days or months) was necessary in order to harmonize the Jewish calendar with the civil Gregorian calendar. The Jewish calendar being a lunar calendar with 354 days in its lunar year, and the civil calendar being a solar calendar in which there were approximately 365 days, there is an 11 day discrepancy.

The Calendar Council of the Sanhedrin, headed by its president, Patriarch Hillel the Second, was concerned with synchronizing the two calendars for the simple reason that the Jewish holidays were based on the solar cycle and had to be observed at their "appointed times" as specified in the Bible. Passover, for example, had to be celebrated in the spring. If adjustments in the calendar were not made, the biblical command to observe the holiday at that time of year would be violated, for if allowed to fall behind by 11 days each year, in a short time Passover would be observed in the winter months.

The annual 11 day discrepancy between the Jewish and civil

calendar was reconciled by adding an extra month (Adar 2) every two or three years (seven times in 19 years). In addition, each year a day was added or subtracted from the months Hesvan and Kislev, as required. These were the "swing" months; in some years they would have 29 days, in some years 30 days.

Exactly how the calendar calculations were arrived at was a closely guarded secret of the Sanhedrin. This was one of the ways in which the Sanhedrin managed to hold on to its power, which it did until the year 359, after which its influence waned and the Jewish community in Babylonia (where the great Babylonian Talmud was being composed) became dominant.

Up until the year 359 the arrival of the New Moon was announced by the Sanhedrin each month based on the testimony of two eyewitnesses who appeared before the Sanhedrin and were questioned about the crescents of the New Moon that they reported having observed. If the Sanhedrin was satisfied with the integrity of the witnesses and their testimony it then checked that testimony against its own (secret) calculations, which had been worked out in advance using mathematical and astrological knowledge. If everything harmonized, the Sanhedrin would send torch signals from mountaintop to mountaintop to notify all communities that the New Moon had officially been sighted. At a later date the Sanhedrin decided to relay the information by messenger rather than by signaling with torches because this had been such as the Samaritans, who did not accept the authority of the Patriarch and his Sanhedrin, were known to send up false flares in order to confuse the message being transmitted.

When the Romans who ruled Palestine had begun to deny the Patriarch some of the freedom he and his court had enjoyed for many years, and the situation had become generally grave for the Jewish community in Palestine, Hillel the Second decided to publish the calendar for distribution to all communities. By this action, the official day(s) of Rosh Chodesh (beginning of the new month) each of the Jewish holidays was fixed; the testimony of witnesses was no longer required. Alfred J. Kolatch, The First Jewish Book of Why, p. 9 (1981)

A special committee of the Sanhedrin, with its president as chairman, had the mandate to regulate and balance the solar with the lunar years. This so-called Calendar Council (Sod Haibbur) calculated the beginnings of the seasons (Tekufoth) on the basis of astronomical figures which had been handed down as a tradition of old. Whenever, after two or three years, the annual excess of 11 days had accumulated to approximately 30 days, a thirteenth month Adar II was inserted before Nisan in order to assure that Nisan and Passover would occur in Spring and not retrogress toward winter. However, the astronomical calculation was not the only basis for intercalation of a thirteenth month. The delay of the actual arrival of spring was another decisive factor. The Talmudic sources report that the Council intercalated a year when the barley in the fields had not yet ripened, when the fruit on the trees had not grown properly, when the winter rains had not stopped, when the roads for Passover pilgrims had not dried up, and when the young pigeons had not become fledged. The Council on intercalation considered the astronomical facts together with the religious requirements of Passover and the natural conditions of the country.

This method of observation and intercalation was in use throughout the period of the second temple (516 B.C.E - 70 C.E), and about three centuries after its destruction, as long as there was an independent Sanhedrin. In the fourth century, however, when oppression and persecution threatened the continued existence of the Sanhedrin, the patriarch Hillel II took an extraordinary step to preserve the unity of Israel. In order to prevent the Jews scattered all over the surface of the earth from celebrating their New Moons, festivals and holidays at different times, he made public the system of calendar calculation which up to then had been a closely guarded secret. It had been used in the past only to check the observations and testimonies of witnesses, and to determine the beginnings of the spring season.[13] Arthur Spier, The Comprehensive Hebrew Calendar, p. 1-2 (1966)

---

13 Both of these sources however talk about "astrological/astronomical" data being used, which must extend beyond the pure lunar cycle and leap months. The other secrets, whether because they became lost/confused by the fourth century or because the rabbis deemed it best they remain untold, were not publicly disclosed by Hillel the Second. This very fact is easily proven when we consider that Tanakh and historical sources from the first century agree the constellations brought in the seasons.

Remembering the Sign of the Fish (Pisces)

Throughout history, pagan elements have attached themselves to the fish. It was used in ancient fertility rights in Babylon, Egyptian and Grecian cultures. The symbol of the fish, of course, also denotes Christianity. Although the lowly fish received a bad rap from paganism, we see in Nehemiah 12:39 that fish were an important staple for Jerusalemites. A gate was so named "the fish gate" on behalf of the lively merchant traders from Tyre.

> "And from above the gate of Ephraim, and above the old gate, and above the *fish gate*, and the tower of Hananeel, and the tower of Meah, even unto the sheep gate: and they stood still in the prison gate."

The nomenclature refers back to the first temple era, while today it is known as the Damascus gate. Scripture tells us of merchants from Tyre who brought fish up to Jerusalem. Zephaniah 1:10-18 also makes reference to these merchants.

There are deeper Scriptural elements about the fish that Scripture and history allude to. We have seen throughout this book how the sign of Aries was enshrined in Israelite memory at the time of the Exodus and how, for example, the historian Josephus felt compelled to reference not just the lunar month of Israel's redemption, but that specific part of the lunar month where Aries returns. That means, by direct reference, that when the Ten Plagues were happening, the struggle to free Israel from pharaoh happened under the sign of the fish, Pisces! But why might that be important to our studies?

The first of the plagues upon Egypt were against the fish in the Nile. But when the Israelites were in the wilderness, they complain and crave meat, but specifically fish: "remember the fish which we used to eat free in Egypt" (Numbers 11:5). Why might they ask for meat but pine for or remember the fish?

Perhaps there was also an understanding that Pisces was their star-sign, and though in bondage, the fish represented the bounty they had given up in order to gain their freedom. They had taken their flocks and herds, but fish don't travel well in a desert. The fish died in the first plague to make way for something else. Their redemption during the one lunar month that Pisces gives way to Aries in the heavens was mirrored on earth with the fish dying. Their freedom, as we all know, was also marked with the sacrifice of a lamb.

In later traditions, the Hebrew Mazzaroth will represent Aries not as a ram, but as a young male lamb, with the word *taleh*. That also preserved the memory that they were freed at the moment the lamb was sacrificed unto YHWH. In Hebrew, "ram" is a separate word, for this very reason.

Another reason why this is important is found here:

> I see him, but not now; I behold him, but not near; A star shall come forth from Jacob, A scepter shall rise from Israel, And shall crush through the forehead of Moab, And tear down all the sons of Sheth. (Numbers 24:17 NAU)

There is only one "star" for Jacob mentioned here, and the power of Jacob begins with his sons being set free from bondage in Egypt, under the constellation of Pisces. While Pisces will remain Israel's sign, technically speaking, they are also warned not to pine for their previous time in Egypt:

> Moreover, he shall not multiply exceedingly horses for himself, nor shall he compel the people to return to Egypt to multiply horses, since YHWH has said to you, *'You will never again return that way.'* Deuteronomy 17:16 (Matara)

In other words, get off the Fish and embrace the Lamb! The triple conjunction of Jupiter and Saturn that announced Y'shua's birth also happened under the sign of Pisces, because, as with the Exodus, bondage was ending and the time of the lamb was at hand. Such is also enshrined in the Torah in another way, another calendar reference:

> You will remember that you were a slave in the land of Egypt, and YHWH your Elohim brought you out of there by a mighty hand and by an outstretched arm; ***therefore YHWH your Elohim commanded you to observe the Shabbat day.*** Deuteronomy 5:15 (Matara)

There is no contradiction that the scientific and astronomical techniques described in this book indicate that the day of the Exodus was a Shabbat. Here we see that the Torah clearly makes that connection as well. That by the stars as they were before, during, and after the Exodus as well as on the weekly absolute Shabbat count, all time cues are keyed to YHWH's redemptive plans.

However, we have also seen that in the not too distant future, the Sign of the Fish will, once again, coincide with the redemptive Sign of the Lamb. In the Gospel of John, Y'shua's disciples made a catch of 153 fish. The only occurrence of 153 in the Constellation Clock is just prior to the 2,000th anniversary of the resurrection, squarely in the middle of the 70th Jubilee since the creation of Adam!

Knowing that the apostles were called "fishers of men" by Y'shua, correlates to the unique occurrence of "153" in the 8,000+ year data set. This could very well suggest that: You have this long to catch followers for Messiah, then time will run out.

Tekufa and Teshuvah
Tracking the Equinoxes in Tanakh

As we saw earlier, Scripture gives us two different terms for the equinoxes in spring and fall, but they are both the same concept. Let's review these terms:

8498 [8499] תְּקוּפָה (Hebrew) (page 880) (Strong 8622) [תְּקוּפָה] **n.f** coming round, circuit; cstr. תְּקוּפַת הַשָּׁנָה Ex 34:22 (JE), adv., *at the circuit* (completion) *of the year,* so 2 לת׳ הַשָּׁנָה: Ch 24:33; = pl. cstr. 1 לִתְקֻפוֹת הַיָּמִים S 1:20; sg. sf. of finished *circuit* of sun Psalm 19:7 (opp. מוֹצָאוֹ; cf. of moon, בתקופתו Ecclus 43:7).

The Scriptures that use these definitions are as follows:

"You shall celebrate the Feast of Weeks, *that is,* the first fruits of the wheat harvest, and the Feast of Ingathering at the ***turn of the year***. (Exodus 34:22 NAU)

The phrase תְּקוּפַת הַשָּׁנָה clearly delineates an end or turn of the year in the fall. However, the same can be said for this phrase describing the spring:

Now it happened at ***the turn of the year*** that the army of the Arameans came up against him; and they came to Judah and Jerusalem, destroyed all the officials of the people from among the people, and sent all their spoil to the king of Damascus. (2 Chronicles 24:23 NAU)

Again the phrase here, תְּקוּפָה, refers to spring when it was customary for armies to renew military campaigns. In a parallel passage we see another word used in the same way:

At the ***turn of the year***, Ben-Hadad mustered the Arameans and went up to Aphek to fight against Israel. (1 Kings 20:26 NAU) [14]

---

14 At the beginning of the spring, Ben-Hadad took his army with him, and led it against the Hebrews; and when he was come to a certain city which was called Aphek, he pitched his camp in the Great Plain. Ahab also went to meet him with his army, and pitched his camp opposite him,

Here is the word being used in this passage:

> [תְּשׁוּבָה] **n.f.** return, answer;—**1.** sf. 1 וּתְשֻׁבָתוֹ הָרָמָתָה S 7:17 *and his*
> *return was* (= he returned) *to Rama.* **2.** esp. cstr. הַשָּׁנָה לִתְשׁוּבַת *at the*
> *return of the year,* i.e. of spring, 2 S 11:1, 1 K 20:22, 20:26, 2 Ch
> 36:10, 1 לְעֵת תְּשׁ׳: הַשּׁ׳ Ch 20:1 (|| 2 S 11:1). **3.** *answer,* pl. abs. תְּשֻׁבֹת
> Jb 34:36, sf. 21:34 תְּשׁוּבֹתֵיכֶם.

Again the phraseology is "at the returning of the year, in the spring".
Same thing here:

> At the ***turn of the year*** King Nebuchadnezzar sent and brought him
> to Babylon with the precious articles of the house of YHWH, and
> he made his kinsman Zedekiah king over Judah and Jerusalem.
> 2 Chronicles 36:10 (Matara)

Undoubtedly, this happened in the spring, especially when we consider
the detailed timeline leading up to the destruction of the Temple itself
in just four months time (2 Chronicles 36:19, comp. to 2 Kings 25:8-
10). This final example receives backing from Josephus as well as the
grammar:

> Now when the king of the Hebrews understood that the Ammonites
> had again gathered so great an army together, he determined to
> make war with them no longer by his generals, but he passed over
> the river Jordan himself, with all his army; and when he met them
> he joined battle with them, and overcame them, and slew forty
> thousand of their footmen, and seven thousand of their horsemen.
> He also wounded Shobach, the general of Helam's forces, who
> died of that stroke; but the people of Mesopotamia, ***upon such a***
> ***conclusion of the battle, delivered themselves up to David, and***
> ***sent him presents, who, at winter time returned to Jerusalem. But***
> ***at the beginning of the spring, he sent Joab***, the captain of his
> host, to fight against the Ammonites, who overran all their country,
> and laid it waste, and shut them up in their metropolis Rabbah, and
> besieged them there. (Antiquities 7:128-129)

although his army was a very small one, (Josephus, Antiquities 8:381)

The campaign begins here in Scripture:

> Then it happened in the **spring** (הַשָּׁנָה לִתְשׁוּבַת), **at the time when kings go out to battle**, that David sent Joab and his servants with him and all Israel, and they destroyed the sons of Ammon and besieged Rabbah. But David stayed at Jerusalem. (2 Samuel 11:1 NAU)

What is particularly interesting, now that we have "returned to the return of spring", is when we combine the first reference in Exodus 34:22 with the "Feast of Ingathering at the turn of the year", with Exodus 12:1-2 which says spring was to be the start/turn of the year! There are only two astronomical events that fit into all these descriptors of returning or starting a year:

> The heavens declare the glory of Elohim; the skies proclaim the work of His hands. ..In the heavens he has pitched a tent for the sun, which is like a bridegroom coming out from his **pavilion**, like a mighty man rejoicing **to run his course. It rises at one end of the heavens and makes its return circle/circuit** (תְּקוּפָה) **to the other; nothing is hidden from its heat."** Psalm 19:1, 5-6 (Matara)

Here is the best description of an equinox in all of Scripture. In addition to having the word *tekufah* where indicated, there are others that make this description, so much so, that I will simply list their definitions from Brown Driver Briggs:

> **Pavilion**[15] **3318** 3319] חֻפָּה] (Hebrew) (page 342) (Strong 2646)
> I. חֻפָּה **n.f.** canopy, chamber (as *covering, enclosing*)—abs. 'ח Is 4:5; sf. חֻפָּתוֹ Psalm 19:6; חֻפָּתָהּ Jo 2:16; —**1.** *canopy,* עלבלכבוד ח'
> Is 4:5 *over all glory a canopy* (for protection). **2.** *chamber,* of
> **bridegroom Psalm 19:6 (metaph. of sunrising);** of bride Jo 2:16
> (חֶדֶר|| of bridegroom).

> **Course 830** 831] אֹרַח] (Hebrew) (page 73) (Strong 734) רוּץ אֹרַח
> run **along a path, fig. of sun Psalm 19:6. 2.** fig. *path, way,* of

---

15 Otherwise known as a *chupa*, which is a half circle of a green bough of leaves that even today Jewish grooms walk under as they have for thousands of years.

course & fortunes of life Jb 8:13, 13:27 = 33:11, 19:8 (נְתִיבוֹת‖)
Psalm 139:3 (נְתִיבָה‖‖) 142:4 (דֶּרֶךְ) Pr 3:6 (דֶּרֶךְ 15:19, 4:18 (both ‖
id.) Is 26:7 (מַעְגָּל‖) so דֶּרֶךְ אָרְחֹתֶיךָ Is 3:12; *plain or even path* א' מִישׁוֹר
Psalm 27:11; in two cases with a special ref. (1) אֹרַח כַּנָּשִׁים Gn 18:11
(J) **of menstruation**[16]; (2) אֶהֱלֹךְ אֹרַח לֹא אָשׁוּב *a path* (which) I shall
not return, I am going Jb 16:22 i.e. to *Sh*ᵉʾól, cf. As. name of lower
world *irsÌit lâ târat, land without return,* v. Jr:10; Jr:65. **3.** fig. *way,*
of mode of living, or of character.

***End* 8657** 8658] קֵצָה] (Hebrew) (page 892) (Strong 7098) קָצֶה **n.f.**
et (pl.) **m.** :Ex 25:18 end (pl. 4 t. **f.** [c. num. masc.], Albr:ZAW xvi
(1896), 93 changes gender of num. in all, or regards as irregular
agreement in gender (Ges:§ 97 c); otherwise Kö:ii. 1, 61, 176);—
abs. 'ק: Ex 25:19 + ; pl. cstr. 1 קְצוֹת K 12:31 + ; sf. קְצוֹתָיו Ex 27:4
+ (so also Ex 37:8, 39:4 Qr; Kt קצוותו, cf. קְצֹת infr.), etc.;—**1.** *end,*
sg. of כַּפֹּרֶת in tabern. Ex 25:19, 25:19 = 37:8 , 37:8; **of curtain**
26:4 = 36:11; elsewh. pl., 37:7 = 25:18 הַכַּפֹּרֶת :ק', cf. 25:19 = 37:8;
of **ephod 28:7 = 39:4, breast-plate 28:23, 28:24 , 28:26** = 39:16,
39:17, 39:19, chins 28:25 = 39:18, grating 27:4 (appar. = *corners*);
tips of wings 1 K 6:24, 6:24; of vine Ez 15:4; הָאָרֶץ :ק' **ends of the**
earth Is 40:28, 41:5, 41:9, Jb 28:24; הַשָּׁמַיִם אַרְבַּע ק' :Je 49:36, cf.
Psalm 19:7; דְּרָכָיו :ק' Jb 26:14, i.e. the mere edge, minute part, of
his doings. **2.** מִקְצוֹת הָעָם = *from the whole of* (fr. among) *the people,*
1 K 12:31, 13:33, cf. Ju 18:2, 2 K 17:32 (v. also Ecclus 16:17, and
3 קֵצֶךְ).[17]

From here, it's not hard to see how these Scriptural terms would be
understood in the historical record.

[116] And the sun, the ruler of the day, making two equinoxes every year,
both in spring and autumn. The spring equinox in the constellation
of Aries, and the autumnal one in Libra, gives the most evident
demonstration possible of the divine dignity of the number seven.

---

16 Since this period of a woman's courses is roughly the same as that of a lunar month, the
celestial linkage in that sense is also very strong.

17 Of particular note here is the "wrapping around imagery" of the places described elsewhere,
such as the tabernacle curtains, as well as the "ends" of the breastplate of the high priest which
we have referenced previously.

For each of the equinoxes takes place in the seventh month, at which time men are expressly commanded by law to celebrate the greatest and most popular and comprehensive festivals; since it is owing to both these seasons, that all the fruits of the earth are engendered and brought to perfection; the fruit of corn, and all other things which are sown, being owing to the vernal equinox; and that of the vine, and of all the other plants which bear hard berries, of which there are great numbers, to the autumnal one. (Philo, On Creation 1:116)

[204] The last of all the annual festivals is that which is called the feast of tabernacles, which is fixed for the season of the autumnal equinox. (Philo, The Special Laws 2:204)

This is the closest that ancient Hebrew could possibly come to describing the equinoxes in the spring and fall.

The Divisions of the Day

According to Scripture, the day begins at sunset, not at midnight nor at sunrise, but this is purely ancient understanding, not later Rabbinical innovation; a truth supported by both Hebrew Tanakh and Aramaic Peshitta. For the vast majority of Bible students, this statement is hardly surprising; however, a small group of people actively argue against this idea, creating division and confusion. Others are unclear as to the Scriptural reasons for the day beginning at sunset and believe it to be a later traditional development.

In the Beginning

"In the beginning Elohim created the heavens and the earth. Now the earth was formless and empty, darkness was over the surface of the deep, and the Spirit of Elohim was hovering over the waters. And Elohim said, "Let there be light," and there was light. Elohim saw that the light was good and he separated the light from the

darkness. Elohim called the light (aur--אור) "day," (yom--יום) and the darkness (khoshekh--חשׁך) he called "night." (layil--ליל) And there was evening (ereb--ערב), and there was morning (boker-- בקר)--the first day" Genesis 1:1-5 (Matara)

From these very famous passages in Torah, we glean many important facts. The plain (peshat) language tells us:

In the beginning it was dark, and, 1: *light* (אור) emerged from that darkness through YHWH's will. As a result, light became separated from that *darkness* (חשׁך).

Then YHWH gave the light another name, that of, 2: *yom* (יום) or "day."

Similarly, YHWH then called the darkness by its alternate title 3: *layil* (ליל) or "night."

When there is evening, 4: *erev* (ערב) followed by morning, 5: *boker* (בקר), this constitutes a fuller version of *yom* which counts as the first day.

Sunrise-sunrise advocates postulate that the Hebrew could read "and there was evening and *then* there was morning, one day." In other words, they assume that the Hebrew language allows for the starting point of the first day to be *boker* (morning), or dawn. Other passages in the Tanakh however, clearly refute this.

Furthermore, just because the construction of the sentence may allow it to read, "and *then* there was" does not mean a separation of the first period from the second. That would be like saying "And there was the sports report *and then there was* weather during the newscast" as though sports and weather could not be part of the same event! As simplistic as this example sounds, it is even more ridiculous to apply this logic to force *"and then there was"* into a pure separation. Not only are there five more occasions where Genesis 1 uses this construction, but many other places in the Tanakh:

*"Hear, O Israel: YHWH is our Elohim, YHWH is one. Love YHWH your Elohim with all your heart and with all your soul and with all your strength. These commandments that I give you today are to be upon your hearts. Impress them on your children. **Talk about them when you sit at home and when you walk along the road, when you lie down and when you get up"** (Deuteronomy 6:4-7).*

There are two evening-morning cycles mentioned here. The order is when you sit at home, which is usually at night, when you walk along the road, which is usually in the morning, when you lie down in evening and then when you get up in the morning again! This statement from the Psalms is even stronger:

*"But I call to Elohim, and YHWH saves me. **Evening, morning and noon I cry out in distress, and he hears my voice"***
(Psalm 55:16-17).

"You must pay (a laborer) his wages on the same day, before the sun sets." (Deuteronomy 24:15).

The reason is that after sunset is, technically, another day.

*"Then I heard a holy one speaking, and another holy one said to him, 'How long will it take for the vision to be fulfilled--**the vision concerning the daily sacrifice**, the rebellion that causes desolation, and the surrender of the sanctuary and of the host that will be trampled underfoot?' He said to me, '**It will take 2,300 evenings and mornings; then the sanctuary will be re-consecrated'"***
(Daniel 8:13-14).

*"And the vision **of the evenings and mornings** which has been told is true, but keep the vision secret because it pertains to many days in the future"* (Daniel 8:26).

These are the same parts of the greater *yom*, a 24 hour period that begins with sunset.

There's no place like Yom for the holidays

םוֹי, 'YOWM', (#3117), *"daylight, 24 hour day, a working day"*, comes from a root meaning *"to be hot."* This can refer either to daylight alone, or to a 24-hour period called the *"day."* An examination of special occasions in the Tanakh reveals the components of a normal day.

> *"YHWH spoke to Moses in the Desert of Sinai in the first month of the second year after they came out of Egypt. He said, '***Have the Israelites celebrate the Passover at the appointed time. Celebrate it at the appointed time, at twilight on the fourteenth day of this month***, in accordance with all its rules and regulations.' So Moses told the Israelites to celebrate the Passover, and they did so in the Desert of Sinai at twilight on the fourteenth day of the first month. The Israelites did everything just as YHWH commanded Moses. But some of them could not celebrate the Passover on that day because they were ceremonially unclean on account of a dead body. So they came to Moses and Aaron that same day and said to Moses, "We have become unclean because of a dead body, but why should we be kept from presenting YHWH's offering with the other Israelites at the appointed time?" Moses answered them, "Wait until I find out what YHWH commands concerning you." Then YHWH said to Moses, "Tell the Israelites: 'When any of you or your descendants are unclean because of a dead body or are away on a journey, they may still celebrate YHWH's Passover. ***They are to celebrate it on the fourteenth day of the second month at twilight.*** They are to eat the lamb, together with unleavened bread and bitter herbs'"* (Numbers 9:1-11).

From here two aspects become apparent. First, it is clear that the celebration of the holiday is keyed to sunset, and there is no indication that it is different from a regular day which one would expect if the holiday made such a shift. And second, here, the "day" includes the night:

> *"**On that same** (Passover) **night** I will pass through Egypt and strike down every firstborn--both men and animals...**This is a day***

you are to commemorate; for the generations to come you shall
celebrate it as a festival to YHWH--a lasting ordinance"
(Exodus 12:12-14).

The question is sometimes asked, "If they are slaughtering the Passover Lamb on the fourteenth at twilight, isn't that really the next day, the fifteenth?" No, because this same Hebrew word (*erev*) may also refer to the sun in the process of setting, which is the late afternoon on the fourteenth. Others suggest that Passover can then be said to start on the thirteenth, thinking that once it is sunset, it marks "the fourteenth day at the beginning of twilight." Again, the answer is no, because the Torah is clear that it is "between the evenings," which is the sun beginning to set after the daylight period of the fourteenth day. The order shown is: night and then day. "The greater yom" includes the night since the "day" is clearly happening after sunset, but before dawn. YHWH adds this confirmation for clarity:

> *"It is a Sabbath of rest for you, and you must deny yourselves.* **From the evening of the ninth day of the month until the following evening you are to observe your Sabbath"**
> (Vayikra/Leviticus 23:32).

To clarify which "twilight" was meant for ancient Israel, i.e., the sunset that marked the beginning of the previous (9th) day, or the one for the day being being discussed (10th), YHWH clearly says to go *through* the 9th day and *then celebrate the Shabbat after the sunset on that day*. This is why Yehudim (Jews) have always adopted this pattern and applied it throughout the Tanakh. In addition, we find the weekly Shabbat also occurring at sunset:

> **When evening shadows fell on the gates of Jerusalem before the Sabbath, I ordered the doors to be shut and not opened until the Sabbath was over.** *I stationed some of my own men at the gates so that no load could be brought in on the Sabbath day. Once or twice the merchants and sellers of all kinds of goods spent the night outside Jerusalem.* **But I warned them and said, "Why do you spend the night by the wall? If you do this again, I will lay hands**

on you." From that time on they no longer came on the Sabbath.
Then I commanded the Levites to purify themselves and go and
guard the gates in order to keep the Sabbath day holy"
(Nehemiah 13:19-22).

Some *"light"* reading

Another way to understand this structure is to remember that, in the beginning:

Elohim called the light (*aur*--אור) **"day"** (*yom*--יום**) and the darkness** (*khoshekh*--חשך**) he called "night"** (*layil*--ליל).

By the direct reference of this verse, we see "light" and "day" are synonyms, as are "darkness" and "night.":

*"And Elohim said: Let there be lights in the firmament of the heaven to divide the day from the night; and let them be for signs, and for seasons, and for days and years; and let them be for lights in the firmament of the heaven to give light upon the earth. And it was so. **And Elohim made the two great lights: the greater light to rule the day[18], and the lesser light to rule the night;** and the stars. And Elohim set them in the firmament of the heaven to give light upon the earth, and to rule over the day and over the night, and to divide the light from the darkness; and Elohim saw that it was good. And there was evening and there was morning, the fourth day."* Genesis 1:14-19 (Matara)

So, if "light" is called "day," and there are "lights" also at night, then it stands to reason that where there is "light", be it greater or lesser, it is part of the *yom*, or "day"! We see here night and then day, darkness and then light, clearly making up the greater unit which is also called day. There is also a special prophetic *Yom* which will not be confined to a day or nighttime period:

---

18 Samaritan: "the abundance of greater light".

"Then YHWH my Elohim will come and all the Set-Apart ones with him. On that day there will be neither light nor cold nor frost. It will be an utterly unique day, without daytime or nighttime--a day known to YHWH. When evening comes, there will be light.
Zechariah 14:1-7 (Matara)

Watches and Hours

In the First Century, the day was divided into twelve equal periods of time, or hours, which were demarcated on a sundial, but "hours" would vary in length according to the time of year. So while the daylight had twelve hours, rarely, would each hour be equivalent to our modern interval of 60 minutes. The word for "hour" (*shaiah*--שעה) is first referred to in the Aramaic portion of Daniel. In some places, a better translation is "brief moment" but that only raises the question as to what "brief" constitutes. The clearest reading is in Daniel 4:19, where the prophet himself is said to have been in a state of astonishment for "one hour." A shorter interval of time, perhaps seconds, is suggested in the Hebrew term *rehgah* (רגע), which is closer to the English word "instant," derived literally from "a winking of the eyes."

A more generic time reference in the Aramaic of Daniel is *iddawn* (עדדן), whose root is more closely associated with a woman's menstrual cycle, but which can refer to a moment or even a year, depending on the context. It is this exact root and word which is used throughout the early Aramaic writings in the form of the word *shaita* (שעתה). Prior to these times, the day and night were divided into watches. Starting with dawn, it would take a few hours for the sun to heat things up; at around the third hour from dawn. This time was generally known as the beginning of "the heat of the day":

*"The next morning Saul put the people in three companies; and they came into the midst of the camp at the **morning watch** (just before dawn -AGR) and struck down the Ammonites **until the heat of the day...**"* (1 Samuel 11:11 Matara)

This verse indicates that the attack began somewhere around 4 AM, and ended about five hours later, when the "heat of the day" began. However, the time period continued from that point until late afternoon. At that time, prior to sunset, we would have "the cool of the day" (Genesis 3:8). Finally, the mid point of this time from dawn to late afternoon was called "midday." The Hebrew word for "noon," *tzohar* (צהר), is from a primitive root that means "roof," or the time when the sun is directly overhead. As for the night, it was divided into three parts. First, there was the period from sunset to midnight:

> *"Arise, cry aloud in the night **at the beginning of the night watches**; pour out your heart like water before the presence of YHWH; Lift up your hands to Him for the life of your little ones who are faint because of hunger at the head of every street"*
> Lamentations 2:19 (Matara).

Then from midnight until the roosters began crowing:

> *"**Now the same night** it came about that YHWH said to him, 'Arise, go down against the camp, for I have given it into your hands'... So Gideon and the hundred men who were with him came to the outskirts of the camp **at the beginning of the middle watch**, when they had just posted the watch; and they blew the trumpets and smashed the pitchers that were in their hands"*
> (Judges 7:9, 19 Matara).

Finally, from the rooster crowing until sunrise:

> *"**At the morning watch**, YHWH looked down on the army of the Egyptians through the pillar of fire and cloud and brought the army of the Egyptians into confusion... So Moses stretched out his hand over the sea, **and the sea returned to its normal state at daybreak,** while the Egyptians were fleeing right into it; then YHWH overthrew the Egyptians in the midst of the sea"* (Exodus 14:24, 27 Matara).

By Y'shua's time, the Hebrews had added a fourth watch, as noted in Mark 13:35.

The many faces of EREV

Erev has many different meanings; the most common ones are "even, eventide, evening, and mixing." It is derived from *arav* which also means "to darken, or to cover with a texture." *Erev* also has several figurative meanings which include the sense of "ending" or "closure"; therefore, it is important to know how to determine a literal from a figurative use of this word. Scriptural evidence also shows *erev* can refer to late afternoon; it is derived from the same root that describes mixing, particularly of shades of light and darkness (Exodus 12:38). It is precisely the mixing of daylight transitioning to night as the sun sets. We will also see later how the meaning "to darken" relates directly to the Aramaic NT and its equivalent term *ramsha*, as we review a passage in Luke. The daylight can be said to start closing or setting, another meaning of *erev*:

> "Prepare war against her; Arise, and let us ***attack at noon***. Woe to us, ***for the day declines*** (*panah*--פנה), ***for the shadows of the evening*** (*erev*--ערב) ***lengthen***!" Jeremiah 6:4 (Matara)

How does the "day" decline, or go into *panah*? Because noon is counted as the mid-point from dawn, the daylight-only form of *yom*. From there it's a very smooth transition to the "going down" or setting of the day period. But notice another aspect to this key verse as well: Erev is defined as the first time that the shadows lengthen past mid-day. Other verses in Tanakh show a clear separation of time between first erev and sunset:

> *"He hanged the king of Ai on a tree **until evening** (erev--ערב); **and at sunset** (bow ha-shemesh—בוא השמש) Joshua gave command and they took his body down from the tree and threw it at the entrance of the city gate and raised over it a great heap of stones that stands to this day. (Joshua 8:29-NAU)*

Once it is sunset, it marks "the fourteenth day at the beginning of twilight." Again, the answer is no, because the Torah is clear that it is again "between the evenings" which is the sun beginning to set after the daylight period of the fourteenth day began, and further Torah instruction makes this clear. The order shown is night and then day; "the greater yom" includes the night as the "day" is clearly happening after sunset but before dawn! YHWH adds this confirmation for clarity:

> *"It is a Sabbath of rest for you, and you must deny yourselves. **From the evening of the ninth day of the month until the following evening you are to observe your Sabbath***"
> (Vayikra/Leviticus 23:32).

"Daylight Savings Time"

Another key fact is this: It was not a normal day as far as *ramsha/ereb* was concerned:

> *"**Now from the sixth hour there was darkness over all the land until the ninth hour. And about the ninth hour,** Y'shua cried out with a loud voice and said, "My El! My El! Why have you spared me?"* (Matthew 27:45-46) *"And about six hours had passed and darkness was over all the land until the ninth hour. **And the sun darkened** and the veil of the temple was torn from its middle"* (Luke 23:44-45).

From these verses we know: 1) It was after the mid-day began, or the sixth hour, when darkness fell over the land. 2) We are specifically told that the **sun darkened**.

> The *question* is, what does Scripture call such an event, and by what term? *"In that day,"* declares the Master YHWH, *"**I will make the sun go down at noon and darken the earth in broad daylight**. I will turn your religious feasts into mourning and all your singing into weeping. I will make all of you wear sackcloth and shave your heads. I will make that time like mourning for an only son and the end of it like a bitter day"* (Amos 8:9-10).

The word used here is *bow* (בוא), which literally means, "to set" and is a synonym for *erev. Erev,* in turn, is rendered into Aramaic as *ramsha.*

Furthermore, we should remember that one of the original meanings of *erev/ramsha* is simply "to darken"! The sixth hour, in three of the Gospels, is being described as the transition time between when the sun darkens and when it sets; only this time it's happening hours earlier.

This scenario was referenced earlier:

> *"Prepare war against her; Arise, and let us **attack at noon**. Woe to us, **for the day declines, for the shadows of the erev lengthen!**"* (Jeremiah 6:4)

This appears to be exactly what the prophets are describing; the time is after the sixth hour, or noon. Then the sun darkens, the shadows lengthen and spread throughout the land! The word used here is *erev* or *ramsha*! Hearkening back to another definition of *erev*, we see this moment of the sixth hour as a "mixing" of light and darkness; a very apt description of what is going on here.

Finally, from a linguistic standpoint, we need to consider the words in Matthew 27:57, *kad hwa din ramsha*, which can be translated as *"now when it was evening."* However, the word *din* also carries several other meanings, including "while", "yet," or even just plain "and." As a result, the simplest reading of the text allows for the clearer rendering of *"when it was still ramsha,"* which would indicate Matthew's viewing of the supernatural darkness as an early *first erev*. That being the case, Joseph of Aramathea had plenty of time from his consultation with Pilate, till seeing his friend Nicodemus who brought spices along with him.

As for logistical considerations, Pilate was very near the execution site, with his "common hall" being in the Antonia Fortress on the grounds of the Temple, while the execution site was just outside the city walls. Pilate was surprised that Y'shua had already died and sent a soldier to check on him (Mark 15:44- 45). This would have added an extra bit of time. A Roman Centurion could have easily made a round trip to the execution area in thirty minutes or less, or within minutes on horseback. The Centurion could easily see that Y'shua was, in fact, dead with the blood and water pouring out on the ground. Therefore, both the death of Y'shua and the granting of permission for Joseph to retrieve the body could have fit within the ninth hour. Pilate's sole concern was to verify Y'shua's death. Armed with the approval, Joseph and Nicodemus went to the stake, probably early in the tenth hour, still allowing sufficient time to prepare and place the body of their Master in the tomb.

What about John?

In John's account, we have the phrase, *beter haleyn Yosip,* or *"after these things Joseph,"* linking the arrival of the counselor to "after" the death of Y'shua on the stake. John is the only writer who was actually at the execution site (John 19:26, 35). Therefore, when he talks about **the arrival of Joseph of Aramathea, he means "at the stake"**, *not about his arrival to Pilate.* Furthermore, Mark 15:42 goes out of the way to inform us it was still daylight but in "evening" or *first erev.* Luke 23:50-55 does the same, but does not mention that Joseph's arrival was "after" anything. The most important details rest with John:

> 1) That Y'shua is condemned about the sixth hour of the *day* of Preparation, which other Gospels say "is before the Sabbath" (John 19:14, compare to Mark 15:42 and Luke 23:54).

> 2) That Y'shua is buried *on that same day before sunset* (John 19:42) but still "at evening" which must mean late afternoon (Matthew 27:57).

When we combine these facts with those in the previous section, it becomes clear that, "after these things," denotes a specific time of the day. In order to synch John's account with the other gospels, Joseph's arrival **at the cross had to be** at the tenth hour. It is at the tenth hour of the day that generally fits the late afternoon time line and specifically fits when we consider that the "first erev" began four hours earlier. Two hours before sunset is still plenty of time to get Y'shua buried, especially since the Gospels tell us the close proximity of the actual tomb.

And the Sabbath was dawning?

Analysis of the context and usage of specific terms indicates the use of dawning and setting as metaphors for opening and closing an occasion. We have seen several examples from Scripture about how that works. Even so, sunrise-sunrise advocates point to a reading in the Greek that says, in two places, "The Sabbath was *dawning.*" The word used for "dawn" is *epiphosko* which literally means "growing light." The idea is that if the Sabbath is tied to the literal dawn, then the day must start at sunrise. However, almost all Greek New Testament primacists recognize this phrase as an Aramaic or Hebraic expression and render it "and the Sabbath was beginning" in their versions of Matthew 28:1 and John 19:31. A quick survey of the two dozen most popular NT translations of those verses more than proves this point. The question is what evidence exists, apart from the general possibilities of meaning that we outlined earlier from Tanakh, to support a *dawning as beginning* idiom? Let's see how this issue, from the Aramaic side which uses *negha* in place of *epiphosko*, is really clarified:

> *"And the Yehudeans, **because it was the eve** (erubata--ܥܪܘܒܬܐ)*
> *said, 'These bodies should not remain on their stakes because **the***
> ***Sabbath is dawning** (negha--ܢܓܗ)'... And they placed Y'shua*
> *there **because the Sabbath was beginning/entering** (ailaa--ܥܐܠܐ)*
> *and because the tomb was near"* (John 19:31,42).

So what we see here are two different expressions that deal with the exact same time frame. The metaphoric use of "dawning" is quite clear in John 19:31, but this is more than clarified by the use of the phrase *"because it was the eve."* Other Gospels make it clear that the crucifixion is in the middle of the day, and yet the word used here in John 19:31 is *erubata,* the same word as *ereb,* and the same meaning as *ramsha!* Even the alternate reading of this phrase: "because it was the setting (of the day)" supports this idea. It's at this point that we remember that *erev/erubata/ ramsha* most certainly has the meaning of "setting" as well as "set." As a result, a day can be said to "set" in the sense that the daylight portion is closing itself out, such as here:

*"And when it became **ramsha d'erubata** (ܪܡܫܐ ܕܥܪܘܒܬܐ) which is before the Sabbath..."* (Mark 15:42).

Some suggest that *erubata* refers to the "Friday" of that week. Sadly, for them, it actually refers to the annual Sabbath of the Feast of Unleavened Bread which fell on a Thursday. This period is just prior to the start of the Feast of Unleavened Bread which is due to start at sunset. However, it should be pointed out that even though there is no conflict between the Greek or Aramaic in naming the day, neither version discredits the plain reading of this verse which is literally: *"and when it became the ramsha that was setting."* So evening itself, whether the first ereb or the second, can be said to set or give way, or close.

When we combine this fact with the dawning/beginning/entering of the Sabbath in John 19:31, 42, this next passage makes a lot more sense:

> *"Now in the **ramsha** (closing/evening) of the Sabbath, as the first of the week was **negha/dawning**, came Maryam of Magdala and the other Maryam that they might see the grave"*
> (Matthew 28:1 Peshitta).

This is how we understand the Peshitta reading above in light of the Greek for this same verse: *"**Opse de Shabbaton** in the dawning of the first of the week..."* (Matthew 28:1 Greek). That phrase may also indicate that while John does not mention the three hours of darkness in his Gospel, he, nevertheless, is aware of it and uses it to synch the time. The phrase *Opse de Shabbaton* is taken to mean, in nearly all translations, "closing/after the Sabbath" as well as "evening" where *ramsha* appears on the Aramaic side. Therefore, the Greek is actually covering and giving witness to both literal and figurative uses. In fact, the Aramaic of Mark 16:1 may reflect an attempt at clarifying Matthew 28:1.

Summary

The only way to allege that a sunrise-sunrise model is supported in the Aramaic New Testament, which should "clarify" the Tanakh's position, is to use terms out of context and not discerning when literal or figurative meanings are intended. There is no Aramaic or Hebrew speaking congregation, (Netzari, Messianic, Christian or otherwise) that studied the sacred text over the last 2,000 years, who would have deviated from the traditional Jewish understanding of what makes up the day and when it begins.

No advocate of the sunrise-sunrise model can prove when and why this, alleged day-switching supposedly happened. If the traditional reckoning of the day was changed, as these folks suggest, then where is the report of the greatest mass conspiracy ever recorded in history? If Mashiyach had advocated or adopted such a practice, it would have angered the Jewish establishment and brought much accusation against him and his disciples, but there is nothing whatsoever found in Jewish writings. Sunrise-sunrise advocates reference a story regarding Rashi's grandson, Samuel Ben Meir, observing that the "day" began with *ereb* and not "night" but the matter is one of pure speculation. There is no evidence that either Rashi or his grandson adopted a view of the day beginning at sunrise.

The Great Year

> Nor is there any better proof than the assertion of the credible historian, of their acquaintance with the *Annus Magnus* [Great Year], the astronomical cycle of 600 years, which brings back the sun and the moon to the same points of the heavens so nearly, that its discovery implies a pretty correct knowledge of the solar and lunar motions.-Encyclopedia Britannica (1888), p. 744

Perhaps one of the most curious statements that the historians make regarding the Book of Signs may be found here:

> Those ancients were beloved of God, and [lately] made by God himself; and because their food was then fitter for the prolongation of life, might well live so great a number of years; and besides, God afforded them a longer time of life on account of their virtue,

and the good use they made of it in astronomical and geometric discoveries, which would not have afforded the time of foretelling [the periods of the stars] unless they had lived six hundred years; for ***the Great Year is completed in that interval***.
(Josephus, Antiquities 1:106)

So what is "the Great Year" and why was it so important that Josephus would say YHWH granted such long lives to the patriarchs in order to make this one important astronomical observation?

The answer may refer to a phenomenon called *Naros* which was probably first written down in ancient Hindu literature almost 5,000 years ago and was also acknowledged by many other ancient cultures. *Naros*[19] refers to the time when a New Moon occurs at the Vernal Equinox, once every 600 years. Regarding its importance, the legendary astronomer Cassini wrote:

> The first luni-solar period, composed of whole ages, is that of 600 years…Though the chronologists speak not of this period, yet it is one of the most ancient ever invented.[20]

And in writing about the famous astronomer Hipparchus, who discovered the precession of the equinoxes, first century historian Pliny says:

> After them Hipparchus proclaimed the *cursum* of each star for 600 years.

The word *cursum* is often debated among scholars. Some believe it to mean: "eclipse" while others believe it to be the daily progress of the moon over a 600 year period. Either way, it still comes down to the same astronomical event at the end of that interval.[21] Having established this ancient knowledge, let's turn to what it means to the Wheel of Stars. Godfrey Higgins explains the Hindu use of this 600 year interval in their

---

19 Also sometimes pronounced "neros" but I have adapted the former spelling throughout.
20 See Anacalypsis by Godfrey Higgins, p. 166. Also noting that the original quote used the word "ancient-est" which has been updated to "most ancient" for the sake of clarity.
21 For more information see: Pliny and Hipparchus's 600-Year Cycle, by Goldstein, B. R. & Bowen, A. C, Journal for the History of Astronomy, p.155-158 (1995).

larger system as follows:

> The first [Hindu astronomical system] is called the Brahma
> Calpa...a Maha or Great Yug or Calpa consists of 2400 years,
> which the Great Yug was divided into four other Yugs of 600 years
> each. The beginning of this 2400 was 3164 years B.C., and it ended
> 764 years B.C. Here, in the division into four, we have clearly four
> ages or yugs of 600 years each. I think the Naros cannot be denied
> here. (*Anacalypsis,* p. 175)

I would contend then that the Hindu system simply borrowed from an
earlier Hebrew model that also used a base 600 pattern. Higgins[22] admits
the following:

> The Sun, or rather that higher principle of which the Sun was the
> emblem or Shekinah, was considered to be incarnated every six
> hundred years. (*Anacalypsis,* p. 176)

In order to see how the Hebrew system of the 600 year Naros cycle
recorded by Josephus differed from its Hindu counterpart, we need only
add one additional Naros to the Hindu date, which brings us to 3764 BCE
and a wider 3000 year cycle.

Before we add the Naros interval, a critical point needs to be made about
the Rabbinic Calendar. The year of 2010 crosses two Rabbinic years,
5770-5771. Year 1 and day 1 of that calendar would bring us precisely,
in Gregorian terms, to September 7, 3761 BCE. However, there is a huge
problem with this date: ***If the Rabbinic reckonings of this as creation
day 1 are accurate, they have the first week of the world beginning
on a Monday.***[23] ***This would contradict the 7-day Shabbat and the***

---

22 Higgins will, from this general point of agreement, go into other associations that I don't
support: such as insisting that the Hindu timing of the flood was superior to that which can be
directly deduced from Scripture. Nevertheless, there seem to be many concordances between
ancient Hebrew and Hindu traditions, along with the significant differences that clearly mark the
superiority of the Biblical model.

23 Actually accounting for Hebrew reckoning, after sunset on Sunday, September 6[th,] but this is
still off by at least a day. We must remember that Genesis 1:19 says, "and it was evening and it
was morning, day one", which is not just a reference to the order of creation but the names of the
days! Even now, Sunday in Hebrew is simply yom rishon (first day) and begins after sunset on

understanding of the creation being on Saturday at sunset or perhaps into dawn on Sunday. However, if we look at what 1 Tishri would have been on the Rabbinic calendar, three years prior, we find 1 Tishri hits precisely on a Shabbat in 3764 BCE.

Therefore, I doubt that it is a coincidence or a small matter to simply demonstrate that:

$$3164 \text{ BCE} - 600 = 3764 \text{ BCE}$$

In other words, we need to look at some bifurcation in the Rabbinic tradition and see that no matter how we parse the dates they choose, their calendar is off the mark. Specifically, some tradition states that 1 Tishri, anciently Yom Teruah and later Rosh Hashanna, was either the birthday of Adam, or of the whole world. In the latter case, Rabbinic opinion is further split as to *when* the creation of the world occured prior to Adam. The majority opinion is that even allowing for the idea that we are not dealing with six 24 hour periods, the calendar would put the First Day on the 25th of Elul. Thus 1 Tishri would be on the 6th day. Other traditions would put the universe's creation anywhere from 6 months to 1 year from 3761 BCE.

What is startling is this: I may have validated this last rabbinic tradition in the astronomy: *While 3761 and 3762 have their 1 Tishri and 25 Elul dates on the wrong days, both 3763 and 3764 have 1 Tishri fall on Shabbat! If that's true, then what we see here is rather elegant. The world or universe is made at sunset on Tishri 1, Yom Rishon (Saturday night sunset to Sunday night sunset) which coincides with the rebirth of the Shekinah/600 year cycle. Then a "year" later, Mankind is also created on Yom Rishon/Tishri 1! "As in heaven, so on earth" indeed!* The Naros cycle also correlates with a few interesting dates in Hebrew history. Let's list all the Naros years from Rabbinic creation forward:

BCE: 1) 3764, 2) 3164, 3) 2564. 4) 1964, 5) 1364, 6) 764, 7) 164

The further back we go in time, the harder it becomes to assign a definite

---

Saturday night.

day and year in modern terms. For example, I think it is safe to suggest that 1964 BCE crosses the general life span of Abraham, but we need additional correlating data. The same is true for 1364 BCE. We know it was during the time of the Judges, but we know little else.

In 764 BCE though, we come to the most likely period of the prophet Amos' most famous prediction, which we will see momentarily.

In order to synchronize this prophecy, we need to look at the reigns of King Uzziah of Judah and King Jeroboam of Israel and where they intersect. Amos 1:1 says that this was "two years before the earthquake". The Jewish Encyclopedia affirms the general time frame:

> The reign of Jeroboam II. lasted forty-one years, according to II Kings, xiv. 23. Though it can not be fixed with certainty, this much may be said, that its termination must be placed between 750 and 740 B.C. Marti ("Ency. Bibl." article. "Chronology," p. 797) fixes his reign between 782 and 743 B.C. The activity of Amos could hardly have coincided with the close of his reign. The fact alone that Isaiah's call can not have happened later than 740, while he so evidently draws on Amos' prophecies, is sufficient for placing Amos not later than 750.

But is there any way to be more precise? According to William La Sor, there is:

> Without a doubt Amos' words were delivered in the days of Jeroboam ben Joash (Jeroboam II), who ruled Israel from 793-753, for the clash between Amos and Amaziah (7:10-17) is an integral part of his message. To excise this passage would leave the book virtually meaningless, Since v.10 therefore, is to be accepted as authentic, there can be no basic objection to the claim that 1:1 also is accurate. Now, since the reigns of Uzziah of Judah and Jeroboam II of Israel overlapped for the period 767-753 (removing portions of each reign that were coregencies with the previous kings), Amos' prophecy can be placed within that period, possibly ca. 760. Old Testament Survey, p. 320

This looks a bit too close to be a coincidence. If the timing is relevant, the prophecy itself must also be:

> Then Amaziah, the priest of Bethel, sent word to Jeroboam king of Israel, saying, "Amos has plotted against you in the midst of the house of Israel; the land cannot withstand all his words. "This is because Amos says, 'Jeroboam will die by the sword and Israel will certainly go from its land into exile.'" Then Amaziah said to Amos, ", you seer, flee away to the land of Judah and there eat bread and there do your prophesying! "But no longer prophesy at Bethel, for it is a Set-Apart place of the king and a royal residence." Then Amos replied to Amaziah, "I am not a prophet, nor am I the son of a prophet; for I am a herdsman and a grower of sycamore figs. "But YHWH plucked me from following the flock and YHWH said to me, 'Go prophesy to My people Israel.' "Now hear the word of YHWH: you are saying, 'You will not prophesy against Israel nor will you speak against the house of Isaac.' "Therefore, thus says YHWH, 'Your wife will become a harlot in the city, your sons and your daughters will fall by the sword, your land will be parceled up by a measuring line and you yourself will die upon unclean soil. Moreover, *Israel will certainly go from its land into exile.*'"
> Amos 7:10-17 (Matara)

So it seems that at the precise moment that the 600 year cycle is renewed, YHWH through Amos, pronounces final judgment on the kingdom of Israel that comes true 42 years later, in 722 BCE!

As for 164 BCE, that is precisely, right at the time when the Maccabean Revolt successfully routs the Syrian army and restores Jerusalem's Temple. The occasion will later become known as Hanukkah!

The next occurrence of the 600 year cycle is in 435, when the Western Roman Empire was in it's death throes. The next two occurrences, 1035 and 1635, do not represent significant occasions for the Jewish people. However, the next future event looms large, as 2235 is part of the 70th Jubilee counted from the entry into Canaan. We should also bear in mind this last reference from Godfrey Higgins on the Hindu system:

I think the four divisions obviously prove, that the sum of 2400 years is only a part of a system consisting of Naroses; and, as we will soon see, of the ten incarnations, in reality Naroses, spoken of in the first chapter and fourth section of the present book of this work. (*Anacalypsis*, p. 175)

"Ten incarnations" of the Naros equals 6,000 years. Since both the Rabbinic and the Naros occasion of 3764 BCE are so close, both are within the same 70th Jubilee on the Long Count. Whether this evidence for a potential 2030 return of Y'shua Mashiyach proves to be credible remains to be seen.

The Paths of Aldebaran

Can you bring forth Mazzaroth in its season?
Or can you stand in the **paths** (נָחָה) of **Aldebaran**?
Aramaic Job 38:32 (Lamsa)

Before we can understand why "Great Bear" in Hebrew is actually better interpreted as Aldebaran in Aramaic, we need to look at some definitions:

6026 [6027] נָחָה (Hebrew) (page 634) (Strong 5148) [נָחָה] **vb.** lead, guide (Ar. *nahÍaÀ go in direction of, turn (eyes) toward*) ; **Qal** *Pf.* sf. נָחַנִי Gn 24:27 + 2 t.; וְנָחֲךָ Is 58:11; נָחָם Ex 13:17; 2 ms. ... Job 31:18, *of guiding constellations 38:32* (הוֹצִיא). –Brown Driver Briggs

1617.0 עַיִשׁ (±ayish) **Arcturus** (ASV and RSV the Bear). Heavenly constellation of which the brilliant star Arcturus is the most easily identified. Occurs only in Job 9:9 and Job 38:32 in connection with kesîl "Orion, " kîmâ the "Pleiades," mazzalot the "constellations," (all of which see). –Brown Driver Briggs

As we saw in the opening section, the 4th century Syrian Saint Mar Ephraim in his version of this passage confirmed the Peshitta Tanakh reading with the word *Iyutha*, which can only mean Aldebaran. All versions of Job mention it by its cluster name in the previous line:

> Can you bind the chains of the Pleiades, or loose the cords of Orion (Job 38:31 NAU)

The name of the star Aldebaran is from Arabic and means "the follower" because it practically stalks the Pleiades cluster! Another Aramaic constellation title other than "satellites" is *Hyades* which refers to the star cluster that Aldebaran belongs.

Lamsa's translation also says ***paths of Aldebaran***. So if following of the Pleiades system is one path, what would be the another path? The only possible answer would be its opposite, Antares, on the other end of the sky. Aldebaran and Antares form a straight line across the entire field of the stars.

Aldebaran and Antares form the main dividing line, or path, from which the Mazzaroth (Zodiac) is divided. It is literally the first line in the Wheel of Stars going east-west. From those co-ordinates the night sky is then quartered with north and south pole stars. The remaining "slices" of the Sky Circle form the entire Wheel of Stars.

Let's look at the other place Aldebaran appears:

> Who commands the sun not to shine, and ***sets a seal upon the stars?*** ***Who alone spreads out the heavens*** and treads down upon the waves of the sea? Who makes Aldebaran, Orion and the Pleiades, and the chambers of the south? Who does great things that cannot be uncovered and extraordinary works without number?
> Job 9:7-10 (Matara)

This language of placing a seal on the stars, but at the same time spreading out the heavens, is a perfect description of the paths of Aldebaran. Interestingly enough, the Wheel itself is further described here:

> Their line has gone out through all the earth and their utterances to the end of the world. In them ***He has placed a tent for the sun,***

which is as a bridegroom coming out of his chamber. It rejoices as a strong man to run his course. Its rising is from one end of the heavens, and its circuit to the other end of them; and there is nothing hidden from its heat. (Psalm 19:4-6 NAU)

The "circuit" refers to an orbit as referenced earlier:

תְּקוּפָה **n.f** coming round, circuit;—cstr. תְּקוּפַת הַשָּׁנָה Ex 34:22 (JE), adv., *at the circuit* (completion) *of the year,* so לִתְ׳ הַשָּׁנָה: 2 Ch 24:33; = pl. cstr. 1 לִתְקֻפוֹת הַיָּמִים S 1:20; sg. sf. of finished *circuit* of sun Psalm 19:7 (opp. מוֹצָאוֹ; cf. of moon, בתקופתו Ecclus 43:7). –Brown Driver Briggs

Here's another key phrase for the Hebrew word for "end":

8657 [8658] קָצָה (Hebrew) (page 892) (Strong 7098) קָצָה **n.f. et** (pl.) **m.** :Ex 25:18 **end** (pl. 4 t. f. [c. num. masc.], Albr:ZAW xvi (1896), 93 changes gender of num. in all, or regards as irregular agreement in gender (Ges:§ 97 c); otherwise Kö:ii. 1, 61, 176);—abs. ק׳: Ex 25:19 + ; pl. cstr. 1 קְצוֹת K 12:31 + ; sf. קְצוֹתָיו Ex 27:4 + (so also Ex 37:8, 39:4 Qr; Kt קצוותו, cf. קְצָת infr.), etc.;—**1. end,** sg. of כַּפֹּרֶת in **tabern.** Ex 25:19, 25:19 = 37:8 , 37:8; of **curtain** 26:4 = 36:11; elsewh. pl., 37:7 = 25:18 הַכַּפֹּרֶת: ק׳, cf. 25:19 = 37:8; *of ephod* 28:7 = 39:4, **breast-plate** 28:23, 28:24 , 28:26 = 39:16, 39:17, 39:19, chins 28:25 = 39:18, grating 27:4 (appar. = *corners*); *tips* of wings 1 K 6:24, 6:24; of vine Ez 15:4; הָאָרֶץ ק׳: *ends of the earth* Is 40:28, 41:5, 41:9, Jb 28:24; הַשָּׁמַיִם אַרְבַּע ק׳: Je 49:36, cf. Psalm 19:6; ק׳ דְּרָכָיו: Jb 26:14, i.e. the mere edge, minute part, of his doings. **2.** מִקְצוֹת הָעָם = *from the whole of* (fr. among) *the people,* 1 K 12:31, 13:33, cf. Ju 18:2, 2 K 17:32 (v. also Ecclus 16:17, and **3.** קָצֶה.

We see that *qatsah* "end" is used in conjunction with *choshen* (the breastplate of the High Priest which held the Urim and Thummim). This is not a casual usage, earlier we saw that both Josephus and Philo described how the twelve stones on the breastplate represented both the twelve tribes and the twelve signs of the Mazzaroth (Zodiac). Josephus continues:

332	WHEEL OF STARS

And for the mitre, which was of a blue color, it seems to me to mean heaven; for how otherwise could the name of God be inscribed upon it? That it was also illustrated with a crown, and that of gold also, is because of that splendor with which God is pleased. Let this explanation {d} suffice at present, since the course of my narration will often, and on many occasions, afford me the opportunity of enlarging upon the virtue of our legislator. (Antiquities 3:186-187)

That description from Josephus is reminiscent of another:

I will bring upon Elam the four winds from *the four ends of heaven*, and will scatter them (as seeds)[24] to all these winds and there will be no nation to which the banished people of Elam will not go. Jeremiah 49:36 (Matara)

The overall picture of the "ends" is of not just the earth but also the sky, it portrays the sun on its annual journey. Once a year the sun leaves its tent and rises from one end of the heavens to the other, completing a *circle* at the *end* of its cycle.

Here are a few more verses about the circle in the heavens and earth:

He sits enthroned above the **circle**[25] (חוג) of the earth, and its people are like grasshoppers. He stretches out the heavens like a canopy, and spreads them out like a tent to live in. (Isaiah 40:22 NIV)

He has inscribed a **circle** (חוג) on the surface of the waters at the boundary of light and darkness. The pillars of heaven tremble and are awestruck at His rebuke. Job 26:10-11 (Matara)

While He had not yet made the earth and the fields; nor the first dust of the world. When He established the heavens, I was there. When He inscribed a **circle** (חוג) on the face of the deep; when He made firm the skies above. (Proverbs 8:26-28 NAU)

---

24 The verb zarah (scatter) is reminiscent of the noun zera in places like Genesis 1:11, though they are different roots and spellings.

25 This word (***khoog***) literally means "to draw around".

Mazzaroth is sometimes translated as "a constellation", which suggests an unnamed star-body. However, it refers to the entire Kosher Wheel of Stars as understood by ancient Israel. Such a reading is supported by the NAS Old Testament Hebrew Lexicon as "the twelve signs of the Zodiac and their associated constellations" as well as here:

> The word Mazzaroth therefore represents the twelve "signs" or, to speak more correctly, the twelve "constellations" of the zodiac. These two terms are often used indiscriminately, but there is a real difference between their significations. The constellations of the zodiac are the actual groupings of the stars, lying along the ecliptic, and are quite irregular in form and length. The signs have no connection with the actual stars but are imaginary divisions of the ecliptic, all exactly equal in length, and they are reckoned from that point in the heavens where the sun is at the moment that it is crossing the celestial equator in its northward motion in springtime. As this point, known to astronomers as "the first point of Aries," moves slowly amongst the stars, taking 25,800 years to complete a revolution of the heavens, the signs of the zodiac also move among the stars, and hence, though at one time each sign bore a rough and general correspondence to the constellation of the same name, the signs have gradually drawn away from them...
>
> There is some probability that in Job 37:9 the same two regions of the heavens are alluded to: "Out of the chamber of the south cometh the storm, and cold out of the north." It will be observed that the complete expression, "chamber of the south," is not in the original, the translators having supplied "of the south" from analogy with Job 9:9. The sirocco comes then from the region held by the mazzal, the "chamber," or constellation of the zodiac, then on the meridian. But the cold, the blizzard, comes from "the scatterers" (Mezarim). Who or what are the scatterers, and why do they represent the north? The late Professor Schiaparelli suggested that by a slight difference in the pointing, the word might be read as mizrayim, "the two winnowing fans," and that this may well have been a native term for the stars which we now know as the two Bears, Ursa Major and Minor, emphatically the northern constellations; the names being

given them from the natural grouping of their chief stars, just as they are known as the two "Dippers" in the United States, or the two "Ladles" in China (Astronomy in the Old Testament," 67-72). -ISBE Bible Dictionary.

Another source adds:

> 2361 **Mazzaroth** 2361.01 Job 38:32, "canst thou bring forth the signs of the zodiac at their respective seasons?" Mazzaloth in 2 Kings 23:5 margin, the 12 lodgings or stopping places (from Arabic menzil "an inn"), in which the sun successively stays or appears to stay in the sky. Gesenius supports margin Job 38:32, "the 12 signs," literally, "premonitions," i.e. "stars that give warnings or presages."-Fausset's Bible Dictionary

While some have suggested that Aries was identified as the first constellation of spring (circa 700 BCE), all sources agree that the constellations were mapped about 3000 BCE. At that time Aries would have clearly been observed in that precise role. Evidence from the book of Job, using Scripture as historical fact, puts it considerably older than 700 BCE.

The term Mazzaroth dates back to the Babylonian creation myth, more than 3,000 years ago, where it is called *mizrata* and defined as such:

> He gave them a starry aspect as **constellations {mizrata}**; he measures the year, gave it a beginning and an end, and to each month of the twelve three rising stars. When he had marked the limits of the year, he gave them Nebiru, the pole of the universe, to hold their course, that never erring they should not stray through the sky. For the seasons of Ea and Enlil he drew the parallel. Through her ribs he opened gates in the east and west, and gave them strong bolts on the right and left; and high in the belly of Tiamat he set the zenith. -Tablet V of the Enuma Elish, From *Ancient Near Eastern Texts*. Translated by N. K. Sandars.

The Babylonian system was itself derived from a much earlier Sumerian one. A carved "animal round" (Zodiac circle) dating back to 3100 BCE features:

> The twelve months on the face of the terrestrial world clock correspond exactly to the twelve signs of the zodiac on the heavenly world clock—the sign of KUMAL (or Aries) is the first and belongs to the month of Nisan.—Hugo Radau, *Sumerian Hymns and Prayers to the God Nin-Ib from the Temple Library at Nippur*, (University of Pennsylvania: 1911), p. 34.

Another ancient witness is that of Egypt. Sources that ascribe a late origin to Aries admit that it was derived from the 36 decade system from Egypt. In that system, each star would rule ten days, for a total of 360 days in all. The same mapping patterns that make up the modern Zodiac have been found as far back as 1290 BCE[26] at the tomb of Pharaoh Seti the First.

So when YHWH asked Job, "Do you know the paths of Aldebaran?" He is in effect inquiring if Job knows the Wheel of Stars.

Understanding the Apocalypse

We live in times of extreme apocalyptic fervor, but there is very little discussion about what "apocalypse" itself really is. The word is derived from Greek and literally means "to uncover truth". It is only in later centuries that it took on its unofficial meaning of "the end of the world" or the age. As sincere truth seekers, we must deeply root ourselves in proper historical and Scriptural context. The Book of Revelation, for example, makes it clear in the first line that this is the "*Apocalypse*" of Y'shua our Mashiyach (Messiah), not of John who is writing it down. Furthermore, in Aramaic the name of this book is *Gilyana*, which is derived from the Hebrew and Aramaic root-word *gela* which means not just to "reveal" but "to manifest". This meaning is further carried over into the one place in Israel that is literally named the Land of Revelation/ Manifestation: Galilee!

---

26 For more information see: Van der Waerden, Bartel: Die Anfänge der Astronomie. Erwachende Wissenschaft. Bd. 2. Groningen, 1965. History of the Zodiac. Arch. f. Orientf. 16.

These elements of lexical cleverness are derived from a Semitic original and a Semitic mindset for this book and the corpus of the New Testament as a whole. It relates squarely, for example, to occasions in Matthew where Y'shua says he came to "fulfill the Torah", but the meaning of that word in Aramaic is not "termination" rather, "to provide proper understanding/revelation". It is in this context that we get phrases like "thus the words of the prophet WERE FULFILLED (understood to mean/ apply to) _____."

Therefore, our "apocalypse" is within our own hearts and minds, as we strive to live a Truthful, Honest, Scripturally based lifestyle and give Father YHWH and His Son Y'shua our best. Whether Y'shua Mashiyach returns tomorrow or in another 10, 20 or 100 years. As sincere people of faith we must never tie our "new" obedience or piety, to fear or even speculation of what may be coming soon. Instead, we have our own personal and intimate "apocalypse" this very day, today, and must root ourselves to eternal life; that's the greatest Revelation of them all.

Illustration

Building the Wheel of Stars

1) Start with the basic Ecliptic Model[27] of the border stars of Aldebaran and Antares, coordinated with the North Star and its point directly below, touching the horizon:

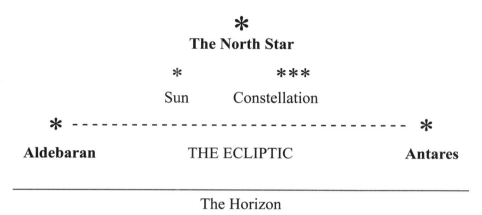

2) Draw a circle between the four main "dots":

3) Divide the circle two more times, so you have 12 equal slices of 30 degrees each:

4) Add constellations as represented by 24 courses of priests along with the Biblical mathematics under YHWH's control.

---

27 For additional illustrations please visit: www.wheelofstars.com

OTHER RESOURCES

Aramaic English New Testament
by Andrew Gabriel Roth

The most definitive Aramaic to English translation that has come forth in nearly 2,000 years. Not only does this Aramaic based New Testament Bible render the Ancient Aramaic in a way that is easy for every English reader to understand, but it investigates nuances, poetry and hidden codes of the New Testament that, until now, have only been available to Hebrew and Aramaic scholars.

The AENT has become an important reference resource for those who want to learn the original teachings of Y'shua (Jesus) and his followers. For Jews who do not subscribe to Y'shua as Mashiyach (Ben Yoseph), there is a world of provocative ancient Jewish thought that is rarely understood and discussed in Jewish circles. For Messianic Jews, there are numerous ancient Aramaic terms and definitions presented with Hebrew cognates from the Tanakh (Old Testament) that sheds much light on difficult or controversial verses. For Christians, there is a wealth of insight and discussion on topics including: the Melchisedec priesthood, the Acharit HaYamin (Latter Days), Grace, Trinity, Virgin Birth, Feminine Attributes, Judaizing, Legalism, Love, the Name of Jesus, the origin of Christmas, Easter and Sunday, as well as insights into Spiritual Anointing, the Rapture and much more... discussed in more than 1700 detailed footnotes and 350 pages of appendix materials.

To Order Please visit:
WWW.AENT.ORG

AENT Scolarship Series DVD Vol. 1
Aramaic Primacy & Textual Comparison

Provides a wealth of information for anyone interested in learning about the original Hebrew and Aramaic language and culture of Y'shua (Jesus) within the original New Testament. This large capacity format includes:

Aramaic Primacy Video

A three part series on Aramaic Primacy that examines some of the beautiful poetry, terms and definitions, and many underlying elements of Aramaic that were embedded deep within the original text. You will also see many graphics that show Aramaic history and archeology like never before. Topics include: **What is Aramaic? What is the Peshitta? What is Estrangela? What is the Church of the East? What are the historical mechanisms of Aramaic Renewed Covenant Primacy? A brief tour of the manuscript record. Why is Aramaic Renewed Covenant Primacy important to you?**

Textual Comparison (Aramaic vs. Greek) Video

This two part series on textual comparison will take you on a 42-Step Journey from Matthew through 1 John. Find out how the earliest Greek New Testament Bibles were, undoubtedly, translated from their original language: Aramaic. Andrew Gabriel Roth takes you through verses in your own Bible and shows how original definitions and ideas evolved from Aramaic and Hebrew into Greek.

BONUS FEATURES INCLUDE:
Aramaic Timeline Video
AENT History & Bible Overview Video
Radio Interviews (2)
Original Aramaic Autograph (Powerpoint)

To Order Please visit:
WWW.AENT.ORG/VIDEO.HTM

AENT Scolarship Series DVD Vol. 2
The Y'shua of History

About 2,000 years ago a shocking claim exploded out of the Middle East that changed the world forever. A Hebrew man named Y'shua, a carpenter from Galilee, was resurrected from the dead as the ultimate validation of his message. Yet, in recent years scholars and detractors alike have cast doubt on whether the man the world calls, Jesus of Nazareth, ever lived at all. Some postulate that his entire story was a re-working of pagan myth. Others are calling first century historical sources a lie based on their "higher" criticism. What is faith? What is fact? What lies between them? What are the historical allegations of Y'shua of Nazareth?

Questions addressed are:

1) How can we know whether the testimony of Josephus the historian is reliable?

2) How do Pagan and Jewish sources who despised the early Nazarenes help validate the Gospel record?

3) Did the Gnostics, an ancient sect rebuked by name, in the New Testament deny the physical existence of Y'shua?

4) What motivated liberal scholars to label the new testament as a fraud?

Join Aramaic scholar, Nazarene historian and translator of the Aramaic English New Testament Bible, Andrew Gabriel Roth, as he sifts through the hype to recover the history of Y'shua that exists outside the Bible.

To Order Please visit:
WWW.AENT.ORG/VIDEO.HTM

NETZARI
PRESS

About the Cover

The front cover features the majestic M51 Whirlpool Galaxy (NGC 5194) photographed by NASA's Hubble Space Telescope January 2005. The smaller NGC 5195 galaxy lies at the bottom spiral arm. Center: Astrolabe plate (altitude / azimuth) below that is the Mazzaroth wheel indicating the Hebrew names for the 12 constellations that relate to the Tribes of Israel.

The rear cover features the magnificent Antennae galaxies (NGC 4038 & NGC 4039; see online article: Colliding galaxies make love, not war). In the center is an ancient Hebrew astrolabe made of brass. Top left is a Celestial Sphere sketch with North, North Star, South, East and West locating bearings. Below is a mosaic with Hebrew inscriptions of the Mazzaroth wheel. Similar mosaics are found in Hammat Tiberias, Huseifa, Susiya, Naaran, and recently at Sepphoris. The ancient Semitic calendar was the platform for the later paganized zodiac. However, a synagogue inscription at En Gedi, Israel, features the names of the Mazzaroth (zodiac) figures in ancient Hebrew and Aramaic writings, without the iconoclastic figures. From right to left of the Hebrew astrolabe is Andrew Gabriel Roth w/shofar, below is Yoseph Ben Mattathias (Josephus), En Gedi inscription, Mar Ephraim, Aries coin, a pic from an Egyptian tomb item representing/standing in for "young Philo" at Alexandria, Egypt, bottom left is a moon phase diagram.

Special thanks to NASA and STScI (Space Telescope Science Institute) for the use of their photographs. Credit: NASA, ESA, and the Hubble Heritage Team (STScI/AURA)-ESA/Hubble Collaboration. Acknowledgement: B. Whitmore (Space Telescope Science Institute) and James Long (ESA/Hubble).

First draft of this book was completed on the Day of the Vernal Equinox March 20th, 2010. Second draft was completed on the 14th of Abib March 29th, 2010 before twilight, on Pesach eve. Seventh draft (and final) was completed on Yom Shishi (Friday) the day after Yom Teruah, 1 Tishri/September 9th, 2010.

Andrew Gabriel Roth